Altering States

Altering States

Ethnographies of Transition
in Eastern Europe and the
Former Soviet Union

Edited by
Daphne Berdahl,
Matti Bunzl, and
Martha Lampland

Ann Arbor

THE UNIVERSITY OF MICHIGAN PRESS

2003   2002   2001   2000   4   3   2   1

A CIP catalog record for this book is available from the British Library.

Library of Congress Cataloging-in-Publication Data

Altering states : ethnographies of transition in Eastern Europe and the Former
    Soviet Union / edited by Daphne Berdahl, Matti Bunzl and Martha Lampland.
       p.   cm.
    Includes bibliographical references and index.
    ISBN 0-472-11058-6 (cloth : alk. paper) —
    ISBN 0-472-08617-0 (pbk. : alk. paper)
       1. Europe, Eastern—Social conditions—1989–   2. Former Soviet
    republics—Social conditions.   3. Post-communism—Europe, Eastern.
    4. Post-communism— Former Soviet republics.   I. Berdahl, Daphne,
    1964–   II. Bunzl, Matti, 1971–   III. Lampland, Martha.

HN380.7.A8 A45   2000
303.44'0947—dc21   00-020478

Contents

Acknowledgments

The nature of transitions in Eastern Europe and the former Soviet Union is the subject of this book. All of the authors conducted fieldwork in their respective countries, examining firsthand the dilemmas, joys, and traumas of altering states of mind, being, and community. They experienced the transition along with those they lived with, spoke with, watched, and recorded. It is perhaps ironic, then, that this book is the product of another set of transitions under way, in this case the widespread use of electronic communities to contact and build relations within the scholarly community. We first hatched the idea of compiling this volume at the American Anthropological Association meetings in 1995. Having witnessed the avalanche of books published in the early 1990s, few of which built upon careful empirical studies, we felt strongly that we would forge a different path and agreed to compile a volume in which ethnographic studies would occupy pride of place. The question then became how to reach those who had been working in the field during the years immediately following the dissolution of socialist states in Europe and parts east. Taking advantage of the well-organized e-mail list of the Society for the Anthropology of Europe, a call for papers was issued on line. It was hoped that this would bring in submissions from scholars living on both sides of the Atlantic. This did not happen, to our dismay. (The issue of epistemological barriers between scholars in different geographical regions is addressed in Martha Lampland's afterword at the end of this volume.) Nonetheless, the contributions do offer a novel view of the transition. Moreover, a variety of issues rarely broached in scholarship on this region is brought forward in the following essays, constituting (one would hope) another transition.

The editors wish to thank Susan Whitlock for her strong support of this project and the anonymous reviewers for the press for their helpful insights and comments.

Introduction:
An Anthropology of Postsocialism

Daphne Berdahl

The essays in this collection examine societies in the midst of rapid and momentous change. These pieces portray life after the collapse of state socialism in Eastern Europe and the former Soviet Union and examine the processes, particulars, and experiences of transition itself. Through an emphasis on the fine-grained detail of everyday life, these essays focus on the contradictions, paradoxes, and ambiguities of postsocialism. They explore the construction and contestation of new cultural landscapes and probe the emergence of new asymmetrical power relations. In a variety of regional contexts and through a range of ethnographic and theoretical perspectives, the authors ask what happens to memory, identity, and personhood in the aftermath of rapid political, economic, and social change. The "altering states" examined here thus traverse multiple intersections of the large and the small: from nation-states to states of mind, from local and individual states of crisis to the crisis of the state.

The collapse of state socialism throughout Central and Eastern Europe in 1989 and the dissolution of the Soviet Union in 1991 are among the most significant major historical transformations, ending the Cold War division of the world and changing the political map of the globe. In many academic studies as well as popular portrayals, this "great transformation"[1] has been described in a discourse of capitalist "triumphalism" that entails a certain linear, teleological thinking in relation to the direction of change: from socialism or dictatorship to liberal democracy, from a plan to a market economy.[2] Not only does this perspective reproduce Cold War binaries and structural oppositions (Kennedy 1994), but it also assumes a particular trajectory of change. The electoral success of former communists in several postsocialist states, the escalating unemployment rates throughout the region, the difficulties in establishing new businesses for many would-be entrepreneurs, the return to a barter (indeed, mafia) economy in the most economically devastated areas, and the slow improvement in most countries' gross national products are but a few examples of the uncertain outcome and ongoing nature of postsocialist transitions that reflect the inadequacy of teleological thinking.

Despite such complications, evolutionary perspectives underwrite many of the "main themes" (Verdery 1996, 11) of the expanding field that has come to be called "transitology." A flurry of scholarly activity across a range of disciplines, particularly in the fields of political science and economics, has produced an abundant and growing literature on such topics as privatization, decollectivization, and the market economy (e.g., Abrahams 1997; Jeffries 1993; Kovacs 1994; Kozminski 1993; Lavigne 1995; Stark 1992), democratization (e.g., Beyme 1996; Pridham and Vanhanen 1994), civil society (e.g., Arato 1994; Karatnycky, Motyl, and Shor 1997; Poznanski 1994; Rau 1991), and nationalism (e.g., Bollerup and Christensen 1997; Gellner 1992; Hockenos 1993). While much of this work is extremely valuable for its illumination of large-scale economic and political processes and institutions, it is an area of inquiry that, as Katherine Verdery puts it, is "saturated in ideological significance" (1996, 10). Indeed, Igor Barsegian has suggested that the term *transition* itself must be viewed as a cultural construct of the "West," informed by Western experience and studies of "Third World" or developing countries: "There is now a real danger of imposing on the postcommunist field the social science categories empowered and backed by Western superiority in technology, politics, and economy. These categories do not describe the field; they prescribe what should be done" (Barsegian, forthcoming).

Urging observers to "suspend judgment about the outcome" of postsocialist transitions, Verdery has similarly pointed to the "rescue scenarios" reflected in images and stories of postsocialism:

> ["Shock therapy"] compares the former socialist bloc with a person suffering from mental illness—that is, socialism drove them crazy, and our job is to restore their sanity. The second implies that (*pace* Fukuyama) history is only now beginning, that prior to 1989 the area was without form and void. While the image of "shock therapy" represents Western advisors as doctors, the "big bang" figures them as God. (1996, 205)

Verdery calls for analyses of postsocialism that question ideologically embedded representations and images of progress. Paraphrasing Rudolf Bahro's famous term, David Kideckel (1995) similarly suggests a notion of "actually existing turbulence" to describe the unique and variable directions of change throughout the region. Just as there were a "plurality of socialisms" (Hann 1993), so too are there diverse trajectories and experiences of postsocialisms. Among other things, this book aims to contribute to an understanding of the multiple trajectories and specificities of the transitions still under way in postsocialist societies.

At the same time, this book is intended as a deliberately ethnographic intervention. Because of a predominant focus on large-scale economic processes, political elites, and evolutionary trajectories, much of the established "transition" literature explains little about how people have actually experienced the dramatic political, economic, and sociocultural changes since the collapse of socialist rule.[3] Even an analysis as insightful, thorough, and sophisticated as the historian Charles Maier's 1997 study of the end of the GDR, for example, is relatively uninterested in the voices and experiences of ordinary Eastern Germans throughout this period of intense transition. What is missing from these macrolevel perspectives is not only an attention to local texture and on-the-ground experience but also the kinds of challenges to certain generalizations, conclusions, and categories of analysis that an acute sensitivity to detail can provide.

Anthropological approaches to the study of postsocialism in Eastern Europe both complement and challenge macrolevel analyses. In this manner, anthropologists have begun to examine the main themes of transitology from ethnographically informed perspectives. Gail Kligman's focus on the process of constructing civil society in Romania (1990), for example, cautions against reifications of state-society dichotomies, while Susan Gal (1996) points to the concept's gendered dimensions. Studies collected by David Kideckel (1995) examine the impact of decollectivization and privatization on local politics, identities, and social organization in rural Eastern European communities, and Ladislaw Holy's (1996) study of national identity challenges certain "vacuum theories" of nationalism that attribute its ascent after 1989 to a need to fill an ideological void left by the collapse of socialism (see also Verdery 1996).

Unlike many observers of the transitions in Eastern Europe, ethnographically grounded scholars frequently emphasize important continuities between socialist and postsocialist societies. Kideckel (1995) and Gerald Creed (1995) point to parallels between certain structures and experiences of collectivization and decollectivization. In a historical ethnography of collectivization in a Hungarian village, Martha Lampland (1995) demonstrates significant similarities between socialist and capitalist political economic practices and illuminates how commodification under socialism in Hungary helped to pave the way for many of the transitions that have followed. In a study of class and social differentiation in a rural Polish community, Carole Nagengast (1991) similarly argues that the reinstitution of capitalism in Poland does not represent a systemic rupture but reflects important "continuities in earlier, class-based *social* relations that masqueraded as *socialist* relations for four and a half decades" (Nagengast 1991, 1). In a discussion of the elaborate social and economic networks formed under socialism's "second society" in Poland, Janine Wedel (1992) also notes how critical these relations will be in shaping Poland's future. More generally, the work of Verdery, who has been at the forefront of theorizing socialism and postsocialist transitions from an anthropological perspective, has been devoted to highlighting continuities in many arenas of social, political, and economic life.

Anthropologically informed studies of postsocialist transitions have also pointed to valuable topics outside of the main themes. Important work on the gender regimes of socialism as well as on abortion debates in many postsocialist societies have contributed to theoretical understandings of the relationship between gender and nation (e.g., Berry 1995; Dölling 1991; Gal 1994; Goven 1993; Kligman 1992; Verdery 1996). In a different vein, analyses of ethnic and nationalist conflicts have demonstrated that eruptions of violence do not simply entail a revival of old tensions suppressed by socialist rule but are hostilities that must be re-created anew (Verdery 1996, 95; see also Bringa 1995; Denich 1994; Hayden 1996). Others have examined the pervasiveness of memory and the uses and burdens of the past (e.g., Berdahl 1997; Hayden 1995; Lass 1994). Another topic of increasing interest to anthropologists (among others) studying postsocialist transitions is the changing cultural meanings and politics of consumption (e.g., Berdahl, 1999; Humphrey 1995; Konstantinov 1996; Merkel 1994; Verdery 1996). Underlying most of these studies, explicitly or implicitly, is the salient question of identity—its rearticulation in altered economic, social, and national contexts (see also Berdahl 1999; De Soto and Anderson 1993; Kennedy 1994; Kürti and Langman 1997; Slobin 1996).

Despite this expanding literature, the ethnographic corpus of postsocialist transitions remains small. One of the central aims of this volume is to augment the ethnographic record while charting new sites of investigation and areas of inquiry. In addition and contrast to the various themes of transitology discussed earlier, the essays in this collection focus on such largely unexplored topics as space, time, metaphor, cultural tropes, symbols, sexuality, environment, neocolonialism, religion, material culture, and kinship.

These topics are not just a matter of supplementing macroperspectives with a local focus, as several ethnographic studies of postsocialism rightly and necessarily do. Rather, these subjects entail a concern for *process*—in the form of transition, construction, negotiation, restoration, subjectification, and contestation. Implicit in this focus on process is a foregrounding of agency. The essays that follow offer a range of viewpoints and theoretical concerns, yet all seek to illuminate certain processes of transition that are most discernible in local practices and individual actions; the authors are interested in how ordinary people make sense of and find meaning in a rapidly changing world. The essays in this book thus offer empirically grounded and ethnographically sensitive analyses of the textures, nuances, and contours of everyday life. Indeed, as several of the pieces point out, cultural categories and foregroundings of the prosaic often frame local experiences and expressions of transition: the Russian notion of *byt* (everyday life) with its connotations of containment and exhaustion, the Armenian concept of *kents'agh* (personal everyday life) transformed in space and time, and the eastern German attempts to recover and display a sense of *Alltag* (everyday life) in the GDR.

In stressing process and agency, however, the authors here are careful not to obscure important contexts of power that frame the social action they describe. Several of the essays, in fact, focus explicitly on the construction, negotiation, and territorialization of nascent, renewed, continuing, and emerging power relations in the New Europe—between East and West, rich and poor, local and national. Rather than viewing these power dynamics in dichotomous terms, however, the writers are interested in the multiple and shifting intersections of power and agency especially visible during moments of social discord.

Another aim of this volume, then, is to suggest different tools and perspectives for the study of societies in the midst of dramatic change. Transition, the authors show, is rife with contradiction. It is an interactive process that both reflects and constitutes a dynamic interplay between large-scale systems and local—indeed, individual—phenomena. One of the most useful methods for illuminating the differential manifestations and experiences of transition, these essays implicitly argue, is to explore how extralocal economic, political, and social processes intersect with the individual lives of people in a community, because it is "in the actions of individuals living in time and place" (Abu-Lughod 1991) that these forces are embodied, negotiated, contested, and potentially transformed. Further, as Michael Herzfeld has pointed out, this ethnographic attention to detail, quickly and "summarily dismissed as mere anecdote" by many disciplines, reveals "what moves people to action" (1997, x, 24).

The ethnographers in this volume have thus listened closely to how people talk about transition, and they have uncovered discursive practices ranging from spatial tropes to neocolonial metaphors; the authors have paid careful attention to what people do with things, focusing on the material culture of exhibits in makeshift museums and living room display cases; and they have remained alert to exercises of power in a variety of contexts, including tourism and landscape design.

The essays in this collection are organized thematically rather than geographically. All are based on extensive field research characterized by a methodology of participant observation, including formal and informal interviews, ethnographic observation, and, quite frequently, long-term residence in a community. In addition to a focus on process, the advantages to this approach are its openness to the unexpected, its attention to the minutiae of everyday life, and its concern for the way in which large-scale processes are interpreted, contested, and negotiated by individuals in a community.[4] In this book, the notion of community has been broadly defined: Roma in Moscow, Jewish communities across Central Europe, gay male sex tourists in Prague, political and environmental interest groups in the industrial center of eastern Germany, kinship networks in the Armenian capital city of Yerevan, a group of individuals in Dresden who struggle to work through the East German past, underground rock musicians in Hungary, and the formerly closed city of Omsk, Siberia. Although it was not the editors' intent to exclude village studies, traditionally the focus of most anthropological studies of Europe, the essays in this collection are drawn from research in urban contexts. In this sense, the volume not only highlights new directions in the anthropology of Europe but, more generally, suggests key concepts for the larger ethnographic study of modernity.

Landscapes of Transition

Throughout much of Eastern Europe, the collapse of socialism was most immediately observable in the landscape: colorful advertisements and neon billboards for Western products that replaced the bland and faded party propaganda, strip malls erected outside of urban centers, and construction projects that in many regions still seem to be everywhere. The unfolding landscapes of Eastern Europe do not merely mirror transition, but, as several essays in this volume demonstrate, they are themselves important and multilayered symbols of change and continuity. Landscape, in this sense, may be viewed as a social process, reflecting and constituting depictions of rapid change in the apparent stability of place.

Alaina Lemon's essay, for example, discusses changing social meanings embedded in the landscape of the Moscow metro. Arguing that the metro is a kind of "place-trope," Lemon examines cultural practices at the metro as well as discursive practices surrounding it to demonstrate how public narratives of transition become grounded in concrete spaces. Indeed, she argues, people have long used public transit to talk about transition in Russia: from the official Soviet discourse in the early days of the metro and dissidents' disdain for its Stalinist associations, to the metro as vehicle for the coup in 1991, to the metro as symbol of commerce and social chaos following the breakup of the Soviet Union. Employed in the service of different interests, depictions of the metro alternately and sometimes simultaneously signify social order and disorder, continuity and transition, insiders and outsiders. The changing landscape of the metro thus constitutes and is constituted by important processes of social, political, and economic transition.

Philip Bohlman's essay on synagogue restoration similarly focuses on symbols that embody transition. For Bohlman, restored, converted, or abandoned synagogues constitute the "historical landscape of Jewish Eastern Europe"; they are metaphors for destruction, exodus, neglect, and return. In addition to constructing an experience and identity of being Jewish, the synagogues and their music have long brought together narratives of fragmentation and contradiction, ranging from nineteenth-century musical forms and aesthetic debates to issues of memorializing and recuperation in the late twentieth century. The act of synagogue restoration highlights these layers of meaning, metaphor, fragmentation, and transition in Eastern Europe's Jewish communities. Furthermore, the post–1989 return to the region of Western tourists, particularly American Jews attracted by a burgeoning "Jewish heritage industry," has heightened the dilemmas of synagogue restoration: what should be done with the empty synagogues of Eastern Europe? Whose narrative voice should be recovered? How does the act of restoration deal with the neglect during the recent (socialist) past? Synagogue restoration has thus often become a trope of uncertainty, haunted by memory.

The return of Jewish Eastern Europe has not only entailed a return of Jewish voices and music, however, but the reinvention of Jewish Eastern Europe through certain practices of cultural colonization as well. Bohlman shows how this return has ironically involved the recuperation, reinvention, and commodification of music manufactured by the West for the East. Like the phone cards sold to help finance the organ restoration in a Budapest synagogue, the mass reproduction of Jewish music through cassettes and compact discs, in addition to the tourist market itself, reflects the way in which Western consumption has been an agent not only for the restoration of Jewish Eastern Europe but for reentering and repossessing Eastern Europe as well (L. Wolff 1994). In this sense, Bohlman's essay highlights Western imaginings of postsocialist Eastern Europe more generally.

Matti Bunzl extends on this theme in his discussion of neocolonial inventions of Eastern Europe following the events of 1989. Focusing specifically on gay male sex tourism, Bunzl demonstrates how a cultural landscape of power is enacted and constituted through bodily and discursive practices. The neocolonial tropes of inventing a distinct "eastern" same-sex sexuality are part of a larger process of producing colonized and colonizing subjectivities. Sexuality and the body are a distinctive realm and privileged site for the invention of an "embodied border" and the asymmetrical construction of Otherness. The neocolonial metaphors that structure practice and experience, Bunzl shows, are the products of unequal power relations between "East" and "West." Indeed, they are part of a reterritorializing process that constitutes Austria's privileged position in the shifting landscape of the New Europe.

Hermine De Soto's essay also focuses on issues of power, specifically in relation to the contested and more literally shifting landscape of a desolate industrial region in the former GDR. The struggles between two "strategic groups" advocating different visions for rebuilding a fractured ecology and landscape have been deeply embedded in the power dynamics of German reunification. Whereas the "Circle" represents the influence of West German corporate interests on local and state-level government and thus the increasingly dominant logic of postindustrial capitalism in the former GDR, the "Reformed Bauhaus" exemplifies an alternative and locally grounded view contesting modernist ideas of progress. As De Soto demonstrates, this debate over landscape design—from which the voices and concerns of local citizens were largely absent—not only concerned the reconstitution of identities in relation to rapid deindustrialization and widespread unemployment in the region. It also concerned the construction and production of memory in relation to a socialist modernity mapped onto a landscape devastated by the logic of socialist monoproduction (Konrad and Szelenyi 1979; Verdery 1996). Indeed, underlying this debate was a struggle over what the new Germany should look like; it was a struggle over what Simon Schama (1995) might call the topography of German national identity.

Unlike the causes and consequences of deindustrialization in East Germany described by De Soto, the deindustrialization in Armenia explored by Stephanie Platz has involved a transition to a "demodernized" rather than postindustrial society. Platz situates her discussion in the context of a catastrophic paralysis of the urban and industrial infrastructure that resulted from an acute energy crisis caused by Armenia's war with Azerbaijan and compounded by the disintegration of the Soviet Union. This radical political and economic change—indeed, rupture—had penetrating consequences for daily life, transforming people's experience of domestic, urban, even national space and time. The landscapes of transition discussed in Platz's essay include metaphors of place that signify distance and proximity in defining both the person and the nation; apartments whose interior spaces seemed to "divide and multiply" (Drakulic

1991) under socialism and then contract in crisis; and urban landscapes altered through an increasing juxtaposition of devastation and affluence. Stripped of the distinctive features that had anchored these spaces as places, domestic and urban landscapes became profoundly disorienting. These spatial transformations have had important implications for personal and national identities.

Making Things Visible

Among other things, the revolutions of 1989 were about visibility—making visible "the people" and their demands for democratic reforms, unveiling contradictions in state ideology and practice, and unmasking the instability of regimes. Following the collapse of socialism, efforts were made to expose and categorize victims and perpetrators,[5] to uncover formerly unsanctioned memories of the past (Watson 1994, 4), to highlight what has changed, and to recover some of what has been lost. In tracing particular practices of making the hidden visible, several essays in this volume illuminate how these processes themselves are most visible in the minutiae of daily life.

In the process and aftermath of transition, for example, making things visible has often entailed opening the most hidden. As Bohlman elucidates, what has become visible—and audible—in the process of synagogue restoration are not only Jewish voices and communities of Eastern Europe but a historical disjuncture unleashed by the effort to "restore the past by connecting it to the present." In the sacred and secularized spaces of the synagogues of Eastern Europe, music gives voice to a history of Jewish presence, disjointed and dissonant but with the potential for suture and repair, if not restoration.

Dale Pesmen's account of opening the most hidden in an era of glasnost and post-Soviet society describes how practices of closedness—ranging from the literally closed Siberian city of Omsk and its blank spots of veiled power to the taking in and hiding of both objects and emotions in a culture of secrecy—reflect the ways in which culturally specific understandings of personhood and national identity are intertwined with and structured by metaphors of space and depth. The openness of glasnost and post-Soviet rule, Pesmen argues, has made visible not only literal spaces like Omsk or "hidden treasures" locked away in museum storerooms but also metaphorical spaces of the soul, where emotions and transformations are lived and experienced most intensely. Whereas closedness and the everyday (*byt*) constrain, openness threatens: by revealing the secrets, depths, and interiors on which the soul paradoxically thrives, by unveiling ugly truths, by opening the "national soul to foreigners, for money." In exploring the cultural meanings and spatial metaphors of the enigmatic Russian soul, Pesmen makes a profound connection between everyday transitions and the depths, interiors, and surfaces—both literal and metaphorical—of people's lives.

In a very different context, Lemon explores a "grammar of surfaces" that is produced in the reading of bodies and the "stark visibility" of trade at the Moscow metro. The new shops that line pedestrian paths, the glass cases that have replaced the draped windows of old metro stores, and the semi-illicit exchanges near metro entrances have "thrown into the eyes" of metro commuters not only a new site of commerce and its attendant, multiple, and ethnicized meanings but also the growing inequalities within Russian society more generally—divisions that can be observed at the metro in particularly bold relief. What is most visible at the Moscow metro are not only processes and products of transition but practices of inclusion and exclusion as well.

Bunzl also focuses on bodily practices as a constitutive site of a new grammar of visibility, deployed, in this case, by gay male sex tourists who come to "see" embodied difference. In the gay discotheques, bars, and guest houses of Prague that have proliferated since the collapse of socialism, and through tropes of availability, passion, and pansexuality, Austrian men searching for the "Prague experience" construct, inscribe, and naturalize "eastern" bodies and an "eastern" same-sex sexuality as distinctly Other. The enactment of this difference in sexual practices, he shows, in turn accentuates the reconstitution of a neocolonial order more generally.

In Elizabeth Ten Dyke's essay, what becomes visible through culturally specific practices of "remembrance work" are memories of an increasingly devalued East German past. A written report about the 1989 demonstrations in Dresden and a museum project containing objects of the vanished state reflect not only how quickly history has been remade into and reshaped by memory but also how the apparent trivialities of the everyday concretize and anchor memory and identity in very significant ways. By evoking stories of the past—ranging from accounts of daily life in an economy of scarcity to recollections of East German coming-of-age ceremonies—the products in the museum are, in a sense, mnemonics, signifiers of a period of time that differentiates Eastern Germans (see also Berdahl 1999). Remembering, Ten Dyke shows, takes work, and this work both reflects and constitutes important processes through which things become invested with meaning and memory.

In her essay on the (anti)politics of art in Hungary, Anna Szemere highlights an issue underlying several essays in this volume: the intense and visible disorientation that can accompany rapid change. Focusing on the life histories and cultural productions of underground rock musicians, Szemere asks what happens to dissident art when the object of opposition (the socialist state) disappears. She explores a profound crisis of identity within a countercultural artistic community, reflected especially in the conversion of numerous alternative rock musicians to new forms of evangelical Christianity. The dissolution of the political context of artistic production under socialism makes visible not only art's contested meanings but also its contextual embeddedness. For Szemere, this visibility suggests important implications for rethinking the relationship of politics and artistic autonomy.

Paradoxes, Ambiguities, Trajectories

As noted earlier, one of the principal concerns of an anthropology of postsocialism has been to challenge teleological assumptions and evolutionary perspectives surrounding a particular trajectory of change. Indeed, many of these assumptions must be viewed as ideologically embedded in the kinds of power asymmetries described in the essays by Bohlman, Bunzl, and De Soto. Particularly relevant for the essays in this volume, as well as for the transitions in Eastern Europe more generally, is a question Bohlman poses in relation to historical changes of the past fifty years for Jews in Eastern Europe: "Transition from what, to what?"

Szemere's contribution most explicitly addresses this issue. Arguing for a processual approach to the study of postsocialism, Szemere cautions against reifying the concept of *transition* and advocates a more nuanced and culturally contextualized understanding of the continuities, subtleties, and peculiarities of social transformation. The unique history of economic and cultural reforms in Hungary exemplifies the highly differentiated experiences and temporalities of postsocialist transitions. The term *transition,* she suggests, should thus be distinguished from *regime change* to differentiate between short and long trajectories of change. Through an analysis of countercultural music and film, Szemere explores how particular transformations were predicted, reflected, and constituted in the realm of art. Szemere thus offers not only a critique of established approaches to transition but an analysis of the processes of artistic production in relation to shifting political and social contexts.

Focusing on the asymmetrical context of German reunification, both De Soto and Ten Dyke highlight profound, although very different, personal and collective ambiguities surrounding postsocialist transitions in the former GDR. The "remembrance work" described by Ten Dyke, for example, reflects ambiguities about both the present and the past. It entails not a construction of "oppositional" memories in defiance of "dominant" ones but an effort to ground a more complicated individual and collective history of opposition, acquiescence, and experience in the GDR through the memorializing practices of everyday material culture. Indeed, as Ten Dyke suggests, such practices reflect the need to transcend dichotomous conceptions of memory. De Soto, conversely, deals with more explicit contestations surrounding the politics of landscape design and, ultimately, the cultural politics of memory in the new Germany. In listening to and amplifying the silenced voices of those most affected by the proposed landscape design, De Soto illuminates the relations of power that determine particular trajectories of transition.

Platz's essay on transformations in space and time in post-Soviet Armenia similarly illustrates the multiplicity of experiences and trajectories of transition. Noting that Armenia's transition from socialism began in 1988 with the Karabakh movement and its demands for national self-determination, Platz challenges top-down theories that stress elite constructions of national identity and shows how changes in kinship practices, once central to the daily imagining of the Armenian nation, reconfigured important intersections of individual and national identities. Armenians increasingly described personal experience through a metaphor of the nation, she argues, and these framings constituted a significant element in the construction and experience of national historical time. The fact that the process of demodernization in Armenia created conditions of intimacy and estrangement, images of rupture and regression, and experiences of expansion and contraction is not inconsistent with this contention. Instead, demodernization's effects reflect the paradoxical, contradictory, and ambiguous nature of transition itself.

This final point is addressed in Pesmen's discussion of the Russian soul. Like metaphor and other cultural tropes (Fernandez 1986), Pesmen argues, the "soul gives form to unwieldy and inchoate pronouns." It is enigmatic, paradoxical, ambivalent, irrational, contradictory, and complex—much like the processes of transition in which the soul is a "vitally important player." In a refusal of closure that mirrors the structure and subject of her discussion, Pesmen shows how the soul distinctively "uses the form of the inchoate to give form to the inchoate." As such, the Russian soul is perhaps the most apt metaphor—both in the lives of the people of Omsk as well as for understanding the transition process more generally—for the inchoate that is the "transition."

Pesmen's point is thus a fitting way to conclude the volume. Like several of the essays, the book as a whole refuses closure. Instead, the authors aim through careful analyses of the contours, textures, landscapes, and utterances of everyday life to illuminate an ongoing and highly differentiated process of altering states. Some of the details of this moment of transition emerge in the ethnographies that follow.

NOTES

Many thanks to my coeditors, Matti Bunzl and Martha Lampland, for their incisive and very helpful comments on this introduction.

1. To use, as do many of these studies, a term made famous by Karl Polanyi (1944).

2. For critiques of this kind of "transition" literature, see, e.g., Kennedy 1994; Kideckel 1995; Verdery 1996.

3. For exceptions to this general emphasis in scholarly and popular accounts, see the work of journalists/nonfiction writers such as Hoffman 1993; Rosenberg 1995; Hafner 1995.

4. For discussions of particular dilemmas of doing field research in a postsocialist context, see De Soto and Dudwick, forthcoming.

5. For an account of this process in four Eastern European countries, see Rosenberg 1995.

Talking Transit and Spectating Transition: The Moscow Metro

Alaina Lemon

A drunken "New Russian" boards a tram and says to the driver: "Let's go to Lesnaja. I'll give you ten thousand bucks!"

"What? Sir, there are no rails!"

"Well, lay them. I'll pay a lemon [a million]!"

So the repair brigade lays rails. The tram moves slowly in the right direction. But when they approach the building there is a problem: the tram's way is completely blocked by mounds of earth, metal, and building materials.

"Oh, I forgot!" The passenger slaps his brow, "Yesterday I rerouted the metro this way!"

(sent by a Moscow reader to *Argumenty i Fakty,* July 28, 1996)

The joke targets the new rich: apparently not satisfied with the mobility afforded by personal BMWs, they want to reroute public transit. The Moscow metro frequently serves as a background to such anecdotes as well as to moral narratives and voracious arguments about what constitutes social order and chaos—especially since the late 1980s, when metro stations became precisely the places where "transition"[1] was most visible to inhabitants of the city. Along with viewing media reportage, riding public transit was how Moscow saw itself, it was where each day the masses encountered thousands of other faces, all somehow marked as belonging to fellow citizen or "alien."

But the structures of the metro alone do not determine all the twists of the tales.[2] Public transit narratives achieve forceful validity not only because they seem to be grounded in concrete spaces but also because they intersect familiar discourses and images depicting authority, culture, and belonging.

There is a long history in Russia of using public transit to talk about transition. Official Soviet descriptions opposed the metro to capitalist transport, which was described as having been built haphazardly for profit. The communists, these official texts bragged, would construct instead a well-planned passage to the future. A 1960s guide for visitors from friendly socialist Hungary recounts how the party opened the first eleven-kilometer section in 1935, contrasting the metro with backward czarist transit: "Before the Revolution, public transport in Moscow was very underdeveloped—there was hardly any tram service" (Kiss 1963, 89).[3] In the present, the tour book continues, everything is "built according to the most up-to-date construction principles" and is "automatic," from laser-equipped token machines to the trains themselves ("an electronic machine drives the high speed train instead of a human driver"—a development that, by the way, remained a fantasy).[4] A guide for English speakers promises that the future will bring "pedestrian underpasses with moving sidewalks" (*Moskovskoe Metro* 1978, 3). These descriptions showcase socialist modernity, the building of an infrastructure to support a future social order: "The Moscow metro will always be among the best in the world" (*Moskovskoe Metro* 1978, 4).

The Moscow metro can still evoke both utopian socialist dreams and "underground" irony about them, as hammer-and-sickle coats of arms remain impressed into the light blue, metal siding of some cars. The same cannot be said about the metro systems of other socialist-bloc capitals, such as Prague and Budapest. While Central European metros followed Moscow's tunnel design and utilized Soviet cars (sans hammer and sickle, however),[5] the stations in Prague and Budapest are uniformly decorated, displaying little or no socialist iconography. Moscow stations, in contrast, exhibit an impressive array of political ornamentations. Adorned by glowing marble, chrome, stained glass, intricate statuary, and mosaic work, each is a lived-in monument to socialism. Seventy meters under Red Square, the most central station, *Ploshchad' Revoljutsija* (Square of the Revolution, finished in 1938), is supported by eighty muscular, larger-than-life sculptures of young Soviets: crouching soldiers, poised athletes, and reading students—male and female—built into the columns. The columns of the 1938 *Majakovskaja* station, named for the futurist poet, are of innovative fluted, slender steel, while round, recessed ceiling mosaics are "skylights" onto parachutists, looping airplanes, blue sky, and orange trees—an homage to the cult of air exploration and to collective farms. The mosaics of the 1954 *Kievskaja* station mark "three hundred years of Ukrainian unity with Russia" and include panels on the "competition between the metallurgists of the Urals and the Donbass" as well as "Pushkin in Ukraine." *Belorusskaja* offers Stalinist, Norman Rockwell–esque murals of round country girls with apples in their aprons.

Hammer and sickle still decorate the carved archways that divide the platform at this station from the train tunnels. Deep escalators and watch booth are in the background.
(Photo courtesy of Nelson Hancock.)

The metro is such an obvious backdrop for political talk about social order or disorder in part because, alongside these older symbols of state stability, highly visible trade has multiplied next to refugees and beggars. While only tourists spend much time peering curiously into the bronze gun barrels dangling from oversized hands of Revolution Square heroes or marveling at the sparkling, mosaic sky at *Majakovskaja,* millions pass through these stations every day; and their readings of those carved and inlaid signs do not register blank. On the contrary, they are subject to change: favorite stations fall from grace, as when rumors circulated that the delicate marble for building *Kropotkinskaja* (prided for softly intricate lighting) had been mined from the Bolshevik-destroyed Church of Christ the Savior, now being rebuilt across the street from the station.

Yet in contrast with maps of former Soviet territory, metro maps have hardly changed. The graphic lines (over a city depicted as invisible white space) have not shifted, though some maps include advertising and may no longer mention that the metro is "named for Lenin."[6] The renaming of

An archway at the Square of the Revolution station (still thus named): a strapping bronze worker holds a jackhammer. The station is below GUM, the State Universal Department store, a nineteenth-century arcade of shops. By the early 1990s, GUM housed several foreign retailers, including Lego. (There is a Lego bag in the hand of one of the waiting girls.) (Photograph by Alaina Lemon.)

some stations on those maps also does not constitute significant change. Many post-Soviets note that they "forget" the new names, offsetting a hypostatized iconoclasm much celebrated in the West. Many station names have even remained untouched, despite echoing the language of Soviet ideology and institutions, such as *Oktjabrskaja* (for the October Revolution), *Shosse Entuziastov* (Enthusiast's Parkway), and *Chkalov-*

skaja (for the pilot-explorer Chkalov). Mocking or affectionately blasphe-
mous nicknames existed all along, such as *Boroda* (beard) for the former
Karl Marx station, but the renamed stations were not actually endowed
with those names—Karl Marx is now *Teatral'naja* (Theater), for example.
The metro in fact continues to regulate many stable social practices,
remaining a reference for calibrating practice to time and place (the auto-
mobile does not reign in Russia, and most people rely on public transit).
People still direct visitors by metro cars and platforms: "Take the Radial
Line, not the Circle Line, sit in the first car from the center, and wait for
me on the platform." The hour it closes (1:00 A.M.) still regulates, though
it does not end, nightly sociability.

Rather than dwelling on iconography *or* iconoclasm in the metro, I
focus here on the metro as a place-trope, a figurative setting in contesting
ontologies of a society in transition, alternately standing for totalizing
glory or uniform repression, social chaos or freedom, conformity or cultured sociability. In pursuing this focus, I stress verbal, visual, and textual
representations that juxtapose social activity with a spatial infrastructure,
often in attempts to "fit" social activity to structure in an iconic fashion.
Such juxtapositions within descriptions of place may suggest De Certeau's
parallel (à la the Saussurian distinction between langue and parole)
between walking and speaking—the former as "actualizing" space and the
latter as "acting out" language (De Certeau 1988, 98). However, while
some of his points are well taken (e.g., that space is multivalent, invested
as place), De Certeau's understanding of speech—as if the main transformative relations were between a speaker and a language structure
("manipulations of the basic elements" [1988, 100])—does not go far
enough. When it comes to social mediations of space, it is necessary to
have more levels of agency than the dyadic relation of an individual to a
built structure. In other words, articulations of space—and practices
enacted within them—draw from diverse spaces, cross media and genre,
and involve many speakers, if even indirectly. De Certeau likewise does
not distinguish discourse inside places from discourse referring to and
naming them and, moreover, does not take up the ways in which referring
to places indexes social relations going on both inside and beyond them.[7]
Thus, besides juxtaposing practices (walking in the metro) to names (talking about the metro), for instance, it is important to consider discursive
practices in and around the metro (talking with others there, talking about
how others walk there, and so forth).

I do not make these distinctions to oppose "direct" to "mediated"
experience. In fact, a theoretical issue I want to unsettle is that mass media
are distinct from face-to-face communication in being less culturally
authentic (see Debord 1994, 67). Public transit, in fact, turns out to be an

ideal site for stressing their similarities. On the one hand, public transport resembles neither mass media nor face-to-face interaction because it seems to offer no bounded "texts" or "local cultures." On the other hand, it resembles both because it simultaneously offers distant social pageantry and interactions with sometimes all too close, flesh-and-blood people. I make distinctions among levels of practice and discourse about public transport because I think this approach will better illuminate how people ground depictions of social change or stability by referring to a kind of place. Media constructions of state infrastructures reproduce material that people remember in face-to-face encounters and cite later, and what is said underground in the metro can reverberate aboveground.

Shifting Metropes, Social Order

De Certeau opens the chapter "Walking in the City" by describing a heady optical euphoria in looking over New York City from the World Trade Center (1988, 91). To perceive the city from a distant height, as an open text, pleasures the understanding. From here, it is not a place but an ideology, an order. But the streets, when not viewed but walked, are nothing like this view; walkers, he says, are "characterized by their blindness" (93). What is more, they are invisible, and

> beyond the reach of panoptic power. . . . Beneath the discourses that ideologize the city, the ruses and combinations of powers that have no readable identity proliferate; without points where one can take hold of them, without rational transparency, they are impossible to administer. (95)

The tunnels of the metro, even more than Moscow's streets, are surely hidden and unreadable from above. But authority works despite this fact; police and informers, like pedestrians, also devise invisible tactics on the ground. Thus, the seeming impenetrability of metro tunnels to panoptic attempts poses a paradox when authority and order are depicted both within and by means of the metro, whether in terms of political utopia or totalitarian repression, ultraconformity or culturedness.

Official Soviet discourse emphasized social stability and unity; the first stations were built by "thousands of volunteers." "Operations never stopped, even during the War" (*Moskovskoe Metro* 1978, 3). The stations already built provided shelter during German air raids, a function memorialized in later films about World War II.[8] The meters added each year signified social enthusiasm, while the building of metros in Prague, Budapest, Sofia, Warsaw, Calcutta, and Pyongyang (with Soviet advisers and plans) testified to a transnational social order. More locally, the metro well fit the Moscow city plan. As tour guides were instructed to inform, "The scheme of the metro corresponds to the plan of the city, repeats its historically laid radial-ring surface plan" (GKPIT, *Moskovskij Metropoliten* 1984). "Like blood vessels, the Moscow metro lines are dispersed in all parts of the city (*Moskovskoe Metro* 1978, 3)." According to the *Great Soviet Encyclopedia,* socialist metro design also fit social needs better than did capitalist city trains—no rattling aboveground structures, no gap, and underground halls designed according to "the method of socialist realism" so that the "impression of pressing weight" is absent and "pylons, columns and arcades emphasize lightness, freedom and spaciousness" ("Moskovskij Metropoliten" 1954, 331). The metro was also cheap ("in the future," public transit was going to be free) and the price of passage remained stable, with the five-kopeck fare not changing from 1935 until 1991.[9]

Many of these proud assertions were fair. Still, dissident and émigré writers disdained the metro as a Stalinist imposition: "The skyscrapers and the Moscow metro, the canals and dams were constructed only for him" (Groys 1993, 122). The "enthusiasts" who built the metro were, in these accounts, forced labor. Indeed, the belief that the metro was "for" father Stalin was reinforced by stories about a secret underground link to the Kremlin from his Moscow dacha (thus explaining the duplicate lines between *Arbatskaja* and *Kievskaja* stations). Besides manifesting Stalin's personal mania for monumental building, the metro, like the Soviet railway network joining all points to the Moscow center, is a trope for totalitarian ordering of modern space and motion, as some also have described the trains of America, England, and the colonies.[10] Svetlana Boym (1994b, 228) likens urban gridding under socialism to "official narratives that cut through the city like the Utopian lines of Stalin's Metro, the most efficient in the world" (the last phrase echoing the official discourse, perhaps tongue in cheek).

More recent accounts of key events in the USSR's breakup parallel these denunciations of dictatorial gridding, even showing contempt for metro passengers as themselves political automatons. For instance, during and after the August 1991 coup attempt, the Western media extolled themselves and electronic information technologies for shaping events, altogether ignoring or eliding the agency of people who lacked direct access to those means and who instead acted on information they gleaned in the streets or on the metro. Foreign correspondents thus emphasized the role of Radio Free Europe, the BBC, U.S. embassy satellites, and CNN, while Russians highlighted their own photocopying and telephone calling. It would certainly be foolish to deny that foreign media affected the content of rumor and information or enabled montages of local and faraway events (Boym 1994b, 217–20). But, mass media accounts of the role of mass media (made and preserved using these same media) remain the authoritative memory, silencing the accounts of people walking the streets and metro paths during those days.

During that August, I was living in a dormitory five bus stops from the station farthest south, *Prazhskaja* (Prague). In the wake of the events, people gathered in small clusters in the station's underpass, as they did throughout the metro and on the streets. Late on the second day of the coup, just outside the turnstiles, a woman returning from the center informed listeners what had happened to Gorbachev. She, too, stressed foreign sources—how the putsch had shut down television was always part of the story—but she had heard this information by word of mouth, on the street. Likewise, multitudes learned to tune into the migrating frequencies of the single, independently broadcasting radio station, *Ekho Moskvy* (Echo of Moscow), because the numbers had been pasted onto metro walls and cars and in the streets, along with Yeltsin's declaration.[11] People read these notices and discussed them on the spot, arguing and interrupting.

Foreign or elite memoirs of the coup, in contrast, described public transport as a site of general apathy or reactionary politics, as did the then director of Radio Free Europe/Radio Liberty:

> Of course, all too many Muscovites kept their heads down, waiting to see which way the wind was blowing before voicing any opinion about events. And there were several in buses and the subway who even argued in favor of the junta, hoping for a return to the Brezhnev stagnation when at least there was something to buy in the shops. (Iain Elliot in Bonnel, Cooper, and Freidin 1994, 292)

The formulaic evidential "of course" arguably reveals more about faith in the Radio Free Europe's mandate to propagate democracy as true representatives of a "free world" than about individual lack of "democratic" conviction within the hearts of the "all too many Muscovites," represented as anonymous riders of public transit. But Russian émigré scholar Gregory Freidin, during an interview with the then deputy of the Supreme Soviet and his sociologist wife, gives a similar, though more ambivalent account. He describes a lone activist on the metro, merely watched by more lumpen passengers:

> The train was half empty (it was 8:30 or so). A youngish, bespectacled man walked silently through our car, holding a pathetic handmade placard with the announcement of the big rally at the White House on Tuesday in condemnation of the putsch. Passengers, poker-faced,

looked at him in silence. There were no gestures of encouragement or, for that matter, hostility. At the next stop, the man walked out of the car and entered the next one. (Bonnel, Cooper, and Freidin 1994, 284)

These various observers had seen the action at the centers of power but had not seen the activity inside the metro earlier in the day. Indeed, had the coup planners shut down the metro, the people who poured from the station nearest the Parliament building (appropriately named *Barrikad-naja* [Barricade], in honor of wars past) could not have arrived to hedge it. Metro travelers can stand for political troglodytes or apathetic drones, but the metro was actually the single reliable vehicle for bringing the crowds to the site of resistance.[12]

At the same time, there is another, in some ways complementary, argument about Russian political nature. Some of the same people who denounce the metro as an emblem of totalitarianism may simultaneously insist that Russians, rather than being the ultimate political conformists, are the complete opposite, embodying resistance and disrespect for order as part of a specific national character bred by a proliferation of unjust and invasive rules. This trope, too, is often represented in terms of transit. Scorn for traffic lights and transit fares are frequently cited as evidence for this nature: "The Russian person, from the very beginning, is raised to disrespect the law, to show contempt for the rules of traffic and to try to get out of paying the fine if the police stop him" (Kirpichnikov 1996, 9). The traffic light example appears in a more subtle account of Russo-Soviet public culture in a vignette remarking the surprise of a Russian who saw an American stop at a crosswalk light moments after a Gulf War protest. Perceived American worship of law is opposed to Russian disdain for rules:

> For the Russian accustomed to routine violations of everyday prohibitions and cynical about the laws because they were part and parcel of the official order, this combination of simultaneous protesting and observing the rules is nearly inconceivable. In Russia, driving through a red light when the police are not watching is an acceptable practice; there, public opinion would be more critical of eating ice cream on the subway, a practice classified as foreign or "uncultured" behavior. (Boym 1994b, 289)

Set on the metro, this example of a resistant spirit that opposes culture to law deserves explication. It is surely doubtful that prohibitions on eating ice cream in the metro arise organically from Russian culture. Rather, such social expectations for public decorum were in fact inculcated by the very socialist programs, policies, and legal definitions that people claim to scorn. These phenomena (such as the liquidation of bad hygiene and illiteracy, among other civilizing projects)[13] remain a source of reference. Distinctions between "complacency" and "resistance" likewise are not always clear (Gal 1995); nor are those between "people" and "authorities" (Humphrey 1994).[14] Rejecting certain explicit rules may be meant to stand for rejecting the socialist order, but others (both explicit and implicit), no less a product of the old order, are accepted as more authentically "cultured."

Looking at some metro "traffic rules," both enforced and self-enforced, will clarify these points. On entering any aboveground station, one faces a row of turnstiles, operated by tokens that can be purchased at a nearby window.[15] Because of extreme inflation, newly fabricated tokens—made of translucent, green plastic imprinted with a metro logo—came into use in 1993. In July 1996, the city began to switch to a magnetic card fare-payment system (lest anyone mistake this change for a sign of transition, the magnetic cards have been in the works since the beginning of the 1980s [GKPIT, *Moskovskij Metropoliten* 1984]). The turnstiles have mechanical arms that open and shut like scissors. Every so often, if a passenger walks through them too quickly for the red laser eyes to register, they clamp shut, which is more frightening than painful, though many people visibly wince as they pass through.

Once inside, there are no controllers of the sort who appear suddenly on Moscow's buses or trams to check tickets punched according to an honor system (as there are in many European subways). On ground transport, fellow passengers can see who punches a ticket and who does not, a situation underwriting a scene in a famous 1970s film, *Gentlemany-Udachi* (Gentlemen of Fortune, a phrase also used to refer to pirates), where the pudgy hero, after rushing to his seat without punching his ticket, fumbles to get out his transit pass, which he waves, announcing to the public, "Edinij, Edinij!" (universal transit pass). The moment is familiar to many, even those who do not "ride rabbit," jumping off when controllers approach. On metro cars, however, there are no such dramas of conscience—people who use counterfeit passes do so at the turnstiles.

Near the turnstiles, in a glass booth, sits an older metro worker wearing a red armband; she watches the vestibule for suspicious activity and checks monthly passes, though perhaps not very thoroughly, as numerous people slip by with counterfeit, borrowed, or incorrectly subsidized discount passes. Most people, however, obey the system, waiting in line to buy the green tokens. When in 1996 I attempted to photograph the "Rules for Riding the Metro" that hung near one such booth, the metro worker emerged to prevent me from taking the picture, informing me that this act

The exit turnstiles at the Kiev station. On the right, Beash (Gypsy) women with children pass through. The sensors only trigger the scissor arms on the way in. (Photograph by Alaina Lemon.)

was forbidden without written permission. None of my Russian friends later interpreted her action as extreme: "she was thinking of terrorists." By that time in 1996, after a rash of bombings on Russian transport, special OMON forces in bulletproof vests also stood near the turnstiles.[16] Since May of that year, the mayor had been setting up brigades to patrol the underground and cars.

Another armbanded woman, armed with two telephones and a microphone, sits in a glass booth at the bottom of the escalators. She is supposed to regulate the escalators' direction and monitor passengers' behavior: when delinquent teenagers roll coins down the banisters or sit on the stairs, she chastises them: if people are blocking a side of the escalator, she issues a warning over the intercom: "Comrades, clear the space to the left." Or at least she used to; by the mid-1990s, in some stations she could hardly be heard over tape-recorded advertising of vacation trips to Egypt.

Still, the passing lane remains clear—hardly anyone needs to be told this rule, and if passengers transgress, those around will loudly tell them to clear the left.

There are no such booths at the bottom of the escalators in Prague and Budapest (they sit elsewhere), and the rule to leave the left clear, written in several languages near the escalators in Budapest, is neither enforced nor much valued there. Another Moscow spatial convention is that in crowded metro cars, people leave space on the bench for an imaginary sixth person; if a sixth person gets up, those remaining do not ooze into the vacated space or even place their shopping bags into it (they hold their bags carefully on their knees). Sometimes even after a fifth person exits, tidy spaces remain just the size for two new people. On benches of the same design in less crowded Prague, people inch over for a sixth person only at the last moment, as if doing a special favor. While working in Prague in 1995–96, I was visited by Russian friends who, seeing this behavior, jokingly declared Czechs to be "dikie ljudi!" (savage people). What people see as valid traffic rules, written or unwritten, differs, at the same time that Russians do not have a monopoly on transgressing those that exist.

Conversely, just as the American stopped for a red light after a protest,[17] the Russians who came by metro to the Parliament building during the 1991 coup did not ride escalator banisters, eat ice cream, or clog the left aisle any more than usual that day. They were not utterly passive and did not break all traffic rules. The extreme case for a peculiarly Russian (or peculiarly postsocialist) distrust of authority and structure seems not to hold, any more than the case for complete political apathy and backward conformism. "Even" in Russia, metro pedestrians can simultaneously protest some rules and observe others.

This discussion of resistance and complacency allows analysis of statements about social order or disorder set in the metro as related to genre and strategy rather than as merely descriptive narrative. While public transit can stand in for the good old—or bad old—order, it can also be a backdrop for social chaos. The mushrooming of commerce around the metro has changed the paths of travel less than it has their social rhythms: hawkers fill transfer tunnels and underground crosswalks, metro pedestrians hesitate over bubble gum or extremist newspapers,[18] combining tactics of shopping and commuting without detouring. The newness of these tactics is threatening to some, and some of the hawkers are perceived as violating licensing edicts or are figured as refugees or foreigners, breaking other conventions. These transgressions are read not as a rebellious Russian national character but as unlawful, inappropriate, and often foreign.

In 1995–96, the media frequently depicted the metro as a setting for the worst of the chaos of transition, a place where unrestrained streams of homeless and beggars sat side by side with the litter and leavings of commerce, where order had degraded:

> Most comfortable for the "businessmen" with outstretched hands is the Circle Line. . . . The Metro, stinking foulness nowadays, piled with trash . . . attracts them with large numbers of people (you always find kind ones), warmth (especially winter), and protection (though order here is not what it used to be, it still holds up). (Modestov 1996, 16)

Social disorders are imagined here in terms of human waste—people out of place. This excerpt framed a journalistic piece calling for the return of movement restrictions, laws prosecuting begging and "leading a parasitic life" that were rescinded in 1993. Metaphoric connections between nomadism and corrupted value remain salient in Russian discourse, figuring ideas about disorder and the loss of values in terms of the actual movements of people.[19] Moreover, the Soviet *propiska* system that required registration of residence with municipal authorities (implemented in 1932 in continuity with czarist regulations) is still in effect, and registrations in large cities like Moscow remain restricted. Economic liberals in Russia and some Western sociologists have argued that constraining population movement is incompatible with market reforms.[20] Advocates of restrictions claimed that the return of harsher punishments for "leading a parasitic life" would restore a lost economic and social order (though, of course, many people evaded those earlier constraints).[21]

Émigré scholar Vladimir Paperny (1993) claims that there is an oscillation in Russo-Soviet culture between movement/fluidity ("Culture One") and stasis/repression ("Culture Two"). As the beginning of a long phase of Culture Two, he cites the first law to settle Gypsies and schemes for urban planning.[22] While Paperny's metaphoric schema seems overly binary, so too do many of the equally figurative political arguments about movement and social order during the more recently presumed transition. In 1996 Paperny's essay was republished in Russian in the new magazine *Itogi* (a joint venture with *Newsweek*). Were later calls for crackdowns on movement read by post-Soviets as a "return" to Culture Two?

Social Pageantry and Moving Montage:
Exclusion via the Visible

> A daily forty-two minutes underground—a wall behind, faces ahead.
> —Russian pop singer Valerij Sjutkin (1996)

In June 1996, a bomb blast in the metro killed several people. One month later, in July, the state unveiled "harsh measures" against criminals, highlighted by beefed-up visa regulations. That same day a bomb exploded on a tram, and another blast occurred the next day. The first blast took place just before the first round of presidential elections and was blamed on "opposition forces" (that is, communists).[23] The second and third blasts took place after the second round, preceded a renewed round of fighting in Chechnya, and were blamed on Chechen rebels. After the third bomb, the mayor of Moscow pledged to sweep out *bomzhej i gastrolerej* (the homeless and illegal guest workers)[24] along with beggars and others. These people were to be identified according to what the mayor called their *vneshnij vid* (outward appearance).[25] That weekend, six thousand people—mainly Asians, Africans, and people from the Caucasus—were arrested for visa and *propiska* violations, and several of these incidents were shown on television.

This notion of *vneshnij vid* and its implication for political and social relations are important. Post-Soviets describe the metro both as a grand spatial structure befitting some ideological order and in terms of sights and interactions occurring there. Although the latter include visceral interactions, they convey brief impressions of outer appearances, as do the mass media. There is no Panopticon here; instances of seeing other people are sequential and fragmented. Moments of quick social interaction, like bargaining or jostling, punctuate the rhythm of the ride, alternating with more quiescent moments, such as watching masses rise up the opposite escalator. Swift as the deep escalators are, the ride is long enough to be hypnotic as the line of faces and hats flow past on the other side, lit by vintage iron lamps set into dark wood paneling between the escalator banks (in stations built by the 1950s).[26] Riding to deep platforms, the height and length of the line can stir vertigo. At the bottom, faces come closer again, belonging to bodies sidestepped, rammed, or accommodated.

The platforms seem calm after the commerce and jostling above. Alcoves and benches give some stations the look of a marble park, where columns carved into elaborate Corinthian leaves nestle Soviet stars. This is where many people meet, reading or watching those who descend gradually or who emerge from trains in abrupt waves. On the cars themselves, the arrangement of seating allows easy observation: padded benches line the car walls, facing each other. One can see what everyone else in the car reads, says, and does.

Pedestrians may later reflect on these brief moments, interweaving them with media images while reciting and constructing social hierarchies. Ethnographers impose readings on social activity. "Natives" can be equally guilty of this imposition, especially on mass transit. The natives of the metro certainly impose all manner of motive on the visible doings of strangers. People claim to know who and what Chechen traders or New Russians are because they have seen them—in passing, but every day— seen how they move, what they read, what they wear. Media images—such as the computer-generated "photo" of the bomber with generic "south- ern" features posted on every tram and bus that summer and speeches such as the mayor's promise to seek out the troublemakers according to *vnesh- nij vid*—enact and produce a grammar of surfaces.

Categorizing people by fleeting surfaces is not peculiar to Moscow. However, what people note has local cultural and historical resonance. Some people claim that the ability to place strangers according to dress has changed. For example, a Russian woman studying stage direction (a pro- fession demanding an acute sense of stereotypes and the ability to deploy them innovatively) explained that a Russian proverb, "Meet by dress, part by intellect," once made little sense to her. She said there had been too few differences in attire to judge by, at least compared to a West she imagined as a site of endless sartorial variety. As she put it, "I read Sherlock Holmes long ago, but we did not understand how he made conclusions about char- acter by a man's trousers or the cut of his coat: we wore whatever they were selling, it never had any connection with character whatsoever" (author's interview 1992). Dress now is said to reflect passing strangers' financial status, though it may have been so previously to a greater extent than some remember. Things that once marked a person as elite have become more commonplace. For instance, furs have become more uni- form, signifying differently than before, since "women no longer save the fur for evenings at the theater, but now wear them even to walk the dog," as I was told by a Russian woman who herself favors Goretex (author's interview 1996). Before the early 1990s, clothes also marked Western for- eigners more clearly. By a few years later, Westerners became less easy to pick out, because more Muscovites were buying imported clothes and shoes.

Not everyone sees such blurring of former markers as proper. In 1991, on an old bus leaving a metro stop far from the center, I saw a grand- mother curse at a Russian family of four dressed in identical synthetic aqua and purple Adidas running suits: "What are you going to do next, speak English?" she spat. Conversely, in combination with complexion, some kinds of imported dress, such as colored silk men's shirts, have become visual signs of internal "foreigners," such as marketers from the "South."

Impressions made on public transit take on additional significance because changes (particularly the rise of commerce at metro stations around the city) are most visible here. Of course, one could purchase official maps that pinpointed state shops next to metros well before 1991. And informally, some stations were long known for what was "speculated" near them. Close to *Akademicheskaja* (Academic), outside the shop *1001 Melochej* (1001 Trifles), one could find hawkers selling faucet washers, doorbells, and plastic planters. Across the street from *Lubianka* (the name of the headquarters of the former KGB and new name of the metro there), the sidewalk outside *Detskii Mir* (Children's World, a gigantic emporium for children's clothing and toys) was home in the early 1990s to one of the largest illicit bazaar crowds within the city proper. By 1996, that crowd was gone, dwindling to a few hawkers of Pampers in the underpass. Near the stations, there always had been newspaper kiosks, ice cream stands, and ticket booths (along with the occasional woman semi-illicitly peddling flowers). A few of them opened onto large, semiofficial produce markets. Still, most commerce in the metro was prohibited until the 1990s, when the underground transfer tunnels became even more dense with small-time hawkers.[27]

One factor that sets metro trade apart from commerce in other venues—and makes it more available for political rhetoric—is its stark visibility. Even by the 1990s, space for shops in prominent or central buildings was limited and expensive. Many of the shops that existed had draped windows or were off the common paths connecting public transport. Only locals knew them. At first, the nonstate kiosks at subway entrances or in underpasses were made of plywood, and trading was conducted on folding tables or cardboard boxes. Some of these edifices remain, but more permanent structures have edged closer to the metro proper, with transparent materials the favorite medium. The newer shops in the metro underpasses and streets just above them are thus not only in highly visible locations but are made almost entirely of glass. Everything inside these shops is therefore immediately discernable; it all "throws itself into the eyes," as a Russian phrase goes.[28]

This visibility of shopping is only somewhat comparable to the much calmer, more institutionalized commerce inside the Prague or Budapest metros. There, one sees display cases for aboveground shops, closed-in newspaper or flower stands, shops set fully into the underpass walls rather than built like barnacles along the sides. There are even full-scale chain boutiques. In fact, most well-trafficked shops there are located safely overhead, within stone walls, and not alongside transport. In Moscow, ever more merchants line the underpass walls with glass casings wide enough for a few goods, a stool, and a salesperson. These glittering surfaces narrow the space for pedestrians.

What is more, these surfaces potentially contrast with the glowing social realism farther down. While the walls of metros in other postsocialist states are covered by advertisements, those down inside the Moscow metro are not; there is no room for them among the statuary, built into the columns themselves. Both communists and democrats, reformists and conservatives, express surprise or outrage that Stalin's metro is the setting for the most visible new sites of commerce as well as for the signs of class division—merchants above and beggars below, sitting under those happy, marble socialist maidens and heroes. Perhaps the platforms housing the monumental murals seem less profane than the transfer passageways, for, as in churches, merchants are not allowed on the platforms, while beggars are not driven off so quickly and even work in the cars.[29] Even liberal authors (such as this one, described in an American press article stressing the slow, stable growth of a "middle class" in Russia) call the juxtaposition shocking, though preferable to the previous order: "We always said we had no homeless, but they were hidden from the public's view. Now we have beggars in the metro. This is terrible, but normal. But to collect war invalids and expel them to a place to die—this is not normal. I prefer terrible freedom to clean totalitarianism" (Alexander A. Kabakov, quoted in C. J. Williams 1996). The reference is to World War II veterans and invalids; declared suspect after returning from the POW camps, many were expelled beyond the 101st kilometer, in accordance with the registration constraints discussed previously. More shocking than seeing those beggars and hawkers in the metro are aboveground legal structures—and social relations—to which such sightings can be connected.

Non-Russians are likewise "visible and audible emblems" for uncomfortable relations, including accusations of past colonialism and present war.[30] The visible aspect of relations between Russians and non-Russians is trade. Many non-Russians, excluded from other kinds of employment, have been visible for a long time as semi-illicit traders in Moscow. It is not unusual to label commodities and ethnic groups as fetishes of each other: "Korean spiced carrots," "Vodka-speculating Gypsies." Such everyday, brief observations are used as points of reference to extend faulty deductions about imagined proclivities invariably seen as dangerous. Russian newspapers thus dispense hints on how to read these proclivities by *vneshnjy vid.* They advise readers to "avoid contact on the street" (Bogartyrev 1996) with unknown women, "especially if they have a vivid eastern appearance" ("Tsygane Shumnoju Tolpoju" 1996). Some of the outward signs of "eastern appearance" may be big earrings, colorful skirts, head scarves, gold teeth, and, most notably, a swarthy complexion. Not heeding these signs is thought to carry the risk of being hypnotized, swindled, cheated, or bombed. Such tropes connecting complexion or appearance to social hierarchies and divisions have a long history, despite official attempts

A bustle of low-end hawking just outside one of the entrances to the Kiev station. A well-heeled (Russian?) woman walks by clutching a Clinique shopping bag. Her gaze seems to fall on the group of Kelderash-Romani (Gypsy) women (gathered center) who trade and do readings at this bazaar. (Photograph by Alaina Lemon.)

at eradicating racism. Well before the breakup of the USSR or the war in Chechnya, slurs such as *chernozhepy* and *negativy* were current.[31]

The first time anyone spoke aloud to me of the charged significance of racialized markers in Russia was, in fact, after an encounter on the Moscow metro in 1990. I was riding with a Romani man, the husband of a Romani scholar. I caught a cold glare from the opposite bench and asked him why those people looked at us with hostility. His answer: "Because I am black and you are white."[32] In 1992 I heard such an observation from the reverse vantage: a young Russian girl was riding with someone who could have been Georgian or Armenian, and my friends clucked in low tones, "Bednaja, ona sebja ne tsenitsja! Chernij on takoj" (Poor girl, she doesn't value herself. What a black one [he is]).

Soviet policies were supposed to "raise the cultural level" of such national minorities. In a Russian monograph published in 1990 a vignette illustrating the assimilative battle against ways of life rightfully "vanishing" is set in the metro:

> In the Metro, at the station *Sokol'niki,* two old Gypsy women entered the wagon. Each had at her back a sort of sack holding babies who could barely hold up their heads, which, like balls, bounced with the jerking of the wagon. . . . Suddenly, a young black-haired fellow in a severe gray suit rose from a seat near us and, attentively peering into the Gypsies' eyes, uttered a few sharp words in Gypsy. The old ladies went dumb and became meek. They got out at the next station. . . . We approached him:
> "Please forgive our indiscretion, but what did you say to them?"
> "I am a worker, a smith, my father was a smith. We always worked for a living and never begged. But those—they are used to begging, their heads are fogged, they don't even understand that they shame themselves and all of us. I told them 'Your children must study, go home and wash them.'" (Druts and Gessler 1990, 311)

This text appeared on the last pages of the book, framing a generalized account of "Gypsy culture." While the vignette made no mention of historical reasons some Roma beg, elsewhere in the book begging is listed in passing as a "traditional" occupation. The idea that Gypsies ignore Russian, public disapproval—and hardly care for the "public opinion" of their "own kind"—dovetails with stereotypes of inherent Gypsy asocial behavior. However, most Roma do partake of Soviet and Russian practices and rules, and when they debate what this participation means, it need not be in such accidental, public encounters. Still, the authors chose to set such a clash in a metro, shifting the significance of debates about assimilation from other possible locales, such as a Romani home. Because the setting was public, the authors could maintain the narrative conceit of framing themselves as the accidental witnesses of a spontaneous event. This technique allowed them to present it dramaturgically as a dyadic clash between a "cultured Gypsy" and his "wild" counterparts, with the passengers, symbolic of the rest of society, reinforcing the lines of this opposition.

Setting reported action or speech in a public space also "deplaced" it, authorizing it as general—a usual occurrence, easily verified—and thus functioning similarly to the way "devoicing" props the perceived objective authority of speech or text.[33] This setting framed Gypsies as representing a general social problem via visceral, visual detail: babies' heads jerking in

unison with the wagon lurches, iconically anchoring the women to a physical metro car.[34]

Many Roma, if they could afford it, avoided public transport in
Moscow during the 1990s, sensing eyes upon them as part of an order
from which they felt excluded. Some "blacks" even kept themselves under
self-enforced house arrest when Moscow Mayor Yuri Luzhkov issued a
"temporary" decree, after the October 1993 White House burning, requir-
ing visitors to pay to register or face expulsion. Subsequent sweeps of the
bazaars by the authorities (OMON special forces) targeted "blacks."[35]
Even before, Roma spoke of feeling surrounded on buses that were full of
"Russians."

One of the most striking stories a Romani girl told me about being
marked as "black" was set on the metro, her narrative tellingly illustrating
the interpenetration of mass media and discursive practices on public transit. In 1991, well before the war with Chechnya broke out, a Moscow cab-
driver was killed by an Azeri; for months thereafter, it was nearly impossible for people with a "southern" (Caucasian) appearance to successfully
hail a cab. The same held true for those Roma who did not look typically
Gypsy and who, because of "European" dress (including designer silk
shirts), were accustomed to being mistaken on sight for other suspect
"blacks":[36]

> Once we couldn't get a cab at all, so we took the Metro. We saw how
> all the *Gazhe* [Russians][37] were reading, and my cousin started saying,
> "What are they writing? What are they writing?" They thought he was
> crazy. All the other black people, Armenians and such, were smiling.
> They knew. "What are they writing about us blacks, eh?" One old
> lady said, "They are writing that we need to kill you all, that you are
> robbing us, and we are becoming poor." Then another black said,
> "We should kill *you.*" My brother laughed and said, "No, no, you
> don't have to kill her—this is a *good, fat, Russian* woman." We
> laughed so hard, we had to get off the train there![38]

These Roma knew how the press described them and evoked a comparable form of visual typing ("This is a *good, fat, Russian* woman") to flip a
newspaper's power to ascribe racialized hierarchies. Usually depicted as
part of the scenery or fauna of public transport, they had no access to mass
media to express their constructions of metro experience. Thus the question, "What are they writing about us blacks?"—a phrase that my Romani
consultant repeated several times—had both immediately amused the
other "blacks" and enraged the old woman.

Although it formally requested information, the intended function of the question about mass media production was to remark on social circumstances, to make a bald metapragmatic comment about ongoing communication within metro space.[39] The deictic, *they,* both indexed a distant center of authority (Russian writers and editors) and implied a proximal *you* (Russian passengers), performatively collapsing a pronominal distinction and implying among several other readings: "What are [you Russians reading] about us blacks?" The question was deliberately provocative.[40] The Soviet public famously prided itself on being the most literate population in the world, on reading everywhere—in queues, on transport. These Roma were in fact literate,[41] but on the metro they watched a (post-)Soviet public read the same newspapers that excluded Gypsies. To ask directly about this reading was to speak of being shut out (in space) by that print (in mass media), to metaphorically index a nonimagined, anticommunity with Russians.[42]

Conclusion

Metro building continues apace in the capital and in the provinces. In May 1996, Yeltsin laid the first ceremonial stone for the first metro station in Ufa, the capital of Bashkirya. Meanwhile, in Moscow, metro construction (costing four trillion dollars in 1996) and architectural renovation projects are at the center of Chicago-style debates, linking corruption, waste, and the mayor's office. For people with an interest in depicting the stability of the current state, public transit can be used as a setting for a benign order that combines new and old. Consider a video clip titled *Russkij Projekt* that aired repeatedly throughout 1996 as part of a series of shorts made for television, varying humor and nostalgia with soft social propaganda: The clip opens with early morning darkness. A famous aging actor plays a tram driver; there are no passengers. A happy golden light fills his tram and lights his features. A beautiful, young, jean-jacketed actress emerges from a doorway on rollerblades as the tram passes and, hooking onto the back of the tram with an umbrella, lets it pull her, the wind blowing her pale, blond hair. She releases her hold as the tram approaches the main building of Moscow State University and skates off into that Stalinist birthday-cake structure. The title of the clip appears under the tram: "This Is My City." Here, sexy traffic-rule breaking combines with a working infrastructural transit order inherited from the past—as embodied by the elderly driver and the Stalinist skyscraper—to produce a patriotic and cozy statement about belonging in the capital.

The examples at hand offer quite varied oppositions (of past utopia to present chaos, of past dictatorship to present opportunity, of wealth to need, of Russia to the West, of patriots to refugees to terrorists). None of these contrasts are generated by some sum of individual encounters with spaces or strangers within the metro (the encounters as *parole* to a metro space as *langue*); immediate spatial experience—contingent as it may be in time or place—underdetermines the construction of ideologies about social order. The oppositions are reproduced by interlocutors who cite from many arenas, including the media, which their experiences even come to resemble as if they were glimpses of some tip of the social mass. Specific oppositions about transit are made in relation to general political and social concerns about movement, money, and people after a regime shift. Talk about transit, its practices and infrastructures, really concerns who should be included in the city, in the nation.

NOTES

Part of the research for this article was conducted under a grant from the International Research and Exchanges Board, with funds provided by the National Endowment for the Humanities, the United States Information Agency, and the U.S. Department of State, which administers the Russian, Eurasian, and East European Research Program (title VIII). I also received a U.S. Department of Education Fulbright-Hayes Doctoral Dissertation Research Abroad Fellowship. I thank several people who took the time to read drafts of this chapter, who suggested angles and turns to consider, and whose comments steered me up the right track: Miklós Vörös, Maria Lemon, Peter Rutland, Richard Handler, and the three editors of this volume.

    1. I use the term with the usual caveats (that it is arrogant to assume a transition from something to something else) but preserve it here as a term used by Muscovites.

    2. See, e.g., Foucault 1984, which argues that architectural structures do not determine social relations or subjectivity but are "rigorously indivisible" (253).

    3. When the metro was still being planned, "to the dismay of many, Moscow was still, essentially, a medieval city—its special layout in no way facilitated the flow of persons and goods. . . . Traffic jams, narrow streets, and floods clearly had no place in the socialist city. In the name of 'socialist efficacy' whole districts were razed, churches were destroyed, and streets were widened" (Bittner n.d.). Bittner notes that these ideals were not peculiar to socialist states and can be found in imperial Russian plans. The point is rather that planners declared the socialist city to be different. See also Starr 1984 on 1930s' debates between urbanist and so-called antiurbanist architects, their schemes of transport, and transportable homes.

    4. Real, living metro drivers enjoy no small power. In recent years, every time they threatened to go on strike, their demands were met immediately, and they make well over the average salary.

    5. The oldest line of the Budapest metro recently was refurbished, and the

non–Soviet style cars that operate on it were used as stages for the 1995 opening. It is worth observing how diplomatic changes will affect public transport infrastructures in the former socialist bloc and the old division of labor in production: Hungary's Ikarusz plant made the buses, Prague made the tram cars, and Moscow made the subway cars. While Budapest sports shiny new Ikarusz buses, many of their counterparts in Russia are decades old, and newer buses there are second-hand Mercedes.

6. Until the 1950s the metro was actually named for Kaganovich.

7. Basso notes that "statements about the landscape may be employed strategically to convey indexical messages about the organization of face-to-face relationships and the normative footings on which these relationships are currently being negotiated" (1992, 223).

8. Such as *Cranes Are Flying* (1959).

9. In 1984, average salaries ranged from 150 to 300 rubles a month. As of 1996, one metro token cost 1,500 rubles, and an average salary was about 700,000 rubles a month at the beginning of the year.

10. De Certeau (1988) devotes a short chapter to comparing train compartments to prison cells. See also Spivak (cited also in Boyarin 1994): the train "is a widely current metonym for the unifying project of territorial imperialism" (1989, 284).

11. The radio station changed frequencies several times a day to escape jamming.

12. Furthermore, parts of the metro itself (sections of escalators) and of other public transit systems (entire tram cars) were important barricade material during the coup attempt.

13. See, e.g., Fitzpatrick 1993.

14. It should be noted, though, that to ethnic or linguistic minorities, metro authorities and the cultured "public" may align as a Slavic majority.

15. For decades, a five-kopeck piece served as a token. One could change higher-denomination coins in metal machines hanging on the station walls.

16. OMON was a special SWAT unit of the police, heavily armed and armored.

17. In general, Muscovites rarely face the choice of ignoring a "don't walk" sign, since most pedestrian crosswalks pass under the streets rather than above them. Moreover, drivers weigh transgression against possible fines, and pedestrians weigh convenience against the chance of serious injury.

18. Several authors have focused on the contents of hawkers' tables in the 1990s, on the fascinating jumble of contradictory, formerly banned stuff for sale. Some of these observations compare this phenomenon to Benjamin's observations of NEP-era commercial license (see Boym 1994b; Condee 1995). Here, I focus on the location of commerce rather than the arrays of things sold or their origin (see Humphrey 1995).

19. Writing on nineteenth-century social thinkers who opposed the physical body to the social body, Catherine Gallagher (1986) finds in Malthus a suspicion of "urban and suburban wanderers" and their "speculation" that did not "alter the material world" and thus added no value (91).

20. "While the operation of the passport and propiska system was quite similar to market-based signals in terms of individual perceptions of costs and benefits, the non-migration functions of the passport and propiska, or registration system, operated in an anti-market fashion" (Buckley 1995, 896).

21. In effect, lack of a *propiska* stopped movement less than it "prevented migrants from integrating themselves into distribution networks in restricted cities" (Buckley 1995, 896).

22. A 1956 Soviet law dealt with nomadic Roma (Gypsies) more strictly. In practice, they were denied residence within the "101st kilometer" of certain cities, along with the déclassé, ex-prisoners, and, nowadays, many refugees. Some of the largest cities closed to such marginals were the ones relatively open to foreign tourists, for example, Kiev, Moscow, and Leningrad.

23. "Reactions to Bomb Blast" 1996.

24. The Western press translated this word as *Gypsies*. Although Roma, like other non-Russians, were in practice also subject to document checks, Mayor Luzhkov did not specifically utter the word *tsygane*. The translation appears to be an imposition of the Anglo sense of *Gypsy* as "traveler." However, the Russian press certainly reinforced such visual connections by broadcasting shots of guards and dogs searching metro cars, with the camera lingering on Romani beggars.

25. ORT, Evening News broadcast, July 12, 1996.

26. This parade of faces moved dissident writer Tertz to close the story *Little Jinx* with a metro image:

> Just imagine for the sake of clarity an escalator in Moscow's deep-sea Metro. [People] were being taxied by conveyor from the world beyond to meet the bloodless party of exhibits while we were plunging down the shaft, finding ourselves powerless to distance ourselves from or merge with the parallel flow, unconsciously scanning the hierarchy of wide browed statues being erected from the bowels of the earth with their tensely propped profiles thrust forward as if they shunned intersecting with or accidentally running into our sinister stream, which was slowly and inexorably dispatching us downward. And who knows? The next time we might have been able to swap places on the conveyor belt; but for some reason that didn't dawn on anyone. Each kept to his own little stair, avoiding the opposite stream. Exchanging glances or greeting with a nod seemed out of the question. (1992, 78)

27. There are practical reasons commerce always has gravitated to the metro. Moscow is a gigantic city. Some groceries were scattered within apartment blocks but were not well stocked (a true cliché). Most people lacked cars and had to ride the metro to find what they wanted. In contrast, hard-currency shops (and later, in the early 1990s, fancier shops specializing in foreign produce) were farther from the metro. The wealthy have cars or ride in taxis. Thus by the early 1990s, small entrepreneurs set up in or around the metro stations, where the masses walked. People might swear about the inflated metro prices, but there was no guarantee of finding the goods at all otherwise. Even by 1996, though well-stocked supermarkets had proliferated and were easier to find, shoppers still had to carry heavy bags

home over public transport, and it remained exhausting to leave one's path to seek goods in this incredibly vast city in which a commute home may take two hours. One of the criteria of a nice flat remains proximity to any metro station. Sometimes the goods offered at the neighborhood metro are even considered better and cheaper than those bought in the store—trucks may pull up with milk fresh from the dairy, and there is no need to add costs for salaries or rent.

28. Foreign products are the most visible; the only domestic goods framed by glass are bread and chocolates. At first, imported luxury goods (designer lipsticks and sparkly shoes) prevailed. By 1995, minidrugstores had opened within every metro station, selling aspirin and Band-Aids, mostly imported. Some people considered this a new convenience, but others complained that these stores did not fill prescriptions, sold nothing "really necessary," and charged too much for everything.

29. Playing musical instruments within the metro system is an offense punishable by fine, but musicians play in the passageways anyway. There, they do not compete with the noise of passing trains and are evicted less quickly.

30. Gallagher's hawkers are "guilty of embodying and hence raising to the surface of consciousness a ruthless struggle for marketplace advantage that Mayhew thinks is going on everywhere unseen." An Irish woman who sells strawberries is a "visible and audible emblem of the sexual and economic exploitation that goes on behind doors and has driven her onto the street" (1986, 101).

31. For example, as documented before World War II by Roback 1979.

32. What is considered "black" or "dark" in much of Russia might be constructed as "olive" or, more euphemistically, "ethnic looking" in the United States. This is by no means to say that Russian-style racism is more extreme but only that the markers are set differently. Generally, the category also includes people from the Caucasus and sometimes from Central Asia. Africans are (in the most neutral terms) called "Negry."

33. Such does not have to be the case. On devoicing, see Silverstein's (1988) critique of Bakhtin and Barthes. On how visual detail (in a text) can elide (realtime) social pragmatics, see Crapanzano (1992). Contentions aside (from Ronald Reagan on) that Russian has no word for "private," the fact remains that metro spaces do not melt into living spaces. In fact, many Russian words can signify different senses of "private" for which English speakers use one word. In any case, as much as values of Russian public-private distinctions differ from those in the United States, they do exist in discourse (on coding women as belonging to the "private" in Hungary, see Gal 1996).

34. See also Appadurai 1992 on how places and cultures come to stand for each other, "peoples" "incarcerated" within places and cultures.

35. See Human Rights Watch—Helsinki 1995.

36. See also Humphrey 1993 for a discussion of how Russians mistook Central Asian refugees for Gypsies.

37. *Gazhe* (plural) can mean any non-Romani people, but most Roma I know in Russia define it as "Russian."

38. This excerpt appears in another context in Lemon 1995.

39. "Insofar as text represents events, particularly events of using languages, the text is explicitly a metapragmatic discourse about such events" (Silverstein 1991, 35).

40. Developing Silverstein's assertion that "natural languages generally only have partially explicit metapragmatics" (1991, 39), Crapanzano (1992) argues that representing the social relations in speech events in bare indexical terms ("metapragmatic indexicality") is awkward—the reaction of the Russian woman and laughter of the Roma may be taken as evidence of this difficulty among strangers in post-Soviet Russia.

41. Gypsies are stereotyped as illiterate, and indeed, official rates of formal illiteracy throughout Europe for Roma can reach 70 percent. These rates supposedly are also high in Russia; however, during my fieldwork, not only were many of the Roma I met literate in Russian, but some could also read a bit of English.

42. This is a pun, of course, on Anderson's (1983) formulation, due respect intended.

To Hear the Voices Still Heard: On Synagogue Restoration in Eastern Europe

Philip V. Bohlman

Prayer at Europe's Largest Synagogue

"It's closed. There's no place to pray."

The voice that greeted me in English, with a discernible Hebrew accent, was gentle, but it startled me nonetheless, as I passed from gate to gate around the Dohány Street Synagogue, hoping to find a lock that someone had forgotten to secure. In 1995–96, I had often tried to find ways to visit synagogues in Eastern Europe, almost always finding someone, official or unofficial, who had a key and could let me visit. I was, however, always uneasy, not so much from a fear of being caught while trespassing as from the nervousness of finding myself alone, with no one to help me understand the abandoned spaces of the synagogues. Budapest, with some twenty-seven synagogues still officially in use, should have been different. Especially at the Dohány Street Synagogue—famous for being Europe's largest synagogue and for occupying the place where the founder of Zionism, Theodor Herzl, was born—it should have been different. It was and it was not.

The Dohány Street Synagogue was at the end of a three-year renovation, and it would open again on the eve of the High Holidays (the first Sabbath services would take place on September 6, 1996). Signs on the entrances and gates announced to all who might want to visit that renovation was under way, but they offered little advice about what to do if one was not simply a visitor or tourist—if, for example, one wanted to pray.

Perhaps because of my nervousness, perhaps because I cannot speak Hungarian but still wanted to dispel some aspect of my foreignness, I guessed that the voice startling me was that of an Israeli. I responded in Hebrew, guessing right, "No, there's no place to pray, but there used to be. I was here in 1991, just at the High Holidays, and they prepared the sanctuary for prayer at that time. Surely, when these renovations are done, there'll be a place to pray."

"Perhaps, but that does not solve our problem, does it?" queried the Israeli, willingly making his problem "our" problem. I realized—which is to say, I had forgotten—that it was Friday, and services for *erev shabbat,* Friday evening, would take place soon. Though I am not Jewish, I do attend Friday evening services on occasion, for reasons both professional and personal. The silence of the Dohány Street Synagogue, baking in the unseasonably hot midsummer sun, was not promising.

We saw a sign hanging from another gate. Advice for those seeking an alternative synagogue in which to observe tradition during the renovation, we thought. As we walked to the sign, however, we realized that it did not address our interests at all. In Hungarian and English, the sign informed us of the possibility of helping "to finance the renovation of the Synagogue and it's [*sic*] Organ" through the purchase of a charitable phone card costing "50$ or 70 DM or 5500Fr."

With the phone card we could call locally or internationally, thereby supporting—as the phone card's paper simulacrum informed us—the "organ fund." Our voices would return the voice to the Dohány Street organ, a grand pipe organ that had accompanied an equally grand mixed chorus. I knew the organ and chorus of the synagogue from cassettes I had purchased at Budapest kiosks five years earlier. Even then, the need for renovation was obvious, but Hungary did not yet have phone cards; no country in Eastern Europe did. For my Israeli companion this was too much. By talking on the phone, one could contribute to a fund for a Jewish musical practice that was not permitted in Israel; there is no place in Israel's synagogues for musical instruments in general, let alone organs, the symbol of assimilation and Christian musical traditions. But could this phenomenon be what assimilation, with its suggestion of sameness and the disappearance of differences between "us" and "them," is all about? After all, the Dohány Street Synagogue, built in 1859 after a design by Ludwig von Forster, is a marvelous example of Moorish style, its evocation of the East, *mizrakh,* as unmistakable as its representation of a mosque (Gruber 1992, 157).

For my Israeli companion, everything began to fit together, just as nothing fitted together. This was Budapest, it was 1996, he stood before one of the great monuments to the European Jewish past, phone cards had returned the voice of Ashkenazic liturgical music to the organ. But there was still no place to pray at the Dohány Street Synagogue.

Entrance to Dohány Street Synagogue, Budapest: *Zsinagóga Felújítás* (Renovation of the Synagogue). (Photograph by Philip Bohlman.)

Ethnography, Narrative, and the Voice of Music

For Jews and Jewish communities, the transitions of the new Eastern Europe are rife with contradiction and paradox. At best, they are to be greeted with trepidation; at worst, they are to be survived with fear. Fundamental to the Jewish confrontation with transition in Eastern Europe is the question "transition from what, to what?" During the Cold War, Jews remained largely invisible, and Jewish communities remained in a quiet,

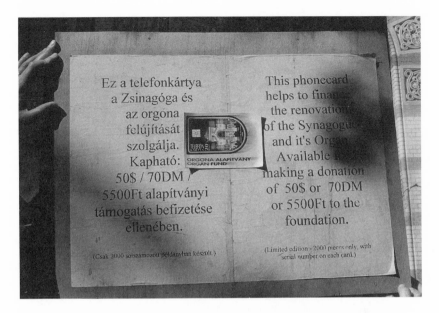

Ez a telefonkártya a Zsinagóga és az orgona felújítását szolgálja. Kapható: ORGONA ALAPíTVÁNY ORGAN FUND 50$ / 70DM / 5500Ft alapítványi támogatás befizetése ellenében.

(Csak 2000 sorszámozott példányban készült.)

This phonecard helps to finance the renovation of the Synagogue and it's Organ. Available by making a donation of 50$ or 70DM or 5500Ft to the foundation.

(Limited edition - 2000 pieces only, with serial number on each card.)

Sign announcing phone card to support renovation of the Dohány Street Synagogue and its organ. (Photograph by Philip Bohlman.)

unnoticed diaspora across a historical, atavistic landscape, much of which—Romania, Poland, the Baltic states—had previously been "the world's Jewish heartland, home to millions of Jews" (Gruber 1992, 2; Kohlbauer-Fritz 1993).

The massive destruction of the Holocaust notwithstanding, many surviving Jews in Eastern Europe attempted to rebuild their communities as well as they could. Initial attempts to return and rebuild communities constitute one of the least documented chapters of post-Holocaust history. Those who chose to return did so, initially at least, in an attempt to locate lost family members—which is to say, to be present if and when they returned. Even in the 1990s, there are Jewish residents in many of the most remote towns and regions of Romania and Ukraine. Most are elderly, and most cannot fully account for their reasons to remain in what they know as their homes. Many serve as caretakers for the Jewish community, tending often to the needs of the synagogue, even when it is rarely used for community functions. All fully recognize that the historical pattern most characteristic of their communities has been that of departure, for the exits of their coreligionists provide the most vivid markers of recent history.

The historical transition during the second half of the twentieth century was exodus or, more precisely, exit: exit from Eastern Europe if the historical dynamic moved forward, or exit into history if it did not (Hoffman 1993). These exits, however, were troubled forms of transition: they settled nothing. "Transition from what, to what?" Prior to communism, there had been fascism and the Holocaust (Dohrn 1991); prior to the Holocaust, there were periods of brilliant cultural achievement punctuated by pogrom (Dohrn 1994). The transitions of the past took place on landscapes with names that do not reflect the political realities of the 1990s: Galicia, Silesia, the Bukovina, the Pale (Applebaum 1994). How could there be a transition to a past that resides only in personal memories and memoirs (see, e.g., *Otsarot Genuzim* 1994; Pollack 1984; Landmann 1995)?

In this essay I focus on one of the two most powerful symbols of the return to Jewish Eastern Europe made possible by the political revolutions of 1989: synagogues—more precisely, the attempts to restore synagogues as an act of transition itself. In the post-Holocaust era the destruction of synagogues was synonymous with the destruction of Eastern European Jewry. Metaphorically, the synagogue represented the community, the *bet knesset,* the "house of gathering." As a structure, the synagogue took on meaning only by containing a community. The narratives of destroyed and closed synagogues have proliferated as a leitmotif through Holocaust literature and ethnography, especially in Eastern Europe. In János Nyiri's Bildungsroman of a Hungarian boy's wartime coming-of-age in Budapest, for example, the novel ends when the family returns to its village synagogue, only to discover that the village's Jews had been killed or had disappeared into the death camps. The boy's mother goes to the village hall to demand that the synagogue be locked and sealed from further use, without any attempt to repair it. The final words of the novel, literally and metaphorically, are the words of the dead, transformed into song but now emanating from beyond the walls of the synagogue. Nyiri's novel is, of course, fictional, but its use of the synagogue as a metaphor for the destruction of Eastern European Jewry arrests readers' attention through its familiarity. For the Holocaust itself is the protagonist's *shul,* his "synagogue" in Yiddish, *Die Juden-Schule* of the novel's German title (Nyiri 1992). The weight of the metaphors of destruction and closure is so great, in fact, that any kind of transition would seem impossible.

The other symbol for the return to Jewish Eastern Europe, the cemetery, might also have served as a focus for this essay, for, like the synagogue, it, too, is the goal of many Jews' pilgrimages to Eastern Europe (Gruber 1994; Dohrn 1994, 19–52). In fact, the two symbols have complementary functions; both embody the transitions of Eastern European Jewish communities, but they do so in different ways. Synagogues confront the policy-making bodies of the new Eastern Europe with a far more complex problem than do cemeteries: Something must be done with the synagogues. Moreover, the fact of their invisibility during the past fifty years requires that something be done with them (Dohrn 1991). Even fifty years after the Holocaust, neglect does something to synagogues, for it, too, articulates a position vis-à-vis the Holocaust (Krinsky 1985). "Doing something," however, creates an even greater dilemma, especially in the post-1989 era when the disjuncture wrought by the Holocaust is exposed again and in new ways. I address the nature of this dilemma in this essay.

The synagogues of Eastern Europe have passed through very different kinds of transitions since the Holocaust—that is, since the destruction of most of the communities that gave them life. Many were demolished after the Holocaust; others were converted to serve other purposes, from private homes to public libraries or cinemas; still others became Jewish community centers, gathering a wide range of services around them. (For a survey of transitions in Germany, see Guttmann 1989.) Synagogues putatively lend themselves to restoration as museums, thus serving the memorializing function of a large monument filled with smaller monuments. (For discussions of the museum adjoining the Dohány Street Synagogue in Budapest, see Benoschofsky and Scheiber 1987). When museums do not adjoin synagogues, museums take over the inner spaces, stylizing them or rendering them as eternal themes, such as the "sanctuary or Torah ark through the ages." The synagogues of Prague's Jewish Quarter are all museums, some officially part time but in reality all full time in one way or another, "worthy of thought," as one popular guidebook title states (Rybár 1991).

As their commodification in guidebooks and museum pamphlets suggests, synagogues have also become primary objects in a Jewish heritage industry meant to attract Western tourists—especially American Jews—to Eastern Europe. The case of Prague illustrates the Jewish heritage industry particularly vividly. As one of the best-known Jewish travel guides— which "now includes the Czech Republic, Hungary, Slovakia, and Poland"—notes, "the spotlight shines on Prague" (Frank 1996, 413). The starting point for the tourist's encounter with Prague's Jewish Quarter is the Staronová (Old-New) Synagogue, which is surrounded by the more recent synagogues-cum-museums as well as the cemeteries that formerly marked the edge of the ghetto. Punctuating all these sites of Jewish history, moreover, are kosher restaurants and convenience stores, which alternate with shops filled with souvenirs and travel agencies where one can book excursions to concentration camps in the Czech Republic (e.g., Terezín).

The journey into the Jewish past has been at once memorialized and commodified through the clear and public definition of its starting point: the Staronová Synagogue.

The restoration of synagogues as museums, however, functions most often as a public trope of uncertainty; guidebooks send tourists to synagogue after synagogue "being converted into a museum." But more often than not, the doors are closed, attesting to mute and indefinite postponements of museum projects. Not infrequently, synagogues in Eastern Europe just stand there, posing questions about what to do with them. There is even unvoiced awareness among local residents that a sacred space cannot simply be eliminated or converted to other purposes without intervention by religious authorities; where, then, to find the proper religious authorities?

On the heels of the changes in 1989, the dilemma heightened. There would be visitors from the West and from Israel who would ask hard questions and seek to involve themselves. The world's Jewish heartland had not gone away, and it would come to attract more and more pilgrims. What, then, should these pilgrims find?

There are other reasons that the restoration of synagogues has come to symbolize the transitions of Jewish Eastern Europe. The synagogue is an ethnographic site, not just a place to experience community but a liminal and border space where one crosses into the sacred spaces of the past. The synagogue is also a narrative space, where the texts that narrate ritual and ritualize history concentrate time and the experiences of being Jewish. It follows that synagogues represent another powerful trope of Jewish modernism, namely, memory. Indeed, memory is monumentalized through the very physical presence of the synagogue (see Yerushalmi 1982). And yet, depending on the ways in which the synagogue is restored, it represents the relation between memory and monument in strikingly contradictory ways that in turn signal a crossing of the historical threshold into postmodernism.

As an ethnomusicologist, I follow yet another distinctive ethnographic path to the synagogues of Eastern Europe. Not only was the synagogue a space of music making, but it was the place in which music—Jewish music—most powerfully ascribed identity to Eastern Europe's Jewish community. It concentrated the voices of the community, transforming voice into a means of listening to the past (see Elbogen 1993, 365–86). Through the medium of the synagogue, through the vessel of music, the historical landscape of Jewish Europe reveals itself. Fundamental aesthetic debates—about whether organs should be allowed, for example—mapped the divisiveness in communities between liberal and orthodox. The cantor-composers in the great synagogues invented more than new musical forms and liturgical rites from the *bima,* or pulpit. They invented Jewish Eastern Europe itself, entering, possessing, imagining, mapping, addressing, and peopling Eastern Europe, to borrow Larry Wolff's metaphors of the invention of Eastern Europe (1994). The music they created assumed a canonized form, the *hazzanut,* which was published for and learned in academies for the training of cantors. It required not just new forms of dissemination but new processes of reproduction. This phenomenon in turn necessitated the division of musical labors within the synagogue itself—for example, between the organist and choir director. Within the community embodied by the synagogue, there was a new community: its musicians.

Such sweeping representational claims notwithstanding, the narratives of Eastern European synagogues are those of disjuncture and fragmentation. The histories and stories of synagogues in the 1990s do not fit together neatly, not least because of the problem of "doing something," of recovering the narrative voice. This essay intentionally recognizes and represents the texture of narrative disjuncture that the dilemma of synagogue restoration unleashes in and for Eastern Europe. I do not move smoothly across the landscape of Jewish Eastern Europe because I cannot. Instead, I have sought out the bits and pieces of narrative disjuncture that synagogues and their music bring together and juxtapose. These fragments of song, these voices still heard, remain trapped in transition, still asking "from what, to what?" They will remain fragments, like the parts for building the Prague Staronová Synagogue, trapped on a "We are changing *Europe!*" postcard, whose narrative and address will be destroyed should someone attempt to cut out the pieces to put them together.

Mikulov: Voice in the Synagogue

> On the first day of Rosh Hashanah, Rabbi Shmelke of Nikolsburg entered the synagogue before the shofar was blown and prayed in tears. "Oh, my God, Master of the world, all people are crying unto you. But what should their supplication really mean to you, for it arises from their sin and not from the exile of *shekhinah,* the diaspora?" On the second day, he came again and wept, "It says in the first book of Samuel, 'Why did my song, Isaiah, come neither today nor yesterday to the table?' Why did the king, the Messiah, not come, not yesterday, on the first day, and not today, on the second of the New Year? And so it is, today and yesterday, the people prayed only about bread for their bodies and for bodily afflictions!"
>
> ("The One Who Prayed and the Messiah,"
> Hassidic tale; author's translation)

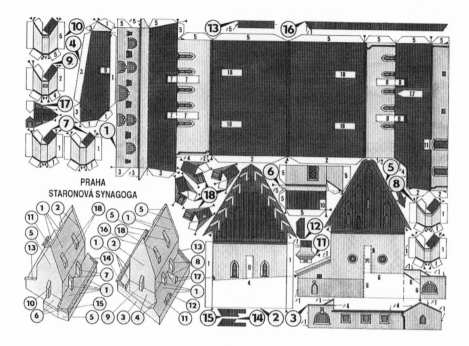

The synagogue as fragments: Praha Staronová Synagoga

Writ large across the tales of the legendary Hassidic Rabbi Shmelke from Nikolsburg is the humanness of voice and music and their power to mediate. In Martin Buber's collection of Hassidic tales (1949), itself a legendary part of Jewish modernism, no other *Wunderrabbiner* (miracle rabbi) communicates so often to his followers with music and with music in so many diverse forms. When he travels to Vienna to ask the imperial court to mollify its treatment of the Jews, Rabbi Shmelke works his "miracles" with song (see "The Trip on the Danube," Buber 1949, 318); when his metaphors connect the internal rhythms of life to the life of the synagogue and the Jewish community in Nikolsburg, Rabbi Shmelke relies on the musicality of the Psalms (see "The Knocking," Buber 1949, 310). The texture of Nikolsburg's Jewish life is the rich counterpoint of music, mystical and metaphorical yet direct and real.

The castle of Mikulov, the Czech name for Nikolsburg, rises majestically from the vineyards of the Moravian plains, a citadel at the border with Austria. Mikulov (population 7,500) is a hive of activity, with workers repairing cobbled streets and painting old artisan shops and new cash stations. The gold leaf on statues has been restored, and the museums that occupy the castle grounds are open for business. By foot, it is possible to navigate the old city of Mikulov (which is to say, the Nikolsburg part) in twenty minutes, circumambulating the entire citadel. There is more to modern Mikulov (which is to say, the real Mikulov part), but it lies some kilometers from the center: apartment blocks hugging factories belching coal smoke—literally redolent of the inefficiency of an industrial economy lingering from the past.

Mikulov's Jewish history is impressive indeed. For centuries it was the seat of Jewish administration for Moravia, home of the legislative councils ruled by the *Landesrabbiner,* Moravia's chief rabbis. The great Moravian chief rabbis holding this office are themselves legendary; in addition to Rabbi Shmuel Shmelke Horowitz, who ruled in the late eighteenth century, Judah Löw ben Bezalel—known best as the "inventor" of the Golem in Prague—was chief rabbi in the mid-sixteenth century. Mysticism shrouds Mikulov's rabbis, and yet this mysticism is always slightly transparent, for it provides a sacred portal through which one passes on journeys between East and West, between the sacred world of Judaism and a secular landscape administered by Prague, Vienna, and the Jewish wine merchants, whose commercial power stimulated the modernization of Jewish life in Moravia.

The mediating power of music and mysticism resided in Mikulov's Jewish community, which hugged the citadel, defining it, in fact, through the synagogues, shops, and ghetto that ringed its base. The mystical power summoned by Rabbi Shmelke with song is not lost on Mikulov's city boosters in the 1990s, for they have taken great pains and spent considerable money to restore the main synagogue. Since 1989 there have, in fact, been at least two phases of restoration, the first intended to convert the synagogue into a museum, the second to transform parts of it into performance spaces. Restoration, in fact, has been a sort of historical norm, for the synagogue, built originally in the mid-sixteenth century, has recovered from various fires and responded to the needs of changing Jewish administrations and the mysticisms of different rabbinical generations. As in Rabbi Shmelke's tale about prayer and the Messiah, yesterday and today are bound together as the shofar— the ritualized musical symbol of beginnings and endings (e.g., at Rosh Hashanah and Yom Kippur)—is blown (Bohlman 1996a). Like the castles and cash stations, the wine museums and tourist shops, Mikulov's synagogue will mediate the many symbols of a tiny Moravian city, the glory of its past not lost on the planners of its future. The shofar connects yesterday to today; Rabbi Shmelke's enjoinder from the Mikulov synagogue that the Messiah will come at some

The synagogue of Mikulov, Czech Republic.
(Photograph by Philip Bohlman.)

future tomorrow remains no less valid for the most recent restoration of the synagogue.

"Viennese Rite": Musical Monuments on the Eastern Landscape of the Monarchy

Music provided the cultural filter that allowed Europe's Ashkenazic Jews to experience themselves as others. By the early nineteenth century the historical gulf between Central and Eastern European Jews was sufficiently gaping that neither possessed a historical memory of the other and neither defined itself in relation to a larger history and culture in which the other participated. The historical transitions of the eighteenth century had not only widened the gulf but had effectively defined Jewish Europe as two distinct entities: Central Europe's *haskalah,* the Jewish Enlightenment, had created a historical trajectory that figured the Jews of the German-speaking lands in opposition to those of Eastern Europe's Hassidism. The borders, it seemed, had become hard and fast.

In the course of the nineteenth century, however, music crossed and redefined the borders. Propelled along a historical path of religious reform and socioeconomic emancipation, Jews of Central Europe struggled to regain some echoes of their own Jewish voice from the East. In Eastern Europe, they discovered "Jewish music," folk song and dance spawned by Hassidism, popular and theatrical musics transported by klezmer musicians, and Yiddish song, the voice of Ashkenazic music (see Bohlman, forthcoming). The other voice of Ashkenazic music belonged to the *hazzan,* the cantor, the specialist-singer of sacred music, who rose from the indistinguishable ranks of *meshoyrerim* (choirboys) to the distinguished ranks of musical stardom (Slobin 1989, 3–26).

The discovery of Jewish music in Eastern Europe was, nonetheless, fraught with paradox. For Central European Jews to take as their own the music of Eastern European Jews, it first had to be collected, colonized, translated, and reinvented for the West. Similarly, it became necessary to reinvent the institutions of Jewish music—both the musicians who constituted such institutions as singers or players and the edifices housing these musicians. The synagogue provided exactly such an institution, not least because it, too, was reinvented in modern forms during the nineteenth century. The humble house of prayer underwent a transformation to the temple, the Moorish-style synagogue, with towering minarets and arabesques enveloping it as the skin of Easternness. Moorish synagogues spread across Eastern Europe along with many other institutions and edifices used by the Prussian and Austro-Hungarian empires to effect colonization.

One of the latest stages in the invention of Eastern Europe, the colonization of Eastern European Jewry had an enormous impact on Central Europe because it was so unsettling: Its imagination of Eastern European Jewish Otherness only intensified the blinding glare in the mirrors of selfness. The selfness encountered in Eastern Europe was, furthermore, a response of eastern Jewish communities to the Austro-German culture of Central Europe. Educated and emancipated Jews in many urban centers chose to speak German, to write and conduct business in German, and to affiliate themselves with a German-speaking social and economic elite. The adoption of musical repertories and styles, such as the Viennese Rite, was therefore another aspect of an Eastern European willingness to embrace the cultural and class advantages that accompanied Central European colonization.

If the Moorish style transformed Eastern European Jewish synagogues from the outside, music transformed the sacred space from within. A new liturgical music emerged with the spread of German-administered empires into Eastern Europe. This music required larger performing ensembles, which became both more specialized and more professionalized as new and more complex music was created specifically for them. During the course of the nineteenth century, to greater and lesser degrees, the distinction between those who performed liturgical music and those who witnessed it grew. The cantors of Central Europe realized the potential of the new Jewish music and recognized, furthermore, a new potential for themselves as composers. The great cantor-composers of the nineteenth century, such as Salomon Sulzer (1804–90) in Vienna, created a new liturgical music, suited to the sacred spaces of the Eastern European synagogues (Avenary 1985). With the published canons of the *Wiener Ritus* (Viennese Rite) at their disposal, the cantors, organs, and choirs of Budapest, Czernowitz, and Bucharest would acoustically redefine the inner space of the synagogues. Prayer books and hymnals published in Vienna and Budapest would fill the pews, centralizing musical ritual much as political and military power had been centralized. The Hapsburg empire would resonate in full voice.

The invention of Jewish Eastern Europe with music was inchoate, however, and its incompleteness in turn has heightened the dilemma of synagogue restoration. Standing at the gates of Budapest's Dohány Street Synagogue, one is struck by the depth of irony: to restore the synagogue, a transition seemingly inseparable from restoring its organ, one recuperates a music manufactured by the West for the East, not unlike the phone card technology of the mid-1990s. The liturgical tradition most favored by the Hungarian *hazzanut* (i.e., its cantors and cantorial institutions, such as the cantors' academy in Budapest) remains that of Sulzer. Contesting these traditions, however, are those of the secular Jewish musics of Eastern Europe, which serve in different ways to recall the discovery of Eastern Europe in the nineteenth century. Modern klezmer ensembles revive the past, and synagogue choirs from throughout Eastern Europe tour in the West, filling the second half of most concerts with Yiddish songs whose traditionality is an invention of the 1990s. In post-Holocaust Europe, the musical traditions that compete to be heard in synagogues continue to reproduce the confused boundaries between Self and Other, between Central and Eastern European Jewry.

Sopron: Restoration as Unending Process

Each time I have tried to visit the "old" and "new" synagogues of Sopron, Hungary—from immediately after the revolution in early 1990 to the summer of 1996—I have encountered the same sign: "in the process of renovation." The two medieval synagogues of Sopron (there is a third synagogue, built in the nineteenth century and now in total collapse) are among the oldest in Hungary, although local residents claim that they are the oldest anywhere in Europe (see Gazda 1989). Age and authenticity are central to the memorialization of Jewish culture in Sopron. On the one hand, the two medieval synagogues (the old dates from around 1300, the new from circa 1350) reflect a thriving medieval Jewish culture; only Budapest claims archeological evidence for a more extensive Jewish presence in the Middle Ages (Gazda 1989; Gruber 1994, 163–66). On the other hand, Sopron's Jewish history has been the result of an unending series of expulsions from Sopron itself; each attempt to rebuild the Jewish history of the city, each attempt to restore the Jewish community to Sopron's history, was greeted with rejection.

It is not likely that the old and new synagogues were used for prayer after the expulsion of Jews from Sopron in 1526. There were other expulsions, especially in 1683, as Ottoman forces laid siege to Vienna, and not until the nineteenth century did Jews return in sufficient numbers to reconstitute a community (Ernst 1987, 233–37). Instead, Jewish communities formed in a large ring around Sopron (called Ödenburg in German), where they grew in importance as the most concentrated rural Jewish area on the border between Central and Eastern Europe. The *shevah kehillot,* the Seven Holy Cities, overshadow Sopron's significance in Hungarian and Austrian Jewish history (see Reiss 1997). Or cutting to the cruel core of the historical paradox, it is because Jews suffered so much in Sopron that they flourished in the Jewish villages that surrounded it (see Bohlman 1993, 1997). It is hardly surprising that the markers of Sopron's Jewish history, the old and new synagogues, were not (re)discovered until archeological diggings unearthed them in the 1950s (Dávid 1978).

The silence of Sopron's synagogues symbolizes a more profound silence haunting the Jewish presence in the city. In the modern era, Sopron straddled the Hungarian and Austrian parts of the Hapsburg empire, literally forming a cultural and political border. Its architecture and urban planning concentrate a welter of differences in the city's center, literally within the ring that recalls, in miniature version, the ring of the imperial capital, Vienna. In Sopron, disjuncture becomes juncture, inconsistency assumes the force of consistency. On the map, Sopron juts into Austria, an Eastern European peninsula surrounded by Central Europe. Sopron held to its Hungarianness, most recently in the Cold War, even as "inland" Austrian trains traveling the north-south axis of Burgenland had no other choice but to pass through Sopron. Resistance to the Germanness of Austria only intensified the resistance to and rejection of Jews, identifiable by their German-sounding names (see Frigyesi 1993). Many Jews who participated in Sopron's cultural life—for example, composer Karl Goldmark, who walked from the outlying Jewish village of Deutschkreutz (in Hebrew, Zelem, and now in Austria) for music lessons—engaged in repeated border crossing to do so. The old and new synagogues, accordingly, could remain buried in the past of the city's center.

The proximity of the border between Central and Eastern Europe now becomes the primary motivation for restoring the synagogue. Were the synagogues to become the museums promised by guidebooks (e.g., Gruber 1992, 182), they would be additional sources for Austrian and German currency. They would provide additional sites for attracting tourists from the West, thereby contributing to the city's design for its own post–Cold War transition. Sopron is separated only by marshes from the Neusiedlersee, a major resort area for Austrians and Germans. The old and new synagogues would be the medieval jewel in Sopron's architectural history. Neither Vienna nor Bratislava, both about an hour from Sopron, could boast such a gem from their Jewish pasts.

In 1990 and again in 1995 and 1996, I spoke with local cultural authorities about the restoration projects. Completion, I was assured in 1996 as in 1990, was imminent. If there had been delays, I was further told, it was because there was no Jewish community to advise and to help. "It's hard to know what to do next," local planners told me, "hard to make sure everything is authentic." I shall have the opportunity to check on the imminence of the restoration in 1999, when I undertake fieldwork in Kittsee, one of the Seven Holy Cities.

Ba-shanah ha-bah—Next year in Sopron.

Jewish Musical Tradition: Oral, Written, and the Space in Between

However one wishes to regard it, Jewish music contests the spaces it fills. In trying to define Jewish music, one must always account for its contradictions, eventually becoming mired in them. The relation of Jewish music to sacred space generally informs attempts to grasp its meanings. Abraham Zvi Idelsohn, the twentieth-century inventor of the canon of Jewish music (see Idelsohn 1914–32), relied on an ethnographic entry into sacred space to provide him with practical boundaries for that canon. For Idelsohn, there was music "of the synagogue" and "not of the synagogue." The music of the synagogue defined a space for tradition, which often contested the music itself. In the synagogue, music existed in both oral and written forms. The text was written, the melodies were not or at least were written only in a flexible if not vague notation (*ta'amim*) that indicated the direction of melody and provided formulas for ending individual passages and sections in a prayer or song text. At all times, Jewish music lends itself to interpretation and contestation. As synagogues spread across the invented landscape of Jewish Eastern Europe, the space of music they embodied spread as well, becoming even more contested (Werner 1976).

At the end of the twentieth century it is not easy to hear synagogue music in Eastern Europe, unless it is imported from the outside. Communities that regularly gather for prayer and services often choose not to do so in a synagogue but rather in a prayer hall next to it or in a community center elsewhere. There are practical reasons for doing so, such as the cost of heating in the winter and the small number of rabbis (Romania has only two, for example). There are musical reasons as well. The music conceived, canonized, and monumentalized for the synagogue's space can no longer be performed appropriately. Not only is there no organ or choir, no cantor or rabbi, but the music itself, the melodies and swelling prayers, does not fit the space. Oral and written traditions exist in disjuncture, and the true dynamic of their disjuncture becomes impossible to maintain.

Prayer books (*siddurim*) and songbooks are inevitably present in the synagogues of Eastern Europe, but they are never used together. Songbooks left lying in pews or stacked in shelves next to the *bima* seem at first to document only the weight of written tradition. Who sings from them, one asks. The songbooks themselves answer this question, but the answer is anything but straightforward. Most piles of songbooks are multilingual—Hebrew, German, Hungarian, Romanian—with imprints that connect them to Vienna, Budapest, Bucharest, New York, or Jerusalem. The bricolage of oral traditions that these books symbolize is no less complex—Orthodox, Neolog/Liberal, stylized Hassidic. Most synagogues contain some songbooks that are very old—from the mid-nineteenth century—and some that are extremely recent, especially those provided by Israel.

When oral tradition disappears, so too must the written tradition that contests it in the space of the synagogue. In February 1996, I entered the Orthodox synagogue of Oradea, Romania. Prior to World War II, Oradea was a city claiming a population that was 80 percent Jewish, perhaps eighty thousand Jewish residents in all; today, about six hundred Jews live here. Piled inside the door of the synagogue were boxes and boxes of books—Jewish books, that is, sacred books that had filled the city's synagogues and the libraries of its enlightened Jewish residents. These boxes had been assembled in the synagogue to be taken to a burial place behind the synagogues and near the cemeteries. "One does not destroy Jewish books," the representative of the community told me. "We shall bury them, so they can be used again." With no trace of irony in her voice she explained further, "We bring them to the synagogue first because our prayer books and songbooks contain the voices of those who came before us."

Slovakia: Litany of Destruction through Renovation

Even in the new Eastern Europe, Slovakia stands out as a nation where the systematic misuse and abuse of synagogues during the Holocaust and

Cold War has given way to an equally systematic neglect of synagogues today. To speak of synagogue renovation in the manner of other examples in this essay would be quite impossible. There are some small Jewish communities, tenaciously asserting their identities in Bratislava and Kosice, but Jewish identity today is not unlike that of Slovak Roma and Hungarians, a historical fact to be eliminated through laws. Successive waves of legislation, intended to bring about a new order in Slovakia, have not been kind to synagogues. Their congregations eliminated or depleted, synagogues contained spaces that were forced to yield to more pressing state needs.

In the early 1990s independent attempts to document the fate of Slovak synagogues were initiated. The documentation from such attempts usually reduces synagogue restoration to lists—indeed, to litanies of facts remarking on the unremarkable. Lucia Benická of Poprad, a photographer engaged in the documentation of Slovakia's synagogues, compiled the following list (1996), which speaks for itself.

Selected Synagogue Restorations in Slovakia

Western Slovakia
Bratislava
The synagogue of the central Jewish Quarter was eliminated in the 1970s, together with the Jewish Quarter, when the city's largest Danube bridge was built. A small synagogue from 1923 still functions on Haydukova Street for the entire community of the Slovak capital.
Trnava
Two synagogues stood abandoned throughout the communist era. One has now been converted into the Galeria J. Koniarika, whose exhibits specialize in "spiritual issues."

Central Slovakia
Liptovský Mikuláš
Converted into a multimedia arts space in the 1990s. Hosts a project called BRIDGES, which brings Jews and Christians together, although there are apparently no Jews today in Liptovský Mikuláš. The city council owns the arts space/synagogue.
Ruzomberok
Property of the city council, which has plans to convert it into a municipal gallery for contemporary art.

Eastern Slovakia

Humenne

Demolished.

Hunconcovce

At the turn of the century there were two synagogues in this regional center for training rabbis. One synagogue became a barn on a cooperative farm in the 1950s; the other was demolished.

Kezmarok

Demolished.

Kosice

A tenacious community in the 1990s that, though largely Hungarian and therefore doubly repressed, has reestablished Jewish institutions. The main synagogue became a book depository when the communists assumed power in 1948, but it now has been restored for use by the Jewish community.

Michalovce

Despite plans to convert the synagogue into an arts space, it was demolished in the 1970s.

Poprad

Converted into a printing company.

Presov

One synagogue was destroyed by fire, and there are plans to renovate the other, despite the long-standing desire of a California congregation to move the structure to the United States (Gruber 1992, 135).

Spisska Bela

Converted into a private dwelling.

Spisska Nova Ves

The Moorish-style synagogue was demolished in the 1950s.

Spisska Stara Ves

Converted into a youth center.

Spisske Podhradie

Converted into a barn on a cooperative farm in the 1950s. Lack of repair has rendered it no longer functional.

To a large degree, synagogue restoration in Slovakia is a matter of representation rather than physical renovation. Indeed, it might be said that photography itself is the most visible form of restoration, for the images of destroyed synagogues appear on many of the most frequently

Postcard from 1996, picturing Bratislava's main synagogue, circa 1905.

purchased postcards in Slovakia. On such postcards, sepia tones and horse-drawn carts create a magical world of pastness, framed by the suggestions of tolerance, as Christian churches provide a backdrop (see, however, Salner 1993).

Hassidim and Organs, or the Undoing of Synagogues

The invention of "Jewish music" transformed the synagogue in the wake of the *haskalah*—the nineteenth-century period of Jewish transition variously called emancipation or assimilation, a period marked by the classicization of Jewish secular culture through the interaction of Central and Eastern Europe and the shift of Jewish culture from private and community spaces into the European public sphere. The transitions that led to a more specified and definable object of Jewish music unfolded—or were driven—along two trajectories. The first shifted Jewish music away from the synagogue. The second carved out a more specific, bounded niche for Jewish music in the synagogue. Both transitions heightened the contestation of ritual, liturgy, and space in the synagogue. Both created a hierarchy of musical specialists and repertories, thereby forging a division of labors between musicians and nonmusicians. And both contributed markedly to the undoing of synagogues.

The first musical transition in the synagogue during the nineteenth century stemmed from the growing awareness of forms of Jewish belief described by some as mystical and pietistic, by others as irrational and fanatic, and subsumed under the name of Hassidism. Although there are many different aspects that definitions of Hassidism must address, two are most relevant for this essay. First, the musical practices of Hassidic Jews take place outside of the synagogue and are largely unconnected to liturgical traditions; Hassidic music, as it was consciously created for ecstatic worship, is by and large in the vernacular language, Yiddish, and its functions are closest to those of European folk song. Second, no music in the New Europe is chosen to represent "Jewish music" as often as Hassidic music (see Bohlman, forthcoming, esp. "Nachwort"); it is, in fact, almost necessary, when organizing and marketing concerts and recordings, to refer to that music as Hassidic or to make it clear that Hassidic music comprises a major part of the performance (Vinaver 1985). For touring synagogue choirs and klezmer revivalists alike, Jewish music is synonymous with Hassidic music.

Whereas Hassidic music moved Jewish music out of the synagogue in the nineteenth century (and back into it in the late twentieth century), the organ and the cantor's transition to composer musically transformed the synagogue itself. As with the creation of Hassidic repertories, the creation of art music for the synagogue was bound up with questions of religious doctrine and practice. New compositions for the synagogue were part of a nineteenth-century reform movement that sought to wrest religion away from the ownership and control of conservative rabbis and mediate it for broader consumption (for an emic history, see Elbogen 1993, 297–333). The new Jewish art music entered the synagogue as its architecture underwent a sweeping transition. With minarets from mosques on the outside (the musical symbolism of minarets was not lost on nineteenth-century observers, for it was from the minaret that the *muedhdhin* performed the Muslim call to prayer, the most common aural symbol of Orientalism), the internal spaces of synagogues became more publicly egalitarian: the women's gallery could serve as a balcony, and women and men worshipers, even when seated on opposite sides of the sanctuary, had equal opportunities to hear the music from the cantor, choir, and organist, all of whom were on the *bimah,* whose literal meaning began to resemble that of its modern Hebrew usage, namely "stage."

As music was repositioned both within and without the synagogue, musical tradition passed through a transition of traditionalization. Hassidic music became an official folk-music tradition; synagogal compositions and performance practices became an official art-music tradition. In the 1990s the traditionalization of tradition underwent yet another refraction, for both Hassidic music and art music became the official traditions of pastness, the monuments to the Jewish voice that was lost. To restore Hassidic song means restoring Yiddish repertories, if not the *Yiddishkeit* (Yiddishness) of Eastern Europe itself. To restore the organ, even through the purchase of phone cards in Budapest, makes it possible to stage the performance of the Jewish past—that is, to put Jewish music on the *bimah* of the present. The music that undid the sacredness of synagogues in the nineteenth century now serves as the medium that will reintroduce the traces of that sacredness to the restored synagogues of the new Eastern Europe.

Suceava: Behind the Carpathians

The Carpathian Mountains—stretching from the Danube at Bratislava, through Slovakia, along the Polish and Ukrainian borders, and finally into Romania, where they resist the pull to the east and retreat through a loop toward the south and west into Transylvania—have long defined Eastern European Jewry in the Western imagination. The Carpathians, even as insurmountable and daunting geological formations, the "dark side of Europe" in Rüdiger Wischenbart's confabulation (1992), connected East to West, providing the route for Hapsburg claims to the East and the path of Jews to the West—Jews whose lives, journeys, and imperial enchantments fill the stories and novels of Karl Emil Franzos, Leopold von Sacher-Masoch, and Joseph Roth. Beyond the Carpathians—or "behind the Carpathians," as modern Jewish authors prefer to put it (e.g., Landmann 1995)—lay the borderless boundary region of Eastern European Jewry, the landscape stretching toward but never reaching *mizrakh,* the East (Pollack 1984; Applebaum 1994).

Behind the Carpathians, synagogues stand in stark contrast to the retreating horizon. The synagogues that remain are modern, built in the nineteenth and twentieth centuries; those that are absent were premodern, traditionally made of wood but now destroyed by fire, the Holocaust, or both. The plains stretching through Moldavia and Ukraine still have sparse Jewish populations. Driving along them, one quickly realizes why it was nearly impossible for the clashing empires of the nineteenth century to lay down borders. The mixture of ethnic, religious, and linguistic groups that continues to characterize the unfolding landscape of villages offered no rhyme or reason to the imperial cartographers charged with the delineation of clear borders (Pollack 1984). Instead, cities were built on the lands of Galicia and the Bukovina behind the Carpathians—Lvov, Czernowitz, Brody—cities that Jews settled in large numbers and colonized with the culture of Jewish modernity (see, e.g., Kohlbauer-Fritz 1993). Synagogues of all kinds sprang up and celebrated the new culture of the East.

The innumerable borders of this borderless region collapse in the one remaining synagogue of Suceava. A commercial center of the Hapsburg empire as early as 1775 and formerly the capital of Moldavia, Suceava now has the thankless task of providing the first (or last) safe haven at the border of Ukraine. The collective memory of the Jewish community of around 200 stretches beyond the border, to Czernowitz (Chernivitsi) in Ukraine, where German was the language of instruction in the best Jewish schools, the language of negotiation with the culture of modernism.

The splendor of Suceava's synagogue belies the history of this frontier of Eastern European Jewry. Built in 1870 and restored in 1991, the synagogue is the sole survivor of a community that worshiped in eighteen synagogues prior to the Holocaust. These eighteen synagogues had survived but then disappeared one by one—victims of Romanian urban renewal, the social redefinition of the urban spaces conceived first by Hapsburg architects. The synagogue must be all things to all Jewish residents in Suceava; Orthodox and liberal (Neolog) Jews alike pray here, together and respectful of their differences.

Music, too, assumes all forms, but quietly, iconically, and ironically. The stylized musical instruments on the ceiling of the main sanctuary are placed at the border formed by the women's gallery. Indeed, the windows of the women's gallery open directly onto the improbable ensemble of harp, guitar, cello, and drum. Iconically, music transgresses the borders of these internally bounded sacred spaces. In Jewish tradition instruments are not allowed inside the synagogue; that they might commingle with the voices of women worshipers, also not allowed in the internal sacred space of this synagogue, multiplies the evident irony. The synagogue of Suceava, however, is all that remains. There are far more pressing concerns than whether women's voices commingle with instrumental voices in the sanctuary of a synagogue behind the Carpathians.

Cassettes: Synagogues Restored for Mass Consumption

The technologies of inexpensive musical reproduction have caught on quickly in Eastern Europe. Jewish music, too, is finding its way to cassettes and compact discs and through these media to the public sphere. I first encountered the mass production of synagogue music in Budapest when

Sanctuary and women's gallery, Suceava, Romania.
(Photograph by Philip Bohlman.)

doing archival research in the cantorial academy in September 1991. Jewish music was making a public appearance again, after quietly persisting in the private sphere during the communist era. Hungarian folk and popular music traditions had enjoyed a share of the market economy that had begun to emerge long before 1989; I intended to take full advantage of the inexpensive cassettes hawked on the streets or hanging in the racks of

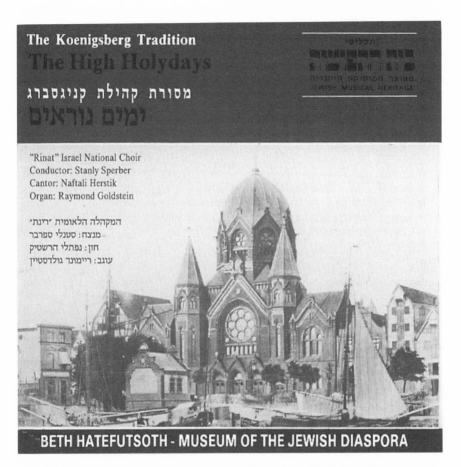

The Koenigsberg Tradition

The High Holydays

מסורת קהילת קניגסברג

ימים נוראים

"Rinat" Israel National Choir
Conductor: Stanly Sperber
Cantor: Naftali Herstik
Organ: Raymond Goldstein

המקהלה הלאומית "רינת"
מנצח: סטנלי ספרבר
חזן: נפתלי הרשטיק
עוגב: ריימונד גולדסטיין

תקליטי

מאוצר המוסיקה היהודית
JEWISH MUSICAL HERITAGE

BETH HATEFUTSOTH - MUSEUM OF THE JEWISH DIASPORA

Cassette of synagogue music from Königsberg (Kaliningrad).

kiosks. What I did not expect, however, was to find cassettes of Jewish music.

Audio cassettes and compact discs are the musical monuments of late-twentieth-century synagogues. Cassettes anthologize and disseminate synagogue music, relying both on bounded canons and unbounded bricolage. Some cassettes contain the music of a single synagogue; the Dohány Street Synagogue tradition was available in 1991 in a variety of mixes and remixes. Other cassettes contain the music of a single cantor. In both genres, there is a commodified medium of *hazzanut*—that is, a local tradition and a cantorial tradition; *hazzanut* is literally the body of music created and reproduced by the *hazzan,* or cantor, and it therefore serves as a metonym for the music culture of the cantor's synagogue and its history. There are cassettes that are historical (e.g., an Israeli recording of the *hazzanut* for Königsberg [now Kaliningrad in the Russian Republic]) and those that are New Age. Indeed, the cassettes of synagogal music modernize and postmodernize tradition. They allow the cassette producer to package the musical space of tradition and reproduce it for mass consumption.

Cassettes and compact discs of synagogal music capture and save the contested sonic spaces of synagogues in Eastern Europe. When synagogue choirs from Russia tour in Western Europe, they bring boxes of cassettes with them, sell them at intermission, and drop off an ample supply at Jewish bookstores. The members of a given synagogue, therefore, are not the primary consumers of cassettes produced by the synagogue's choir or cantor. Instead, consumption takes place elsewhere, on choir tours or at kiosks frequented by tourists, for example. The Russian cassette pictured here was even produced by the Joint Distribution Committee, a Jewish development agency whose presence is now ubiquitous in Eastern Europe.

Through sonic representation, cassettes and compact discs act as powerful agents for the restoration of synagogues. At one level, they themselves are acts of restoration; this fact is not lost on their producers, who usually place a picture of the synagogue or its *bimah* on the cover. At another level, cassettes force an acceleration of restoration processes; the organ must be repaired, or the choir's music library must be put in order. At still another level, cassettes make synagogue restoration a public phenomenon; it is no longer limited to the sacred space of the synagogue but is rather something to which anyone can contribute.

Cassettes and compact discs also relocate restoration in ways that render the deployment of tradition part of a postmodern transition. The local emerges only from a mixture of old and new styles. Variety is an indispensable component of marketing, making it necessary to layer one holiday's music on another's. The space of the synagogue becomes a hybrid space where traditional forms of contestation give way to transgression of the sacred. Once restored, however, the voices of synagogue music are packaged and distanced from the space to which they traditionally gave meaning.

Cassettes, phone cards, and the campaigns of local and international cultural agencies remain only truncated forms of commodification. A synagogue choir may earn enough through cassette sales to finance part of an international tour; local arts agencies may cobble together enough donations to organize an exhibit or to bring in a few Jewish musicians for workshops; and benefit concerts may stave off urban planners hoping to cash in on the potential of transforming urban ghettos into quaint "old city"

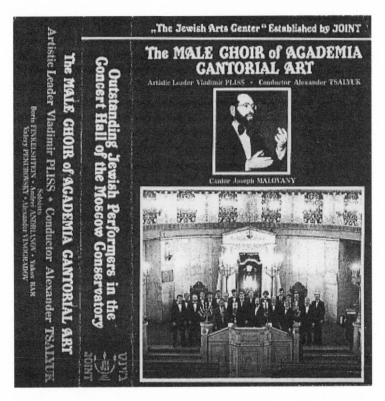

Cover of a cassette by the Male Choir of the Moscow Academia of Cantorial Art (mid-1990s).

malls. The danger of total commodification of synagogues may loom on the Eastern European economic horizon for some, but in fact the voices recovered by cassettes and disseminated through choir tours deflect the tendency toward total commodification. Again, the crucial question of "transition from what, to what?" in Eastern Europe encumbers the path of commodification.

The cassette culture of Eastern European Jewish music does not rush headlong into a market economy but rather coalesces around the cultural spaces of in-betweenness that the restoration of synagogues articulate. Cassette sales respond to the immediate financial problem, not least because they concentrate musical tradition from the past. Restoring it for the future is an entirely different problem: the voices needed to make it heard again are too few. The dilemma of transition "to what" is not solved through commodification, which becomes strikingly apparent when one goes in search of the new. There is no new music in Eastern European synagogues, only traces of the old that occasionally lend themselves to postmodern mixing—notably, the penchant for using Hassidic folk songs in every concert, even those emphasizing the sacredness of the synagogue. The commodification of Jewish music puts the synagogue "in transition"—that is, in a zone of historical in-betweenness that indeed perpetuates transition while ultimately falling short of complete restoration.

Cluj Napoca: Radio Sonic in the Women's Gallery

I hurried with my meal at Cluj's kosher lunchroom to avoid being late for my tour of the synagogue, which was just around the corner, visible through the lunchroom windows. I had an appointment for the tour, and it was important to be on time. The synagogue on Parisu Street had been restored—"very modern" (I was warned), and the head of the offices in the new synagogue would take great pride (I was further warned) in showing me what could be done with Romanian synagogues in the new era of market economy. After several days in Transylvania's utter poverty, accentuated by the bitter winter of 1996, I could not imagine how this promise of a modernized synagogue could be kept. With nervous trepidation I searched for the entrance and failed to find it—which is to say, I failed to find the entrance to the sanctuary, failed, in fact, to find any traces of it having been opened or entered in recent memory.

"Around the back," a voice enjoined. "There's a parking lot around the back, and you can get into the studios from there."

Now late for the appointment, I ran to the back and spotted the huddle of Dacia automobiles, nudging as closely to the synagogue's backdoor as possible, the door to the women's gallery. Still uncertain about whether this was the correct door, I hiked up the freshly painted steps and stepped into an eerie silence. The director of Radio Sonic stepped through the door, speaking in perfect English, "You must be the American music professor. Welcome to the studio of Transylvania's first privately funded radio station."

The director of Radio Sonic had every reason to be proud. With entrepreneurial skill and hard work, he and his coworkers had created a space for Western popular music in Transylvania. Programs were the products of individual hosts who brought their own compact disc collections; the host of the live program broadcasting at the moment came over to shake my hand, beaming as he pointed to his shelf of heavy-metal compact discs. Radio Sonic, moreover, managed to broadcast at certain times

External view, Parisu Street synagogue, Cluj Napoca, Romania. (Photograph by Philip Bohlman, courtesy Institut für Volksmusik-forschung.)

in Hungarian, the language of Cluj under Austro-Hungarian domination and still the language of one faculty of the city's Babeş-Bolyai University and theaters. "Nothing political, just trying to address Transylvania's minority groups."

"Broadcasts in Romany?" I asked, referring to the area's massive Roma population. "Gypsies aren't really a listening public for us," the director answered.

"Yiddish or German," I queried, "for the Jewish residents?" I followed with a tasteless attempt at humor, "After all, you broadcast from a synagogue."

No answer. The question made no sense. To break the silence, the director responded, "Most of all, we want to shift as much as possible to English so that we can build a bridge to the West."

I expressed my appreciation of this gesture to reach out to me, the visitor from the West, at the same time that I began to display nervousness in the maze of broadcast studios, poking my head into one office door after the other, looking for the restored synagogue.

To dispel my nervousness, the director quietly remarked, "I'm afraid

Internal view, Parisu Street synagogue, Cluj Napoca, Romania: Radio
Sonic. (Photograph by Philip Bohlman, courtesy Institut für Volks-
musikforschung.)

I don't know anything about the synagogue. It's downstairs. Radio Sonic
just has the second floor, where the extra seats used to be. You can't get
downstairs. It hasn't been used for years."

It is not by chance that this essay ends as it began. The closing ethnographic moment in Cluj is not the same as that in Budapest, but they narrate transition in Eastern Europe in similar ways. One is standing outside
the doors, as it were, of synagogues restored and yet not restored. Voice
has returned to these synagogues, even if the voices are the disembodied
voices of a nineteenth-century organ in Budapest and a rock-music radio
station in Cluj. Thanks to local and international investment in the new
market economies, the recovery of these voices was possible.

Restoration, nonetheless, remains incomplete, though in reality not
entirely for want of investment. If Radio Sonic could cover the women's
gallery in Cluj in drywall, it could probably scrounge up enough money to
clear the piles of plaster off the floor of the sanctuary below. But synagogue restoration in Eastern Europe is not truly about plaster and drywall.
It is about restoring the past by connecting it to the present. Such continuity, such processes of transition, however, cannot be undertaken effectively. The historical disjuncture is too great. It is, nonetheless, precisely

this historical disjuncture that can be sutured and repaired, if not restored. It is a historical disjuncture voiced by music competing for the spaces, sacred and secularized, in the synagogues of Eastern Europe. It is the voice of disjuncture that Rabbi Shmelke heard in the shofar of Rosh Hashanah in Mikulov. The sonic space of that disjuncture embodies questions about the Jewish presence in Eastern Europe, past and present. Restoring the synagogues of Eastern Europe makes it possible to hear that voice of history, if not occasionally to listen to it and to shudder at the deafening dissonance that it makes so palpable.

ACKNOWLEDGMENTS

Research for this article was made possible in 1990–91 by a grant from the Alexander von Humboldt Foundation (Forschungsstipendium) and in 1995–96 by a short-term grant from the International Research and Exchanges Board and by a Fulbright Guest Professorship (Council for the International Exchange of Scholars) in Musicology at the University of Vienna. I would like to express my gratitude to all these foundations and institutions. An earlier version of the article was presented in October 1996 at the Ethnomusicology Workshop of the University of Chicago, and I am indebted to the many helpful criticisms and suggestions offered by the workshop participants. The final version has benefited particularly from the insights of Matti Bunzl.

With deepest respect, moreover, I extend special thanks to the Jewish communities in Eastern Europe with whom I shared the experiences that made it possible to write this essay. The everyday experiences of these communities since 1945 and then again since 1989 profoundly narrate the transitions of Jewish life in the new Eastern Europe.

The Prague Experience: Gay Male Sex Tourism and the Neocolonial Invention of an Embodied Border

Matti Bunzl

As the train was approaching the Czech border following a little over an hour of quick and smooth riding from Vienna, one of my travel companions warned me, "Just wait until after the border! The train will slow down and it will take forever until we actually get to Prague. It happens every time!" I inquired into the reason for these delays. "Oh I don't know. I guess they're trying to fix the tracks, or something—trying to get them up to Austrian standards." Indeed, shortly after we passed the border markers, the train stopped for a few minutes, only to resume its northwesterly course to Prague at a markedly slower pace.[1]

In the context of the shifting cultural landscapes of post-1989 East-Central Europe, this concern over the train's deceleration marks a common metaphoric enactment of a border crossing whose complex tropes structure the sociospatial actualizations of the region's geography.[2] Thus, while Prague is located more than one hundred kilometers west of Vienna, my fellow travelers would frequently remind me that we had just entered the "former Eastern bloc" (*ehemalige Ostblock*), the "Eastern countries" (*Oststaaten*), or—in the most common figuration of a local topography always already bearing the imprints of diffuse yet powerful spatialized oppositions—simply the "East" (*Osten*).

I had boarded the train to Prague in May 1996 following the invitation of two Viennese acquaintances to accompany them on one of their frequent weekend trips to "gay Prague" (*das schwule Prag*). They had asked me to join them when I mentioned my interest in learning more about Prague's gay scene and its current status as the preferred site for Austrian gay male sex tourism. My own curiosity about the phenomenon had been piqued by a 1995 article in *XTRA*, Austria's most widely circu-

70

lated lesbian/gay publication. Written under the pen name "Petronius" (1995), the piece chronicled the author's experiences during a recent trip to the capital of the Czech Republic under the title "Prague Experiences" (*Prager Erlebnisse*). In vivid terms, Petronius (re-)created a story whose narrative structure mapped a transfiguring journey into a "heart of darkness."

Leaving the security of Vienna's environs, the author braves the "fucked-up Czech railway cars, which [Austrians] discarded in 1945" to approach Prague—an "Eastern bloc metropolis" (*Ostblockmetropole*) where he fearfully expects to encounter the remnants of the "worst times of socialism." Once there, however, Petronius finds himself pleasantly surprised. The bed-and-breakfast recommended to him by Austrian friends who had already made the trip to gay Prague turns out to offer all the "Western standards" the author desires as a "discerning gay tourist": large double bed, mini bar, and satellite TV.

From his room, Petronius, however, is quickly hurled into the exoticized world of the "Prague scene," from whence he emerges, after successfully negotiating the unfamiliar sociosexual terrain, with a young boy whose "broken German" is marked by the "cutest Czech accent." To Petronius's astonishment, the eighteen-year-old readily returns to the bed-and-breakfast, where—after eagerly consuming such amenities as the contents of the mini bar and the straight soft-porn beamed over the satellite—he engages Petronius in the most "passionate love-making of his life." As the author notes, "It was incredible and unbelievable; a young boy, who earlier seemed to be straight when he got all excited over the cheap hetero sex flicks, was now making more passionate and hotter sex than any gay youth I have had in my life."

Within the economy of Petronius's account, this moment of sociosexual disjuncture required an explanation intelligible to the author and the story's Austrian (gay male) audience. Rendering the boy's voice after "a repeat in the morning," Petronius circumscribed his encounter under a localized trope of sexual availability and uninhibited passion: "That is normal. Most Czech people are bisexual. I like sex, so I do it." Having thus conquered (both physically and discursively) Prague's sexually embodied heart of darkness, Petronius's article—which was illustrated with a nude photograph of a very young, skinny (presumably Czech) male in a sexual pose signaling availability—closed with the author's fantasy of settling permanently in the "golden city."

Petronius's account, which I read while preparing for several months of ethnographic research in Vienna, seemed to constitute what, in the context of colonial travel writings, Mary Louise Pratt has called "imperial meaning-making." In that sense, the text recalled the hegemonizing logic by which narratives of exploration fashion a conceptual matrix for the metropolitan creation of the "domestic subject of Euroimperialism" (1992, 4).[3] If Petronius's chronicle thus emerged as a sociodiscursive site of contemporary, neocolonial knowledge production, it pointed to the sexual politics of imagined empire as a principal arena for the embodied negotiation of the shifting boundaries of the New Europe. Viewed from that perspective, Petronius's narrative bore an uncanny resemblance to the discursive motifs circumscribing the sexual dynamics of imperial experience.[4]

Even more to the point, perhaps, the account's focus on same-sex sexual erotics recalled the body of texts Joseph Boone has analyzed under the rubric of the "homoerotics of Orientalism" (1995b, 89). Boone's readings of selected Western imagings of the Near East continuously reveal a pervasive sexual subtext premised on "the West's fantasies of an eroticized, decadent Arabic world whose perverse pleasures are matched only by its pansexual acrobatics" (Boone 1995a, 150). As the "geo-political realities of the Arabic Orient" thus "become a psychic screen on which to project [Western] fantasies of illicit sexuality and unbridled excess" (Boone 1995b, 89), the "Orient" effectively emerges as a sociosexual landscape of embodied Otherness.[5]

In the context of these critical analyses of the Western colonial/sexual imagination, I decided to go to Prague to investigate gay male sex tourism as a site of the neocolonial reterritorializations occasioned by the transition from "state socialist" to "capitalist" social orders. Following Pratt's lead, I conceived the sociogeographic space of Prague's gay scene as a "contact zone" (Pratt 1992, 6)—a (neo)colonial location where formerly separated groups come into ongoing physical relation, predicated on complex structures of economic, social, and symbolic inequality.

The Prague Experience: Tourism in the "New Europe"

Arriving in Prague after more than five hours on the train, we were greeted at the platform by several elderly women offering private accommodations to arriving tourists. "Never take them up on their offers—you don't know what you're getting into," Peter, one of my traveling companions, told me. "Just stick with me. I've been here so many times. I know how to deal with these people."

We also avoided the taxis parked outside the train station. "They always overcharge. They know you're from the West, and they just cheat you out of your money." We proceeded by foot, flagging down a cab on the street a few minutes later. Peter approached the taxi driver in German, inquiring about the price for a ride to our pensione. After a few minutes of debate, a sum was agreed on, and we boarded the taxi.

We traversed Prague's inner city, arriving, after twenty minutes or so, in one of the outer districts. There, the taxi stopped in a residential neighborhood in front of an inconspicuous, modern two-story building blending into an area characterized by recent construction. Other than the two Mercedes with German license plates parked outside the residence, nothing announced the building as the pensione Haus Hans, one of the preferred accommodations for gay male sex tourists in Prague.

As I quickly learned, Hans, the pensione's eponymous owner and manager, was a middle-aged German entrepreneur. He had initially visited the city in 1992 after hearing of the sexual possibilities Prague afforded gay men from the West. Charmed by what he found and recognizing the lacking infrastructure for gay male Western tourism as a business opportunity, Hans decided to relocate and open a guest house catering to a gay male clientele. With specific advertising in gay Western publications (Austria's *XTRA* among them) and listings in such gay male travel guides as *Spartacus,* Haus Hans proved an enormous financial success. At the time of my visit, reservations for a weekend stay in one of the pensione's six rooms required at least three months' notice, and Hans had just acquired another building to be converted into a second, larger, and even more luxurious pensione.[6]

As we were shown to our rooms, Haus Hans's allure for gay male Western tourists became instantly apparent. In a familial atmosphere, the predominantly middle-aged patrons—mostly German and American at the time of my visit—freely associated with a number of young Czech men who seemed to be hanging out at the pensione. As I was told, not only were guests of Haus Hans welcome to bring tricks and hustlers to the bed-and-breakfast, but their presence during the day was in fact encouraged. They were invited to take their meals with the guest house's patrons, and several amenities—ranging from video games to a bar—were provided specifically for their entertainment. In consequence, every day a different set of young men would populate the pensione—procured, I was told, in nightly excursions to Prague's gay locales.

As the evening approached, Peter and Alexander (my other traveling companion) readied themselves for the night's tour. As they explained, there were a number of different venues where available boys could be found. At first, they considered heading to some of the train stations and video game parlors where they had picked up young men in the past, but in the end they decided to go to the Acapulco—a gay bar and discotheque that had a reputation for a young and willing clientele. "And you will see," Peter told me, "it doesn't have that Eastern feel at all."

After paying a minimal cover charge, we entered the Acapulco. In the large, dimly lit room that opened before us, a number of slot machines dominated the scene. Two adjacent rooms housed a dance floor and bar, respectively. Michael Jackson blared over the sound system, but the dance floor was deserted. The bar, however, was filled to capacity. Most of the men sitting there were middle-aged or slightly older; Peter immediately identified them as Western tourists looking for "sex with boys." Indeed, several of the older men were engaged in conversations with Czech youths. Most of the Czechs—ranging in age from around sixteen to twenty-two— were grouped around the slot machines. Occasionally, an older patron would approach a young man, usually by offering to buy him a drink. Such invitations were almost always accepted. At other times, a middle-aged German man acted as matchmaker, introducing Western patrons to boys they had identified as desirable.

Peter and Alexander quickly gauged the situation. Among the boys at the slot machine, they recognized several former tricks. Recalling past experiences with some of them, they proceeded to decide on their choices for the night. Peter approached a youth previously unknown to him. During a drink, terms were quickly established, and within thirty minutes, Peter headed back to Haus Hans. Alexander left shortly thereafter with another young man in tow.

The next morning, I encountered them during breakfast at the guest house. The two boys had spent the night at the pensione, and now, at around 11:00 A.M., Peter and Alexander discussed options for the day. Eventually, they decided on a shopping trip, inviting along the two boys, who willingly accepted.

As Peter told me later, the boys had refused money in return for their sexual favors. But since it was assumed that some form of reciprocity other than free lodging was to take place, he and Alexander had decided on the shopping trip, where they would buy their tricks a number of goods. "Stuff here is so cheap for us anyway. It's really no problem," he explained.

Colonizing Histories, Postcolonial Analytics

Ultimately, this essay is concerned with the representational apparatus sustained in the interstices of such "Eastern" ethnographic realities and the "Western" experiential tropes through which they are at once constituted and apprehended. In this sense, I take some conceptual cues from Larry Wolff's remarkable intellectual counterhistory of Western European constructions of Otherness. In his book *Inventing Eastern Europe: The Map of Civilization on the Mind of the Enlightenment,* Wolff effectively locates the origin of "Eastern Europe" in eighteenth-century fabrications of a demi-Oriental sphere that cohered contradictory Western projections of cultural difference and backwardness into a self-contained sociogeographic entity.

As such, the opposition between Western and Eastern Europe was not grounded in a "a natural distinction, or even an innocent one, for it was produced as a work of cultural creation, of intellectual artifice, of ideological self-interest and self-promotion" (L. Wolff 1994, 4).[7]

Within the realm of the Hapsburg monarchy, the constructed fault line between East and West signified and reproduced the social geography of internal strife.[8] Until the inception of mass-based Slavic nationalist movements in the 1870s, the imagined universality of German cultural ideals had underwritten the ethnic hegemony that had characterized the Austrian empire. But if Slavs had been able to attain a viable German identity according to a logic of normative German *Bildung* and refinement, the situation changed in 1879, when the German liberal party was defeated at the elections to the Reichsrat, leading to an Austrian cabinet controlled by clerical, conservative, and pro-Slav parties. In that situation, the threatened German minority populations at the margins of the empire embraced a virulently nationalizing project. As Pieter Judson (1993) has shown, this project had overtly colonial undertones, replete with colonialism's constitutive tensions. On the one hand, the efforts of German nationalists were marked by the universalizing sense of their "civilizing mission" among the Slavs, a conception often directly modeled after European colonizers outside Europe. On the other hand, the nationalist project sought to give coherence to a previously undefined German identity by reimagining non-Germans as fundamentally different. As Judson puts it,

> In a geographically peripheral region of Austria, where German speakers represented a numerical minority, [German] nationalists . . . wanted local Germans consciously to reflect on the differences which supposedly separated them from their Czech neighbors. In time, these incidental differences would become understood as insuperable, and would yield a clearer sense of their own identity to all German speakers. (Judson 1993, 48)

In turn, the overtly colonial logic enabling the initial constitution and fortification of German- and Slaviceness in the Austrian empire authorized the seemingly self-evident ascription of the former to a progressive, forward-looking West, the latter to a backward and primitive East. If such powerfully vested distinctions at once mapped onto and underwrote the political realities of the Cold War period, Wolff, for one, is quick to note that the demise of the state-socialist order hardly effaced the conceptual boundaries circumscribing East and West in contemporary Europe. On the contrary, he intimates that the altered political landscape would afford a sociodiscursively privileged West the occasion to imagine "new associations to mark [their] difference" (L. Wolff 1994, 14). In this sense, the process of inventing Eastern Europe emerges as an ongoing phenomenon—a principal site for the negotiation and constitution of the sociocultural realities of the New Europe.

To date, few social scientists, however, have endeavored to trace Western (re)inventions of Eastern Europe engendered by the transitions in the formerly state-socialist countries.[9] This project attempts to amend this situation. Through the analysis of contemporary Austrian figurations of Czechness, I seek to elucidate the neocolonial Western project of charting and thereby inventing a new, posttransition Eastern Europe. In the face of the colonial history indexed by the ethnographic configuration being examined, I hold that this process is at once predicated on a long-standing Western intellectual and social project of Othering its Eastern counterpart and the immediate impetus generated by the events of 1989.[10] Following Boone's effective elucidation of the "homoerotics of Orientalism" as an integral part of the West's colonial imaginary, I focus on the embodied domain of male same-sex sexuality as a principal site for the (neo)colonial project of assigning socioculturally stratified locations within the New Europe. This emphasis on sexuality and the body as locations for the invention and negotiation of cultural distinction in the post-1989 world is not intended to foreclose other avenues of inquiry into the complex deployments of difference in the New Europe. On the contrary, I ultimately view the neocolonial constitution of an embodied border as part of a larger sociocultural apparatus whose representational dimensions range from mass-mediated images (such as the ones found in commercial films like *Mission Impossible*) to figurations of economic and political developments (ranging from the marketing of Eastern commodities and narrations of joint ventures to debates about EU and NATO expansion).

At the same time, I ultimately side with such scholars as Anne McClintock and Ann Stoler in thinking of sexuality and the body as privileged domains in the investigation of (neo)colonial orders (McClintock 1995; Stoler 1995). For if one takes seriously Foucault's (1978) analysis of the sexualized body as the primary interface of competing sociodiscursive and political agendas and thus the main site of post-Enlightenment subjectification, and furthermore, following the leads of George Mosse (1985) and Sander Gilman (1985), if one understands constructions of sexuality and the body as the arena of cultural differentiation and Othering in the modern world, then it seems worthwhile to focus on figurations of Eastern bodies and sexualities in an attempt to elucidate the West's ongoing negotiation of post-1989 Eastern Europe. The focus on gay male sexuality as an inroad to the problematics under question is, in turn, intended as a twofold corrective of ongoing analytic practices: On the one hand, I seek to restore from the usual ethnographic oblivion the active and specific contributions of gay men to larger social processes of cultural constitution and differentiation. On the other hand, I hope to augment the sparse literature written at the intersection of lesbian/gay studies and postcolonial criticism, thus pointing to the fields' mutual relevance and the need for continued inquiry along their various crossroads.

Concretely, I propose to read Austrian gay male sex tourism in Prague as a historically and culturally circumscribed practice whose ethnographic realities underwrite some of the discursive manifestations sustaining the larger project of reinventing Eastern Europe.[11] Like Wolff, who privileges the often sexually veiled accounts of travel into eighteenth-century Europe's heart of darkness in his reconstruction of the Enlightenment's mental map of the continent,[12] I argue that contemporary Austrian men's narratives of same-sex sexually motivated travel to the "contact zone" of Prague similarly function as part of ongoing negotiations of Europe's social and cultural topography. As I will illustrate in my analysis of these discourses, they effectively enact conceptions of an embodied border through constitutive metaphors of (same-sexed) sexual Otherness.

To substantiate this argument, the remainder of this essay is structured as follows: First, I will consider some of the salient parameters circumscribing Prague's (and the Czech Republic's) same-sex sociosexual field, followed by a discussion of some of the specificities of Austrian gay male existence. I will then turn to narratives of the Prague experience, analyzing how gay male Austrians enact recurring tropological fields that underwrite the construction of a (same-sex) sexually embodied border. Invoking the voices of a dozen Austrian men who have offered me lengthy accounts of their travels to Prague, I will initially examine the neocolonial tropes underlying the narrative figuration of Eastern border crossings and the pragmatic constitution of Western same-sex circles in Prague's sociosexual field. I will then analyze the sociodiscursive invention of Czech same-sex sexual Otherness, focusing on the tropes of availability, passion, and pansexuality. Following an examination of these tropes' narrative naturalization, I will, in conclusion, turn to the question of sociosexual subjectification, arguing that—in the case of Austrian same-sex sexuality—it bears the traces of a neocolonial economy, fortifying the colonizer's sexual subjectivities through constitutive disavowal of the fantasized sexual Other.

Before I can proceed, however, I need to further locate the epistemological basis of my argument. I am by ethnographic and linguistic competence an anthropologist of contemporary Austria, not the Czech lands. This article is thus written from a distinctly Austrian perspective, giving voice to the cultural work of Austrian gay men rather than their Czech interlocutors. In this sense, the essay deliberately eschews the trappings of an ethnographic panopticism (Rosaldo 1986)—a mode of inquiry and textual representation that constructs the anthropologist as an omniscient figure. Rejecting the colonially veiled and culturally decontextualized apparatus of third-party translation (see Tomas 1991), I do not purport to comprehend the social world of the Czech men who associate with Western sex tourists. In limiting this article to the reconstruction and interrogation of the Austrian experiential tropes generated in the environs of the Prague experience, my ethnographic stance thus admits to its own partiality (Clifford 1986a). However, this partiality remains strictly faithful to my interlocutors' "native point of view." After all, Austrian gay male sex tourists experience the Czech Republic as a site of sociosexual Otherness, a situation that structures their narratives of the Prague experience as vehicles of situated cultural (in)comprehension—the exact process, in other words, that this essay seeks to elucidate.

Beyond advancing an epistemology of ethnographic partiality, my focus on the Austrian dimension of the Prague experience enunciates a more general argument about the transitions in Eastern Europe. Other contributors in this collection have interrogated the directionality of transition (Stephanie Platz) or questioned its conventional dating (Anna Szemere). My essay, in contrast, seeks to complicate its standardized localization. While the existing literature tends to trace the effects of the transition exclusively within the previously state-socialist countries, this piece documents the transition's relevance on the other side of the former divide. I argue that in terms of the reorganization of cultural orientations and practices, the transition occurred (and occurs) not only within the boundaries of the former Eastern bloc but also in the West, where the sudden access to the East and its commodities, be they goods or bodies, profoundly altered the state of social and cultural affairs.[13] In this sense, my analysis of the Prague experience only begins to chart the complex dynamics of transition in the West.

The Sexual Politics of East and West

In recent years, the liberalizations in the formerly state-socialist countries have spurred the growth of relatively public gay male scenes in several major cities. For socioeconomically advantaged Western travelers, this development occasioned the proliferation of potential sites of sexual opportunity, often figured—to use Boone's term—as an imperialist "economics of boys" (1995b, 99). This gay male touristic fascination has recently been chronicled in American novelist Stan Persky's journalistic travelogue *Boyopolis: Sex and Politics in Gay Eastern Europe* (1996), which follows the geography of the author's sexual exploits, taking the reader from East Berlin and Warsaw to Budapest and Zagreb.

While Prague does not figure in Persky's autobiographical account, the city has come to occupy a prominent place in Western travelers' imagination of Eastern Europe's same-sex sexual topography. Beyond Prague's obvious touristic attraction as "one of the most unspoiled historic city centers in Central Europe," *Spartacus* also extols the city's ability to develop according to Western standards (1996, 179). The guide's sentiment that "Prague is booming" while "other eastern and central European cities are finding the new economic climate difficult" (1996, 179) recalls commonly held perceptions of the Czech Republic as a rapidly and properly Westernizing country (see, e.g., Matouschek, Wodak, and Januschek 1995, 238). *Spartacus* is also quick to figure Prague and the Czech Republic more generally as particularly tolerant and licentious social spaces—a notion that is echoed, albeit in a heterosexual context, by such prominent chroniclers of the New Eastern Europe as Eva Hoffman (1993, 120–88). Indeed, the country's current legislation of same-sex sexuality is among the most liberal in Europe. A statute setting the age of consent for male and female same-sex sexual relations at eighteen was abolished in 1990, leaving fifteen as the general legal age limit for mutually consensual sexual activity (Graupner 1995, vol. 2).[14] In this light, it should not be surprising that Prague has quickly become a fixture in the gay world. A burgeoning center of gay male pornography, the city also boasts a continuously expanding gay infrastructure. A recent addition is a franchise of American-owned Drakes—a twenty-four-hour gay erotic center that advertises its location to Western tourists through a geographically deployed trope of sexual allure: "Discover Prague, the new Amsterdam" (*Spartacus* 1996, 181).

By contrast, Vienna—Austria's largest city and the home to an overwhelming number of the country's open lesbian/gay population—features a quiet, predominantly local gay male scene. While the city's same-sex sexual politics of everyday life are marked by tensions between an urbane laissez-faire attitude and powerful remnants of hostile Catholic doctrines, the country's gay men continue to be the victims of an overtly discriminating legal code. While two paragraphs respectively interdicting "propaganda" for "sexual relations between persons of the same sex" and the formation of "associations" intended to "facilitate same-sex sexual relations" were abolished in early 1997 following years of lobbying by lesbian/gay organizations, Austria's infamous Paragraph 209 remains on the books to this day. That piece of legislation prohibits same-sex sexual relations of male persons over the age of nineteen with their fourteen- to eighteen-year-old counterparts regardless of mutual consent. In the absence of equivalent statutes outlawing heterosexual and lesbian relationships (both legal at fourteen) in these age brackets, Paragraph 209 not only constitutes a symbolic act of marginalization and disenfranchisement but presents a very real legal threat in light of dozens of convictions each year (Bunzl 1997; Handl et al. 1989).

While the existence of Paragraph 209 undoubtedly plays a role in rendering the Czech Republic a desirable travel destination for gay male Austrians (especially those with sexual interests in younger partners), the allure of Prague clearly extends beyond the lower age of consent. None of my gay male Austrian interlocutors, for example, indicated that they would cease their regular visits to Prague if Paragraph 209 were abolished (which is a possibility, given a slightly altered political constellation). For many of the men I interviewed, the Prague experience has simply become a constitutive aspect of gay life in contemporary Austria. Indeed, I estimate that among the several hundred gay men in my Viennese circle of acquaintances, around 75 percent have traveled to Prague over the past five or six years, while at least 30 percent visit the "golden city" as sex tourists with some degree of regularity. Because Prague has thus become by far the most popular single tourist destination for gay Austrian men, the narratives of these trips not only structure the neocolonial invention of an embodied border but circumscribe the experiential horizon underwriting the actualization of sociosexual subjectification in the New Europe.[15]

Narrating the "Eastern" Other: Czech Bodies, Czech Sexualities

Without exception, all narratives of the Prague experience collected in the course of field research are anchored in culturally resonant accounts of border crossings in the New Europe. As such, they are sustained by a field of colonizing tropes, signifying and (re)constituting Austria's privileged position—socioeconomically grounded and popularly imagined—vis-à-vis the "emerging democracies in the East" (see Matouschek, Wodak, and Januschek 1995, 245). The main discursive site of this neocolonial construction is the metonymic linkage of Prague qua the East as an unknown and inherently foreign heart of darkness to be conquered by the Western traveler. This trope is in turn underwritten and augmented by the socially scripted reactions to the cultural realities of the Eastern Other, which are almost invariably figured in constitutive opposition to a Western Self.

Petronius's account of the Prague experience can serve as an ideal type for the colonial underpinnings structuring narrativizations of the journey to the East. Just as the continent's sociopolitical realities discouraged him from entering the East during the state-socialist period, none of my interlocutors reported any immediate familiarity with the Eastern countries prior to their sexually motivated forays to Prague. And much like Petronius, they figured their venture into the contact zone as a perilous quest. "Of course I was a little scared to go at first," one Viennese man told me. "After all, I didn't know *what* to expect there; so when a friend initially asked me to come to Prague with him, I was very defensive. 'No,' I said, 'I don't want to leave my familiar surroundings [*Umfeld*].'"

The familiar surroundings of Vienna thus stand in constitutive opposition to a diffuse set of dangers—a trope at once predicated on the neocolonial semiotic structuring contemporary Austrian discourse about the East and generative of the expectational horizon of Prague's sex tourists. In this light, the East's sociocultural realities invariably signify in a hierarchy that figures Austria qua the West as a normative marker of proper development. As one frequent sex tourist to Prague put it, "When I started going to Prague three years ago, it was still pretty much communist. Just awful, really in Eastern bloc fashion [*ostblockmäßig*]. It was just like Vienna after the war [*Nachkriegszustand*]."[16] Only very recently, my interlocutor opined, had Prague begun to approach Western standards.

If such inherently hierarchical encounters in the contact zone fortify Western subject positions by engendering the patronizing approbation underlying neocolonial demands for "improvement," they also produce a specific neocolonial knowledge situated at the intersection of socioeconomic privilege and structured misrecognitions of local realities. Thus, the narratives of gay male sex tourists in Prague are permeated with various conspiracy theories clustered around diffuse fears of falling victim to one's own Otherness. My interlocutors repeatedly told me that the Czech bureaucracy, police, and military operated like a mafia, singling out Western tourists as potential prey. In the final analysis, only an intimate familiarity with the abject Eastern terrain could truly protect Westerners from harm. One man's account of his dealings with Czech taxicabs illustrates the neocolonial dimension of this territorial knowledge:

> Even the taxi drivers are a mafia. They take advantage of you whenever they can. If you look stupid enough—and they think every foreigner is stupid enough—then you pay three or four times as much, because you don't know how much it is supposed to cost. And when you've been cheated like that, you will begin to learn what to look at. You will know how they manipulate the taximeters. If you've been there long enough, they won't be able to get you.

Ultimately, this ready ability of Austrian gay male sex tourists to lay prolonged territorial—as well as epistemological—claim to Prague's social geography at once evidences the neocolonial underpinnings of their sexual ventures into the Czech Republic and underwrites the powerfully vested construction of embodied Otherness. For in the final analysis, an instance of neocolonial knowledge production structures the invention of a distinct Eastern (same-sex) sexuality.

In the context of the economies of gay male sex tourism in Prague, this neocolonial project finds its spatial anchoring and practical enactment in such localized microcosms as Haus Hans. There, in effect, congregates a gemeinschaft sustained by the neocolonial possibilities Prague affords gay male Western tourists. The centrality of such an immanent community of colonizers to the pragmatics of gay male tourism is evidenced in the frequent invocation of Haus Hans as the central site of the Prague experience. Many of my interlocutors—nearly all of whom had stayed at Haus Hans on one occasion or another, with a majority returning on a regular basis—noted the pensione's friendly and familiar atmosphere as gay Prague's main attraction.

Such narratives most often figure Haus Hans as a shelter against the diffuse threats posed by an underdeveloped and potentially hostile environment. If Petronius thus emphasized the Western amenities available at the guest house, one of my interviewees linked that trope to the pensione's function of protection:

> Haus Hans is very, very pleasant. It really is something sensational. Hans is such a nice man who always has everything under control. He has been there for such a long time. And he is always very attentive when there could be anything dangerous [*der sehr aufpaßt wenn was gefährlich sein könnte*].

In essence, Hans is constructed here as a trusted, because ultimately Western, figure whose prolonged familiarity with the Eastern Other renders him a logical focus of neocolonial expatriate community building.

But if the physical (and cultural) security afforded in Haus Hans's haven of Western tranquillity remains a major draw for Austrian sex tourists, the pensione's main attraction lies in the effective sustenance of a gemeinschaft of gay Western men who share a common neocolonial relation with Eastern bodies. In this sense, most men commented on the constant presence of Czech boys (and the possibilities enjoined by that situation):

> That's what's so great about Haus Hans—to be able to meet a boy over breakfast—a boy, who was brought to the pensione by two friends who happen to be staying two rooms down. . . . That does not go in the direction of group sex, but more like, a bunch of

young Czech men on the one side, and a bunch of foreign johns on the other.

Ultimately, this figuration of Eastern boys vis-à-vis Western men not only signals the socioculturally sustained directionality of the Prague experience (with the Eastern boys brought to the guest house by and for the enjoyment of Western men) but underwrites the strict conceptual and symbolic separation that governs its sexual economy. This economy enacts an ethnicized form of homosociality that ties Western men to Eastern boys through shared vectors of desire while simultaneously foreclosing erotic bonds within the hierarchically privileged class of men (see Sedgwick 1985). In sociodiscursive practice this foreclosure is transported in a strict linguistic regime that renders other Western johns—German, American, or Dutch—as potential or actual friends and buddies while relegating Eastern men to the status of boys, a deliberately deindividuating denomination signaling their position as circulating commodities.[17]

Even more important in this project of homosocial regulation, however, is the neocolonial invention of a distinct Eastern sexuality—a sexuality that, more fully than any linguistic regime, enacts the delineation between Eastern and Western bodies in the narrative practice of their (re)constitution (a process extending from casual comparisons of a boy's performance in Haus Hans to accounts of sexual encounters provided in such neutral settings as an ethnographic interview). The following analysis focuses on the tropes of availability, passion, and pansexuality as the privileged coordinates in gay male sex tourists' negotiation of their embodied border crossings in the New Europe.

The colonial trope of sexual availability has been noted repeatedly, albeit in heterosexual contexts, in the critical analyses of sexualized figurations of the West's various Others (see Said 1979, 190; McClintock 1995). Much as in Boone's account of the literary homoerotics of Orientalism, however, the figure is readily transposed into colonial same-sex sexual fields, particularly those structured around a hierarchizing binary between colonizing men and colonized boys (Boone 1995b, 99–104). In Prague's neocolonial context, the trope prominently reappears in the narratives of gay male sex tourists. There, it is often embedded in an implicitly comparative framework pitting the ready availability of Eastern men against difficulties encountered in approaching potential sex partners at home:

When we first went to Prague, we didn't dare to do anything. We hadn't yet realized how different things really were there. The second time I went, I still didn't do anything on the first day. But then on the second day, I gave myself a kick and I approached one of the boys in the gay disco. He was sitting at a table by himself, and I just sat down next to him. I was surprised that he didn't mind, and we immediately started talking—was all sweet and friendly and totally interested in talking to me. And then another guy joined us. It was a revelation.

Most narratives of gay male sex tourists contain similar moments of revelation engendered by the perception of Eastern men's willingness to readily associate and engage in same-sex sex with Westerners. Most narratives figure this initial surprise as a precursor to a more seasoned understanding of Czechs' general interest in sexual relations with Western men. Reflecting a variance in individual tastes and expectations, such relations are thought to include one-night stands, little affairs, holiday flings (*Urlaubsabenteuer*), and long-term relationships:

It's just really simple with the Eastern boys—getting to know them, I mean, and to develop something. It's real easy to have more than a one-night stand if that's what you want. It can last for a couple of days, even longer sometimes. It might not be a real relationship, but you get the feeling like it is.

In such accounts of sexual availability, the potentiality of monetary exchange is invariably bracketed. In a neocolonial context marked by highly stratified purchasing powers, prostitution (even if the term should apply on a technical level of sexual favors extended in return for remuneration) is not figured as an economic burden. If one of my interlocutors, for example, told me that "boys can be easily acquired over there," it ultimately remained unclear whether that notion signified the boys' status as prostitutes. Most of my interlocutors were careful to emphasize that their tricks were not in fact prostitutes (a status that confers little symbolic capital in the neocolonial communities sustained at such sites as Haus Hans). At the same time, it is always understood that Western johns trafficking in Eastern boys compensate their sex partners materially in the form of money, gifts, and/or the provision of meals and lodging for a specific time.

If the specter of prostitution fails to alter sex tourists' figurations of the always sexually available and willing Eastern boy, it is in large part due to a closely related sexualized conception of Czech bodies as distinctly passionate and sensual. Many of my interlocutors, for example, argued that the sexual energy exerted by their Czech lovers was proof of their genuine desire to be with Western men, regardless of any material arrangements that might frame the encounter:

The boys in Prague are always so very active in bed. I couldn't believe it at the beginning. Even at times when money was involved, they would behave in bed just like a gay lover. As passionate as you can only imagine. And then most of them will tell you immediately that they're in love with you—it's so nice. They might be seeing people on the side, but that just doesn't matter.

For other Austrian gay male tourists, Czech men's sexual Otherness is expressed less through their passionate bearing in bed than through a mysterious, sensual intuition that is said to guide their behavior. Figured in opposition to an unmarked Western sexuality, it is an image that surfaces in accounts of Eastern boys' ability to service Western men: "I had never seen anything like that at home. He didn't have his own agenda, but was totally attentive to me. We couldn't really communicate, of course, but somehow he could feel what it was that I wanted. And he just did that."

This imagined sociosexual context of unencumbered passion and enigmatic selflessness renders the Prague experience a primary site for liminal sexual experiences. Citing the absence of inhibitions, a number of Austrian sex tourists described their encounters in Prague as a space for sexual experimentation and unknown pleasures. One Austrian man recounted the following episode:

I really don't think I had ever had such incredible sex. And that was also the first and only time in my life where I was a "top" during anal intercourse. That is something I always long for. I really want to, but normally I just don't dare to do it, even though it's the hottest thing for me.

So we were in bed and at first everything was unclear. His body language signaled that it would be possible for me to take him, but I thought, "Better not. It just won't work." But he just insisted on fucking. So I thought, "OK, I'll just let him fuck me." But then he signaled, "No, the other way around." And I was just perplexed. But then it was just so hot.

A similar narrative thematizing the transcendence of sexual boundaries in conjunction with figurations of Czech men's passion was offered to me by another sex tourist: "I went to Haus Hans with this guy. He was just like a wild animal. He fucked me so hard that I came without any immediate stimulation. That had never happened to me. I hadn't even known that that was possible."

If Austrian gay male sex tourists figure the Eastern bodies they encounter in the course of the Prague experience through the tropes of availability and passion, they also fit them with a distinct sexual subjectivity—a kind of pansexuality that is believed to underwrite Czech men's sexual practices. On a narrative level, this pansexual subjectivity is realized as a sociocultural site of embodied difference, surfacing as a naturalized omnisexuality. The following account illustrates the sexual indefiniteness that characterizes Western figurations of Czech men's Eastern sexuality:

> In their conduct, Czechoslovakian[18] boys are much, much more open to the topic of homosexuality. There, it is never automatically: "Oh no, get away from me, I'm not gay." Especially in the Czech Republic, the readiness and self-evidence [*Selbstverständlichkeit*] to have sex, even boys with men, is just so much greater than I have ever experienced in Vienna. It's just not a problem for them to have gay sex, even when they otherwise only sleep with girls. In fact, most of the boys I have encountered seem to prefer women, but that's just never a problem.

While such accounts of Czech omnisexuality serve as an explanatory scheme for Eastern men's willingness to engage in same-sex sexual activity with Westerners, the indeterminacy of this naturalized pansexuality also occasions demands for a more rigorous and culturally resonant sociosexual categorization. Several Austrian men, in fact, recalled attempts to determine the sexual orientation of their sex partners. More often than not, however, such inquires failed to yield tangible results: "So when you then ask them if they are gay or hetero, they usually don't respond in a straightforward way. They just never say, 'yes, gay' or 'hetero,' but they will give you a percentage, like, 'I'm 30 percent gay.' I find that strange and endearing at the same time." In this light, most Austrian gay male sex tourists figure the men they encounter in the course of the Prague experience as bisexual. At the same time, my interlocutors noted the term's radically different valence:

> Well, I guess most Czech boys are bisexual. But it is just not the same as in Austria. There are so few bisexuals in Vienna, and most of the ones I know are either gay and only pretend to also like women, or they've had affairs with girls years ago. Sure, there are a few people who really like to go to bed with men and women, but it's really rare. Most people want to do one or the other.
>
> In Prague, things are totally different. They are just so openly bisexual. Just about all the boys I've had sex with there had girlfriends, but they were into having sex with men as well. At the same

time, there are hardly any real homosexuals, who only sleep with men. I really think they just like to have sex—boys, men, women—it just doesn't matter. They're just not afraid of their sexuality, and so I've always gotten what I wanted.

In such narratives of sexual conquest in the New Europe, the tropes of availability, passion, and pansexuality ultimately congeal into a topography of embodied Otherness. Constructed on the neocolonial terms of a Western gay male subject seeking adventures in an exoticized East, they delineate a sociosexual field structured by an economy of Eastern supplies for Western demands.

This sexual geography's neocolonial structuration is at once sustained and heightened by the narrative suppression of its constitutive socioeconomic inequalities. Analogous to Pratt's notion of colonial "anticonquest"—the "strategies of representation whereby European bourgeois subjects seek to secure their innocence in the same moment as they assert European hegemony" (1992, 7)—Austrian gay male sex tourists tend to systematically misrecognize the sociosexual positionalities engendered by the Prague experience. The main discursive vehicle of this structured misrecognition is the constitutive negation of the socioeconomic realities circumscribing the ongoing transition in East-Central Europe. In this regard, none of my interlocutors volunteered observations on standards of living, purchasing power, or currency exchange. Even when prompted through specific questions, the Austrian sex tourists I interviewed were by and large unprepared to reflect on the socioeconomic underpinnings of the Prague experience. In this light, the realities of Czech infrastructures entered conversation only through appraisals of the presence or absence of specific Western amenities—a recurrent, neocolonial trope that gauges the East's developmental trajectory against normative Austrian standards.

The constitutive suppression of the socioeconomic differences underlying the Prague experience finds its sociosexual correlate in the figuration of the sexual groupings sustained in its environs. Concretely, Austrian gay male sex tourists tend to negate the structured inequalities engendering the encounters between Western and Czech men. Rather than viewing the encounters as predicated on the entrance of a socioeconomically privileged group vis-à-vis an underprivileged population, they are routinely constructed in universalizing terms that obfuscate specific inequalities through recourse to notions of mutuality. In this regard, Austrian sex tourists always resist the figuration of their Czech sex partners as prostitutes, notwithstanding their self-evident remuneration in one form or another. In a typical statement, one interlocutor illustrated the Prague experience in opposition to an imagined scene of Thai gay male prostitution:

Yes, of course, I give a boy money or buy him clothes or something like that. But that doesn't mean he's a prostitute. I think I would have grave moral problems if things in Prague were like they are in Thailand. I mean, I've never been to Thailand, but I hear that you just make your selection, go to your hotel for an hour, and that's it. There is just no affection like there is in Prague, where the boy really wants to be with you and where you can have much more than just a one-night stand.

Such exteriorizations of the specter of prostitution not only disaffirm the tangible reminders of the material inequities sustaining the Prague experience but effectively foreclose any recognition of the socioeconomic privileges enjoyed by Westerners in this neocolonial setting.

This suppression of the socioeconomic dimension of the Prague experience in turn underwrites the naturalization of the Eastern body and its sexuality in terms of timeless cultural difference. For, in the negation of socioeconomic inequalities as an explanatory model for Czech men's willingness to engage in same-sex sexual activity with Western tourists, their behavioral and embodied characteristics are readily ascribed to a primordial Czechness: "I really think that Czechs are very free about their sexuality. I don't really know why that is. Maybe it's something about their culture [*Kultur*]. It probably has been like that for a long time, and now that communism is gone, it can come out again." In this socially deployed narrative context, the tropes of availability, passion, and pansexuality are effectively grafted onto a dehistoricized system of cultural differentiation.

In the final analysis, this construction of Czech-embodied Otherness indexes a sociosexually veiled geopolitical landscape where cultural specificities are distributed according to a neocolonial logic. In reiterating and refracting older colonial regimes of nationalist separation, it is part of a sociodiscursive system that effectively demarcates and constitutes a distinct Eastern body in the transitory interstices and metropolitan pleasures afforded in the New Europe.

Neocolonial Subjectifications

In many ways, this figuration and sociodiscursive naturalization of a distinctly coded Eastern (same-sex) sexuality recalls Homi Bhabha's groundbreaking analyses of the operative principles of colonial discourse. As Bhabha notes in his article "The Other Question: Stereotype, Discrimination and the Discourse of Colonialism," the construction of colonial subjects in and through discourse is predicated on the "exercise of [a] colonial power" that not merely facilitates but in fact "demands an articulation of forms of difference" on "racial and sexual" grounds (1994, 67). Bhabha's emphasis on embodied conceptions of difference underwrites an analytic intervention that effectively refigures colonial (and neocolonial) discourse as a generative representational apparatus. Rather than interrogating (neo)colonial images for their specific qualitative valences, Bhabha enunciates a Foucauldian project, proposing to focus on the *"processes of subjectification* made possible (and plausible) through [the] stereotypical discourse[s]" sustaining (neo)colonial projects. In this manner, (neo)colonial discourse becomes intelligible as a moment of *"productive* ambivalence"— a site that generates colonial fields of power and knowledge as well as the colonizing and colonized subjectivities produced in their conceptual environs (67). In this sense the (narrative) domain of sexuality ultimately occupies a privileged if intrinsically ambiguous position in (neo)colonial discourse, interpolating both colonizing and colonized subjects in inherently stratified positionalities.

Indeed, the fortification of a specifically Western gay male subject position is continuously effected in the environs of the Prague experience, rendering it a privileged site of sociosexual subjectification in the New Europe. In the ethnographic context of this essay, the ubiquitous comparisons between Czech (qua Eastern or Slavic) and Austrian (qua Western) sexual subjectivity underwrite the latter's demarcation by way of the former's constitutive abjection. In this regard, the conspicuous trope of Czech pansexuality occupies a specifically vested position. As it is imagined in the narrative practice engendered by the Prague experience, it is figured against the backdrop of an Austrian sociosexual system pervasively stratified according to the hetero-homo binary. As one Austrian gay male sex tourist put it: "Over there, things are just totally different. You can sleep with men, women, whatever. They just don't seem to feel any pressure to decide what they want or who they are. In Vienna, you're either hetero or homo, and if you like to do both, most people think you're kind of weird." While such statements suggest the subversive potential implicit in a sociosexual system structured above and beyond the hetero-homo dyad, the Prague experience ultimately occasions the reification of its sociosexually scripted stratification. For, notwithstanding the marginalization and oppression effected by the strict enforcement of the hetero-homo binary in Austria's sociosexual field (Bunzl 1997; Handl et al. 1989), the gay male sex tourists I interviewed in the course of researching this essay thoroughly exteriorized their imagined notion of Czech pansexuality, constructing it in abject opposition to a stratified site of Austrian gay male subjectification:

I love to go to Prague. It's so close to Vienna, but at the same time it's a totally different world. People are just so loose sexually. It's almost like there is no order. When I'm with a boy, I just never know if he's gay, straight, bi—it's really strange. Something like that would never be possible in Austria. And actually I'm glad. I really think people are either hetero or homo—it makes things a lot easier.

Through such abjectly exoticized constructions of Czech pansexuality, the narrative field underwritten by the Prague experience ultimately sustains the fortification of Austrian gay male subjectification according to the normalizing principles of the hetero-homo dyad.

If the Prague experience functions as a principal site for the production and reinscription of a normative Austrian same-sex sexuality, it also engenders its constitution as a distinctly neocolonial subjectivity. In particular, the communal interstices sustained at such neocolonial sites as Haus Hans occasion a sociosexual subject position marked by Western privileges over Eastern bodies. As Austrian gay male subjectivity is reproduced and fortified in such spaces, it is thus ultimately reconstituted as part of larger processes of subjectification that construct distinctly Western sexualities in constitutive opposition to the East's embodied Otherness.

The grounding of these Western sexualities in the realities of neocolonial power differentials, in turn, underwrites their production beyond the specificities of the Prague experience. For the sociosexual field circumscribed in its environs ultimately reaches beyond Prague's gay male spaces to include various other topographies of Eastern sexual Otherness. As Persky's travelogue, among other recent accounts, amply demonstrates, the Eastern frontier of the New Europe affords numerous sites of Western sociosexual subjectification—sites always already marked by the micropolitics of neocolonial privilege. The current preponderance of Hungarian, Slovakian, and Czech prostitutes offering their services in Vienna's gay male scene only underlines the translocal dimension of this geopolitically stratified process of sociosexual subjectification.

If Austrian gay male figurations of embodied Czech Otherness thus become intelligible as the colonizing traces of a distinctly Western sociosexual subject position, much ethnographic work needs to be done on the other side of the Prague experience. Whether Czech sexual subjectivities should be conceived as inherently colonized entities or as sites of resistance against hegemonic sociosexual regimes (or both, as Bhabha's theorizations of colonialism's constitutive ambiguities might suggest) remains to be debated in light of evidence documenting Czech negotiations and figurations of Western sexualities.

NOTES

For their helpful comments and valuable insights, I thank Daphne Berdahl, Martha Lampland, Susan Gal, Billy Vaughn, David Churchill, Chad Heap, Mark Blackbird, Helmut Graupner, Stefan Dobias, Michael Toth, the members of the Anthropology of Europe Workshop at the University of Chicago, and the two anonymous readers for the University of Michigan Press.

1. Conceived in the environs of a full-scale ethnography of gay Vienna, fieldwork and interviews for this article were conducted during eight months of ethnographic research from April to November 1996. Following anthropological convention, all proper names used in this article are fictitious.

2. For another ethnographic account of border crossings in the New Europe, see Bohlman 1996b.

3. For other critical accounts of the intersection of travel narratives and colonial knowledge, see Mills 1991; Spurr 1993; Blunt 1994.

4. Since the publication of Edward Said's pathbreaking *Orientalism* (1979), questions of sexuality and the body have occupied a privileged space in postcolonial theory and criticism. Said himself famously reflected that the dynamics producing "typically Oriental" women for the Western imagination "fairly stands for the relative strength between East and West, and the discourse about the Orient that it enabled" (1979, 6). If the construction of exoticized sexualities thus emerges, in Said's analysis, as a salient metaphor for the (neo)colonial process of circumscribing and subjugating the Other, several other critics of Western imperialism have identified the domain of sexuality as the principal site of the colonial contest. In this manner, British colonial historian Ronald Hyam holds that "sexual attitudes" not only "influenced the lives of the imperial elite as well as the subjects of empire" but in fact "crucially underpinned the whole operation of British empire and Victorian expansion. Without the easy range of sexual opportunities which imperial systems provided, the long-term administration and exploitation of tropical territories . . . might well have been impossible" (Hyam 1990, 1). If such analyses of the imperial (hetero)sexual field map phantasmic sexualities on colonized spaces, literary critics such as Anne McClintock have recently focused on the domains of gender, sexuality, and respectability to document colonialism's metropolitan realities. In this framework, modern "Western" identities (racial, sexual, and so forth) emerge as always already constituted in abject relation to the exoticized Others of the colonial contest. As McClintock effectively puts it, "imperialism is not something that happened elsewhere" (1995, 5). Rather, as a mechanism triangulating between such intertwined dimensions as colonial power, money, sexuality, race, and gender, it is figured as the central component in the conceptual field of metropolitan subjectification. It is in that sense that sexualities emerge as privileged sites for the constitution (and analysis) of (neo)colonial relations. Within the discipline of anthropology, Ann Stoler's work has rendered the problematics of colonialism and sexuality as a central area of inquiry. In several influential articles (1989; 1991; 1992), she has scrutinized the colonial histories of French

Indochina and the Dutch East Indies to "suggest that the very categories of 'colonizer' and 'colonized' were secured through forms of sexual control that defined the domestic arrangements of Europeans and the cultural investments by which they identified themselves" (1989, 634–35). More recently, her book *Race and the Education of Desire* (1995) deploys a critical reading of Foucault to frame the history of European sexuality itself as a constitutive reflection of colonial domination. In this analytic context, the domain of sexuality and the complex forms of its normalizing deployment emerge as privileged sites for the anthropological engagement with (neo)colonial situations across the ethnographic spectrum. On the gendered and sexual dimensions of the German colonial experience, see the work of Lora Wildenthal (1993; 1994; 1997).

5. Taking its conceptual cues directly from Said's *Orientalism,* Boone's work remains one of very few attempts to problematize same-sex sexuality in the context of the colonial contest. For Boone (following Said), the "Orient" essentially functions as a site of "sexual promise," offering the realization of illicit gay male fantasies. As Boone puts it, "the fact remains that the possibility of sexual contact with and between men underwrites and at times even explains the historical appeal of orientalism as an occidental mode of male perception, appropriation, and control" (1995b, 90). In thus extending Said's critique of the sexual subjugation of "Oriental women," it is not surprising that Boone emphasizes gay male Western figurations of the Near East, focusing in particular on North African sites such as the Moroccan Tangier (1995b, 99–104). In part, this article was conceived as a reformulation of Boone's project in an intra-European context. In this sense, I hope to add to and complicate the understanding of the (homo)sexual dimension inherent in the "West's" contradictory figurations of its "Eastern" Others. Other work on the subject includes Lane's (1995) Lacanian analyses of images of masculinity and gay male desire in British colonialist literature and Bleys's (1996) account of the history of same-sex sexuality in the ethnographic imagination of a colonializing Europe. Given this limited literature, the relation between (neo)colonial regimes and gay male sexuality (not even to mention lesbian desire) remains insufficiently appreciated.

6. Haus Hans is one of roughly half a dozen bed-and-breakfasts in Prague that cater to an explicitly international gay male clientele. While most Western sex tourists choose to reside in one of the gay-identified bed-and-breakfasts when in Prague, some affluent travelers do prefer large hotels with established international reputations.

7. On the "invention" of Eastern Europe, see also Maria Todorova's work on the Balkans (1997).

8. In this brief discussion, I am focusing on the colonial and representational dynamics of the Austrian empire (or as it was officially termed, "the Kingdoms and Lands represented in the Reichsrat," a territory that encompassed present-day Austria as well as the predominantly Slavic-speaking areas of Bohemia, Moravia, Galicia, Bukovina, Carniola, and Istria). I am thus bracketing the complex linguistic and cultural politics in the kingdom of Hungary, where Hungarian and German hegemonies existed in highly compartmentalized forms.

9. A notable exception to this trend is a group of Austrian sociolinguists who have begun to chart the complex strategies and diffuse assumptions underlying the ongoing sociodiscursive construction of an Eastern European Other. In their book *Notwendige Maßnahmen gegen Fremde? Genese und Formen von rassistischen Diskursen der Differenz* (Necessary Measures against Foreigners? Genesis and Forms of Racist Discourses of Difference), Bernd Matouschek, Ruth Wodak, and Franz Januschek scrutinize Austrian mass-media coverage in the wake of the events of 1989, proposing that the proliferation of powerfully sanctioned discourses about the countries and peoples of the former Eastern bloc occasioned a reconceptualization of their "nature" while simultaneously locating Austria—qua the West—in a refigured position of superiority (1995, 12, 59). Focusing on the changing discursive constructions of Romanians—from an initially empathetic figuration of a disenfranchised and destitute population to a paternalistic conception of a people in need of Western tutelage to a racist construction of radical Otherness and immediate threat to Austrian national stability—they not only document the volatility of contemporary Western imagings of the East but highlight their salience in changing understandings of Western selves (1995, 243–49). Given Austria's historical, geographical, and conceptual proximity to the East, the latter is a particularly relevant motive, enjoining the continuous repositioning of Austria within a privileged realm of Western Europe (see also Gal 1991).

10. Insofar as powerfully vested Austrian representations of Czech Otherness reproduce and refract the colonial impulses of late-nineteenth-century nationalism, I feel justified in figuring contemporary constructions of a distinct Czech sexuality and body as a neocolonial practice. Moreover, Wolff's notion of the ongoing "invention" of Eastern Europe clearly gestures to a (neo)colonizing logic of subjugating the Other. More generally, I hold with Bart Moore-Gilbert that a postcolonial theoretical engagement is warranted in the analysis of "cultural forms which mediate, challenge or reflect upon the relations of domination and subordination—economic, cultural and political—between (and often within) nations, races, or cultures, which characteristically have their roots in the history of modern European colonialism and imperialism and which, equally characteristically, continue to be apparent in the present era of neo-colonialism" (1997, 12). Bracketed in my analysis of the West's neocolonial figurations of Eastern Otherness in the wake of the transition is the colonial dimension of Soviet hegemony during state socialism, a dimension that tends to dominate "indigenous" discussions of colonial experience.

11. In this manner, this article is also intended as a contribution to the anthropology of tourism. Since its inception as a distinct subfield within the discipline (Smith 1977), the anthropology of tourism has retained a relatively marginal position, focusing on such issues as the commodification of culture, the representation of authenticity, and the uneasy overlaps between the social identities of tourists and anthropologists (see, e.g., Boissevain 1996; Nash 1996; Lanfant, Allcock, and Bruner 1995; Harkin 1995). Within the anthropological literature on tourism, the question of (heterosexual) sex tourism has been almost completely bracketed (but see Truong 1990 and O'Connell Davidson 1996 for accounts on Southeast Asia

and Cuba, respectively). Gay male sex tourism, conversely, has not entered the anthropological literature to date.

12. Following Said and other proponents of postcolonial studies, Wolff emphasizes the historicity of the body as a sociodiscursive location for the fixing of Eastern European Otherness. In his account, the Eastern body (and Western ways to talk about it) repeatedly emerges as a principal site of distinction in the Enlightenment invention of Eastern Europe, a motive that, as L. Wolff documents, is closely tied to such sexually colonizing conquests as the ones recalled in Casanova's autobiographical account of his mid-eighteenth-century voyage to Russia, which turns on the purchase and subsequent "domestication" of his Russian mistress Zaire's sexual, Eastern Otherness (1994, 31–32, 50–88).

13. In Austria, for example, the transition had profound effects on consumer behavior and on eastern Austria's local economy. In the years following the initial liberalizations in Hungary and then Czechoslovakia, hundreds of thousands of Austrians reoriented their shopping patterns, regularly traveling to the towns across the border to stock up on cheap groceries. To this day, many people continue these ritualized excursions notwithstanding relative currency alignments. What continues to provide an incentive for "shopping in the East" is the recent emergence of Austrian-owned malls (the most famous being the "Excalibur-City" in the Czech border town of Haté), which thrive on low building and maintenance costs and lure customers through grand "experience shopping" (*Erlebnisshopping*). Within Austria's border regions, the economic effects of the persistent revenue losses have been dramatic enough to force the Austrian government into the recent enactment of protective legislation designed to safeguard the economic foundation of local retailers.

14. With the age of consent at fifteen, the Czech Republic and Slovakia have two of the more liberal legislations in Eastern Europe. Only Slovenia's penal code, which allows commencement of male same-sex sexuality at fourteen, is more permissive. Croatia and Hungary, by comparison, set the age of consent at eighteen (Graupner 1995, vol. 2).

15. On the mutually constitutive relation between embodied categories of social belonging and their narrativizations, see Bunzl 1996.

16. Vienna's *Nachkriegszustand* (a reference to the damage caused by the Allied bombings of 1945) is a widely circulating trope marking an urban space in ruins. Concomitantly, it invokes the subsequent period of successful *Wiederaufbau* (reconstruction), thereby indexing a triumphant presentist teleology.

17. The German term for "boys" is *Jungs*. While other than in English the term has no overtly racist connotations, it indexes the rigidly hierarchical binary *Männer/Jungs* (men/boys), a socially veiled distinction that reflects and reproduces the homosocial field of Haus Hans, where relations among men are triangulated through the bodies of boys. In this sense, the terms do not signify their bearers' age but serve to reference, bestow, and fortify neocolonial status. Rather than their actual age, it is thus their location in the cultural economy of the Prague experience that reduces Czech men to boys while elevating even very young sex tourists to the socially privileged status of men, a position they would not occupy in Vienna's gay

male environs, where their age would exclude them from the socially prestigious friendship circles of more mature gay men. In this context, it should be clarified that the reason for gay male Austrians' repeated travel to Prague nearly always inheres in the desirable age and social dynamic of the sexual field. Gay male Austrians do not travel to the Czech Republic in search of sexual encounters with equals, whether in age or social standing. In consequence, I know of very few situations in which relations between Austrians and Czechs transcended the neocolonial circumscription of the Prague experience.

18. Misrecognizing local realities, my interlocutors repeatedly invoked the obsolete *Tschechoslowakei* (Czechoslovakia) and *tschechoslowakisch* (Czechoslovakian) when describing their experiences in both the Czech Republic and Slovakia.

Contested Landscapes: Reconstructing Environment and Memory in Postsocialist Saxony-Anhalt

Hermine G. De Soto

Introduction: A Postsocialist Problematic

Over the past 150 years the industrial urban region known as Dessau-Bitterfeld-Wittenberg was one of Germany's most important industrial belts. Located in the new federal state of Saxony-Anhalt (Sachsen-Anhalt),[1] in the middle of the former German Democratic Republic (GDR), the region—home to 450,000 inhabitants—was an important mining area long before the former socialist rational redistributive economy began to mine it for brown coal according to the logic of rational, socialist-modernist monoproduction (Konrad and Szelenyi 1979, 47–63; Verdery 1996, 19–38). The first coalfield, Auguste, opened in 1837, and the Goitsche,[2] which began mining in 1949, continued operating until German reunification. At that time, the Goitsche's brown coalfields extended over a landscape of sixty square kilometers. Following the reunification contract's stipulation that mining and chemical production would be curtailed in the Dessau-Bitterfeld-Wittenberg region, coal production closed in 1990, transforming the region's landscape overnight.[3]

In his book *Landscape and Memory,* Simon Schama argues that "inherited landscape myths and memories share two common characteristics: their surprising endurance through the centuries and their power to shape institutions that we still live with." Schama further observes that "landscapes can be self-consciously designed to express the virtues of a particular political or social community" (1995, 15). During the process of rebuilding the landscapes of postsocialist eastern Germany, the Dessau-Bitterfeld-Wittenberg region became the contested site of such practices, whose politically charged reinvention of a distinctive landscape of postsocialist Saxony-Anhalt self-consciously imagined and designed social community.

The region's abandoned and desolate but still fascinating landscape had been built and rebuilt by socialist industrial production over the previous decade. As natural water flows were rechanneled for industrial usage, the area's rivers foamed with pink and white chemicals discharged from industry, while ubiquitous coal dust settled on cars, furniture, plants, animals, and humans. Such environmental exploitation resulted in a fractured ecology as the groundwater that supplied the region's drinking water became toxic from decades of absorbing industrial wastes.

Reflecting on five years of reunification and the onset and triumph of capitalism in eastern Germany, East German economist Christa Luft has noted that reunification was not based on a

> dominating drive to grow together two German parts and to create in the eastern part, as Chancellor [Helmut] Kohl promised, "a blossoming landscape." On the contrary, competition was prevalent in which the desire for private property dramatically changed into euphoria and lust. Among the new managers, or those who fashioned themselves as such during the frantic first years of restructuring, a frightening decline of values and ethics took place. Anonymous industrialists and businessmen snatched up millions of marks, while smart and crude adventurers took advantage of the chaos of restructuring to make fast money. In many places in eastern Germany, East Germany's property became literally part of a monopoly game. (C. Luft 1996, 174)[4]

In Dessau-Bitterfeld-Wittenberg, the question of industrial restructuring became part of this "monopoly game," staging the competition for the rebuilding of the region in the form of contested discourses of environment, ecology, and culture. During the first phase of restructuring, in 1990, one of the most urgent tasks was the creation of new visions for reconstructing a devastated environment and its social and economic infrastructures. The production of new concepts for the fractured environment, however, proved more complex than anticipated. Nevertheless, in the initial chaos of transformation and cultural paralysis, two major "strategic groups" (Jessop 1983) publicized their visions, unique insights, and concerns for the degraded industrial environments.

This essay examines how these two strategic groups—the *Initia-*

tivkreis Bitterfeld/Wolfen e. V.[5] (the Circle) and the *reformierte Bauhaus*
(Reformed Bauhaus)—began to imagine the reinvention of the environment, ecology, and regional identities in the specific postsocialist context
of German reunification. I will illustrate and explain how these two groups
entered a politics of culture and how they competed for discursive space
through the employment of different ideas of modernity in regard to
reconstituting the region and confronting its environmental problems.
Based on Rudolf Bahro's observation that in postsocialist environments
there remains a lack of impulses for small, reform-oriented, behavioral
changes at both the bottom and the top (1995), I will juxtapose and analyze citizens' perceptions of the strategic groups' politics of culture in light
of their distinctive visions of inclusion or exclusion of women and men in
the rethinking of the environment, ecology, and regional identity.

Key Actors in the Politics of Culture, Environment, and Ecology

Most nonrevolutionary cultural processes and their various forms
(regional, national, transnational, global) are also political processes and,
as such, are often contested and frequently negotiated (Handler 1988;
Featherstone 1995). During revolutionary times, such as the postsocialist
transformations, however, there is a specific "high level of awareness of the
importance of culture," because in such exceptional moments, culture
becomes an essential "base and guide for change" (Whisnant 1991, 192;
Brown, forthcoming). Other scholars who have examined the importance
that culture might gain in radical upheavals have focused on how, in such
accelerated times, cultural processes of formalization and ritualization are
involved in the invention of new traditions that are "characterized by reference to the past" (Hobsbawm 1983, 4). Anthropologists who study public culture have recently begun to ask about which groups may enter the
production process of culture, who will invent which tradition and which
cultural understanding, and how and to what ends will the produced cultural understanding be put to use (B. Williams 1991; De Soto 1996). In
such a conceptual framework, culture is seen as a "site of multiple contests
informed by a diversity of historically specific actions and intentions"
(Stephens 1995, 22). And, based on such an understanding, the politics of
culture consists of "processes of conflict and maneuvering that go on both
internal to communities of this kind of cultural producer[s] and between
them and the political sphere" (Verdery 1991, 12).

Such an understanding—in which the analytic focus is on competing
political practices of culture—is useful for this study of why two strategic

groups were interested in advancing their respective cultural understandings and how they envisioned and articulated their understandings of how to rebuild environment, community, and identity after socialism. In the Dessau-Bitterfeld-Wittenberg region, the key actors—the Circle and the Reformed Bauhaus—both entered the postsocialist cultural site of contest to "strive through discourse to suppress alternative messages and capture 'ears' crucial to gaining the resources that would facilitate a broader hearing for their message" (Verdery 1991, 12). Examining politics of urban landscape and space in Russia, Blair Ruble suggests that such processes "emerge in sharpest relief at those moments when the very mechanism for determining society's winners and losers undergo rapid and thoroughgoing transformation" (1995, 2).

The Circle, consisting of a mixed membership of eastern and western German constituents, was supported by Sachsen-Anhalt's office of economy and office of traffic and development and the city of Bitterfeld's magistrate's office. Other associates of the Circle were Bitterfeld's mayor and city administration and a former West German city administrator who had become mayor of the eastern German city of Wolfen after reunification. (Wolfen and Bitterfeld had been integral parts of the former socialist industrial landscape.) Further supporters of the Circle were major West German industrial representatives, including Bitterfeld GmbH, the multinational company Deutsche Babcock AG (which after reunification owned forty new factories in eastern Germany), and the multinational company Bayer Bitterfeld GmbH.

The Circle was founded in 1991 with the slogan "Bundle together and coordinate initiatives, and apply these initiatives with reason to the development of the region Bitterfeld." By 1994 the Circle had grown from the original twenty associates into a 117-member group. During that time the main representative of the Circle announced that his association would enter its visionary future model for regional environmental restructuring and renewal in the upcoming competition for the world exhibition, Expo 2000, to be held in that year in the western German city of Hannover.[6] In the regional newspaper, the representative announced that the international audience visiting the region in the year 2000 to see design in the making in this specific postsocialist landscape would gaze at "a dream that is becoming true. The region, desolated by chemical production, industrial waste, and pollution, transforms itself into a thriving land. Bitterfeld refurbishes its nature. In six years, this area will be a huge recreational park, a land of a thousand lakes" ("Bitterfeld möblelt die Umwelt auf" 1994).

The other strategic group, the Reformed Bauhaus, primarily comprised East German urban professional experts (including regional planners, urban sociologists, landscape designers, and architects), academics, and state representatives from Saxony-Anhalt. Other members included urban experts and representatives of the city of Dessau and representatives from the federal government. In addition, the Reformed Bauhaus established a network of international and interdisciplinary board members called the academic council.

This Reformed Bauhaus has both ties to and differences from the Bauhaus school that reached international fame in the 1920s. The former Bauhaus's concept of modernity was based on a progressive understanding of industry and culture, and it aimed to reunite arts and crafts as inseparable parts for a distinctive style of urban building and living. The potentials for cultural development of this cutting-edge concept never bore fruit in Dessau: the Bauhaus was silenced under the Nazi regime, and some of its founders emigrated to the United States. After World War II, the Bauhaus's various ideas of modernity became distinctively instrumentalized in Cold War politics (Betts 1996), and after the founding of the two separate Germanies, a New Bauhaus was founded at the Institute of Design in Ulm in the Federal Republic of Germany, while the leader of the GDR, Walter Ulbricht, officially denounced the former Dessau-based Bauhaus concept as "bourgeois formalism" (Betts 1996, 87; see also Betts 1995; Halter 1991).

In the post–World War II GDR, the buildings of the former Bauhaus in Dessau were used for multifunctional purposes—for storage, for museum exhibitions, and for various socialist meetings. In the early 1970s, lingering changes in Cold War politics also introduced reforms in the Bauhaus in Dessau. In 1976 a keen, younger team of East German academics, urban planners, urban sociologists, architects, and engineers began to restore the Bauhaus's modernist buildings and initiated a rethinking of the Bauhaus's concept of modernity. However, only during the collapse of socialism, in 1989, did this previously lesser known East German Bauhaus group gain publicity and transform the Dessau-based Bauhaus into a foundation (*Stiftung*). Also during this time, the Reformed Bauhaus familiarized the public with the concept of the *Industrielle Gartenreich* (Industrial Garden Empire).

While I was staying at the Bauhaus, one of the leading theoreticians of the Reformed Bauhaus explained to me, "We will continue the former Bauhaus School's tradition of being a future-oriented institution. Yet we will also critically examine the former Bauhaus's perception of modernity to develop new concepts for the present regional problems." By questioning the progressive understanding of the positive power of mass industrialization, by pointing to industrial developments after the 1930s and to the environmental and ecological calamity caused by socialist large-scale industrialization, the Reformed Bauhaus was trying to resynthesize, through the idea of the Industrial Garden Empire, the domains of culture and environment, which were disconnected by industrialism and were now in urgent need of reconnection. In doing so, the Reformed Bauhaus aimed to employ those practices of the former tradition that it regarded as essential for the production of a new culture: critical thinking, creativity in regard to place and space, risk taking in the name of experimentation, and loosening of administrative rules on regional design and planning so that new visions for environmental consciousness could develop. Interested in public attention for its vision of the future, the Reformed Bauhaus, like the Circle, entered the competition for Expo 2000 with a model for regional development—the idea of the Industrial Garden Empire.

Diverging Imaginations, Inventions, and Inscriptions

According to Benedict Anderson (1983, 15), "all communities larger than primordial villages of face to face contact (and perhaps even these) are imagined." In Dessau-Bitterfeld-Wittenberg, both the Circle and the Reformed Bauhaus began to create their distinctive styles and contextual imaginations of how the postsocialist "community," or region, ought to be renewed. Processes of reimagination of community are not specific only to the postsocialist region in Sachsen-Anhalt. In his study of the post-Soviet city of Yaroslavl, Ruble found similar processes where "Russians [use] the pretext of the end of Soviet-style socialism to reimagine their towns and cities, with conflicts arising over procedures for privatizing housing, policies governing historic preservation, and land-use decision-making" (Ruble 1995, 12).

The Circle

As it entered the public discourse in competition for public attention, the Circle profiled itself as the propagator of a distinct imagination for reconstructing the postsocialist region. Through public announcements (in local newspapers, on television, at town meetings, and at county office meetings), representatives of the Circle presented its imaginations, inventions, and inscriptions of cultural meanings in regard to the local environment, ecology, and history. The Circle's principal position holds that the environmental problems of the region can be solved only in a joint venture between industry and local political leaders and that the unemployment problem would be addressed most effectively through short-term employment in the restoration of the Goitsche coalfield and the demolition or reconstruction of former factories. By the year 2005, the environment is to be transformed into a new chemical industrial park that, combined with lakes (created by flooding the Goitsche coal mine), natural reserves, and recreational facilities, would significantly raise the quality of life of the region's inhabitants.[7]

In their strategies for a managed environment, the Circle calls for the creation of a positive image of the degraded environment so that industrial and financial investments will be forthcoming. This is especially important since approximately $200 million in federal support has already been invested since reunification. To receive still more support from the European Community and from federal and state governments, the Circle seeks to demonstrate how new environmental technologies can help clean up the environment while serving as useful tools for teaching citizens about restoration. The Circle tries to implement this vision through a variety of projects ranging from structural and management development (privatization and the hiring of efficient, western German managers) to the development of a regional industrial history through the production of brochures that illustrate the accomplishments of more than one hundred years of industry.[8]

The Circle's final strategy—a new vision that has yet to be fully articulated—focuses on cultural renewal after socialism. The ideas underlying this strategy imply that future *Vereine* (voluntary associations), such as sports, rifle, and singing clubs, would be the ideal transmitters of a new culture in this region.[9] The Circle believes that the promotion of regional identity through social history, a vision that the Reformed Bauhaus promotes, would hinder the process of restructuring; instead, the Circle advocates that by the year 2000, citizens should come to forget that coal mining once severely injured the environment and ecology of this postsocialist region.

The Reformed Bauhaus

The members of the Reformed Bauhaus have developed a model through which they attempt to alert society to the dangers of flooding the Goitsche coal beds: the inadvertent rise of groundwater would contaminate any future lake and would poison the drinking water, and the contaminated lake would be harmful for swimmers and for fish. The Reformed Bauhaus also warns of the possibility of soil contamination through the flattening of the Goitsche and the lack of humus reproduction in the region because of decades of soil removal in the course of mining. The Reformed Bauhaus further argues against the obliteration of local memory in relation to industrialization and its concomitant creation of ecological and environmental calamities, raising such questions as whether an artificial lake is worth the destruction of memory; whether planned economic, environ-mental, and cultural violence should be forgotten; where the region's con-taminated burial sites are, sites filled with chemicals for the past 150 years; and whether past events can be reflected on and understood if historical memory is not kept alive.

Based on such questions, the Reformed Bauhaus illustrates its new vision of a differently imagined region with its reinvented concept of the Industrial Garden Empire. In part, this concept expresses what Schama has figured as "a way of looking; of rediscovering what we already have, but which somehow eludes our recognition and our appreciation. Instead of being yet another explanation of what we have lost, it is an exploration of what we might find [in landscapes]" (Schama 1995, 14). This new vision seeks to create a different social consciousness through a particular process of cultural renewal based on practices of reflection and self-recognition.

Regional identity construction through landscape memory and con-sciousness-raising stems from the Reformed Bauhaus's affinity with the ideas of the reform-oriented Duke Leopold III, Friedrich Franz von Anhalt-Dessau (1740–1817), whose designs for "Gardens of Liberty" (Rotenberg 1995) resemble garden landscapes of the Enlightenment in the Netherlands and in England (Schama 1995), symbolically expressing the duke's eighteenth-century understanding of the Enlightenment and its environmental philosophy. Leopold III called this English- and Dutch-style landscaping the "Dessauer-Gartenempire."

The Reformed Bauhaus's reinvention of this tradition—based on Leopold III's translation of a new cultural movement into environmental renewal programs in which human beings and the rest of nature interacted reciprocally and harmoniously—is best illustrated in the appropriation of the old term *Gartenempire,* which reappears as the Reformed Bauhaus's new concept of the *Industrielle Gartenreich* and in the use of this concept as a cultural medium through which negative and positive (deconstructive and constructive) historical regional processes can be brought into public and political debate. Only through such a challenge can environmental and social-historical structures become conscious and comprehensible.[10]

For the Reformed Bauhaus, the twentieth century has been marked by three distinct and environmentally consequential moments of modern-ization—in 1900, 1930, and 1960—all of which were based on a common belief in planned rational growth, risk taking, and the utilization of natural resources until environmental and ecological boundaries were reached. Convinced that the postsocialist environment will not survive a fourth thrust of modernization, the Reformed Bauhaus warns that even environ-mentally friendly technologies, such as the ones envisioned by the Circle, cannot cure the fractured environment. Instead, for the natural and cultural environment to renew itself, the present environment needs to be protected: factories, urban houses, and working-class settlements need to be restored rather than destroyed, and the region's economic renewal should focus on use-value-oriented work and subsistence production compatible with the environment.[11] Only after such restoration can a regional identity be constructed to replace the one lost in the collapse of the former economic and sociocultural system.

Finally, although the Reformed Bauhaus and the Circle both maintain that institution building is still lacking in the region, the Reformed Bauhaus champions regional institutions that foster democratic representation and support ecologically oriented reform. During my research in the early summer of 1995, a first symbolic step toward institution building was undertaken by the Federal Environmental Office (*Bundesumweltamt*). To demonstrate the practice of federalism in eastern Germany, federal state representatives began to move the main office from the metropolis Berlin to the regional city of Dessau. With this symbolic move, local people hoped that the presocialist, modernist, industrial buildings would be saved from demolition, but the environmental office did not preserve these buildings, especially the *Gasviertel* (industrial gas works).

Interpreting Diverging Cultural Inscriptions

As noted previously, the most significant postsocialist deprivation for the local population of the Dessau-Bitterfeld-Wittenberg region remains the loss of work-generated selfhood and identity. As in many other regions of the former GDR, the situation in this industrial zone has a specifically gendered dimension (Behnk and Westerwelle 1995; Arbeitsamt Dessau 1995). During my interviews people often said things like "Our identity came through our work," and "With the loss of work, our identity was broken."[12] Thus, the groups that enter the politics of culture in regard to environment and ecology must display visions that not only incorporate ideas of how to rebuild the local environment, ecology, and economy, but also—and equally important—illuminate how to imagine the construction of regional identity and history in relation to work or employment after the break with former socialist industries and previous work-related identities. How do the Circle and the Reformed Bauhaus respond to these challenges in their imaginations and landscape designs?

The Circle entered the politics of culture with a vision that resembles in part the ideal-type concept referred to as the dominant social paradigm (Cotgrove 1983; Dobson 1990). This vision inscribes cultural meanings that represent values similar to those that Grove-White (1993) calls the "orthodox official environmental discourse." In its vision, the Circle expresses values that have been the norm of rational industrial systems in both capitalist and socialist societies: history as progress is epistemologically embedded within an uncritical modernist position in which boundaries are drawn between culture and nature (Grove-White 1993). Thus, environmental problems are understood as natural problems and need to be solved and regulated with natural scientific methods, with the newest technological inventions, and with restructured capitalist industrial and economic growth.

Such a conceptual separation of culture and nature does not yield an unobscured imagination for regional identity and history. The Circle's suggestions for building regional identity are based on the concept of a "managed environment" (Redclift 1994, 128) in which sterile future lakes would fulfill recreational needs while contemporary environmental and ecological calamities would fall into their flooded oblivion and where mythical celebrations of regional history would depict the last century as one of uninterrupted industrial progress and accomplishment.

Conversely, the distinctive Reformed Bauhaus vision exemplified in the reinvented concept of the Industrial Garden Empire resembles both an "ecocentric" position (Redclift 1994) and what has been called the new environmental paradigm (Cotgrove 1983; Dobson 1990). In this vision, the Reformed Bauhaus offers a challenge to both capitalist and socialist rationalities, industrialization, and modernization. The modernist orientation of progress is contested with a notion that sees people as participants in the natural environment, which should be valued for its aesthetic qualities rather than for its pragmatic and instrumental functions. In such a sustainable society, consumption needs should be balanced according to the limited availability of natural resources, and technology should be used for promotion and improvement of small-scale economics. Further, such a society should be legitimized with new institutions that favor the development of personal fulfillment and self-expression in which citizens direct the course of society.

The Reformed Bauhaus's Industrial Garden Empire would constitute such a new institution—a reinvented tradition (Hobsbawm 1983) occasioned by the abrupt introduction of a postindustrial capitalist system and the resulting revolutionary break with previous regional identities. With this strategy for identity formation—linked, as it is, to a contemporary critique of modernity—the Reformed Bauhaus has followed a position similar to approaches that have been reported from less-developed countries. For example, such "'ecocentric' positions seek to rediscover what existed before the colonial embrace distorted their development process [and imply] building 'bridges to the past.'" In contrast, "in developed countries [such as Germany] the emphasis is rather on what we usually term 'post-industrial' society, and what this implies for work, leisure and culture" (Redclift 1994, 126).

Where Are the Citizens?

During my fieldwork in the early summer of 1995, the unemployment rate in villages of the Dessau-Bitterfeld-Wittenberg region averaged between 20 percent and 22 percent and was remarkably higher and faster-growing for women than for men (Arbeitsamt Dessau 1995).[13] Citizens of the region were distressed by unemployment, social insecurities, and insolvent retirement pensions. Both older and younger generations were embittered by the loss of their previous public cultural meeting places, which, as they expressed, formed an integral component of transmitting local identity. Some village mayors tried to extend their local services, but the ones I interviewed said that they had no solutions for how to deal with the current problems. During my visits and interviews, city and village mayors conveyed that "nowadays old people are remaining in the villages, while younger people become labor migrants and move to bigger cities and to western Germany." Village mayors also mentioned that there are no recreational facilities for younger people, that the previous youth clubs, kindergartens and day-care centers (*Tagesstätten*) were gone, and that all the other social security services that had been provided by the socialist county office were now the responsibility of individual villages. "But what should we do without money?" one mayor exclaimed.

Villagers with whom I discussed the issues complained "that politicians are not interested in our situation." Several unemployed women remarked, "We are afraid of the future because we do not know what will happen to us. Nobody asks us what to do. As unemployed women, we are considered worthless, less than dirt." Another woman, Rosie,[14] joined our discussion, commenting,

> We women are in trouble because the new industrialists are afraid that they have to pay health insurance for our children. Now they want us to sign a paper in which we agree to give our children away if they get sick. This is the reason why we decided not to have any more children. For us, the transitional short-term employment [*Arbeitsbeschaffungsmaßnahmen*] is a straw we hold onto before we drown. New employers favor men for employment.

For Rosie, "Our village has lost its social character. Nothing is there anymore—public community houses, movies, and restaurants—everything is gone." And Christian, a retired coal miner, said,

The basis of our humanity has been taken from us. We don't understand the new rules, and all protest does not help us now. Most politicians have never visited our villages. For us, five years of German reunification have meant a growing and bigger rift between East and West Germany. We are simple working-class people and are now in total apathy. And we lack trust in the political process because there is only emptiness and nothing happens.

Citizens were also disillusioned in regard to participation and inclusion in their region's project developments. For them, both the Circle and the Reformed Bauhaus projects were abstract entities that seemed to exist independently of everyday lives and worries. Although the Reformed Bauhaus is alternative in its vision in regard to environment, ecology, and identity reformation, many unemployed female citizens I spoke with during my fieldwork stated that its vision excludes "concrete ideas about employment," a perception that is a real concern for the large population that became unemployed after the close of the giant socialist industrial complexes in this area. Emma, a woman responding to the ideas of environmental renewal and the closing of previous factories, told me, "We'd rather trample three daisies than lose one job."

As M. R. Redclift (1994, 126) has observed, such visionary shortcomings in regard to employment and the market seem to be an analytic deficiency in "ecocentric" positions: although for these ecocentric positions "sustainable development is the objective of many perspectives on the environment, . . . the role of the market in defining its various historical stages remains obscure." In a village where I talked with people about their perceptions concerning environmental renewal, Birgit noted,

We are afraid since our work was taken away from us. We like the ideas of the Reformed Bauhaus, but these ideas do not translate into work for us. Among unemployed women, there is a rise in psychological illnesses. Women retreat into privacy and often talk about violence in the family.

In addition to these citizen concerns about unemployment, a man I interviewed questioned the selective reinvention of landscape tradition for identity formation. Mr. Schwarz was concerned that the Reformed Bauhaus concept, although alternative in its representation, could be misused for the purpose of conservative "historical manipulation," and he was especially critical of the idea of a "reformist" historical development of the region:

What kind of history is transmitted to us? Do they mean Duke Franz, Hugo Junkers,[15] and the Bauhaus? What about the other history of the region? Or the time before Duke Franz, until 1758? Or was Duke Leopold, the "Old Dessauer,"[16] also a reform-oriented duke? Perhaps in 1997 this story will be told to us in honor of the duke's 250th birthday! That Duke Franz truly succeeded in his reforms is rather doubtful and seems to be based on a widely circulating legend. His successor was an archconservative duke who was suspicious of all renewal and used the help of Prussia to reverse previous reforms. The *Halbabsolutismus* [half absolutism] existed in this region until the overthrow of the monarchy in 1918. Is it forgotten that the *Freistaat* [free state] of Anhalt only existed from 1919 to 1932 and that the Nazis had already come to power here in 1932? Is it forgotten that the citizens who were loyal to the duchy expelled the former members of the Bauhaus? . . . Can such a selective picture of history rebuild new identities? I will try not to let myself be manipulated into such a picture simply for the sake of an identity.

While citizens of the Dessau-Bitterfeld-Wittenberg region expressed concerns about the Reformed Bauhaus, they also criticized the Circle. Some villagers referred to the representatives of the Circle "as the marionettes of West Germans [*Wessies*]."[17] At a town meeting I attended, a local mayor and proponent of the ideas of the Circle declared that at this point in regional development, citizens' participation was unimportant because local leaders first needed to develop adequate concepts, projects, and clarifications about finances "before it is time to talk with citizens." But while this mayor noted "that citizens would be welcome to further the Circle's projects until then," local women representatives of ORWO[18] have been prevented from joining the Circle's debate regarding the representation of the Dessau-Bitterfeld-Wittenberg region at Expo 2000. At one meeting, the local male administrators and male representatives of the Circle silenced critical women's voices with such statements as "Women's ideas lack substance and are impractical for policy implementation."

At yet another meeting I attended during my fieldwork in the county seat, citizens' representatives and county administrators discussed which postsocialist projects ought to be shown at the Expo 2000. One women's group tried to convince an official body of the Circle to include their project, *Frauenintiative Wolfen-Bitterfeld e. V.: die ökologische Landwirtschaft* (Women's Initiative of Wolfen-Bitterfeld e.V.: Ecological Farming). In this project unemployed women were working to restructure an old estate into an ecologically run farm. When another woman entered the dialogue to explain the importance of showcasing at Expo 2000 women's projects addressing the economic situation of women in postsocialist East Germany, a male administrator interrupted, saying "Women lack ideas, and women don't have concepts for solving conflicts." When the same woman sharply replied, "We don't even have a chance to participate. We are excluded," a West German environmental expert working for the Circle broke into the discussion and remarked, "We first need to discuss whether it is even legitimate to have special projects for women." After a long silence, another woman responded that

> 67 percent of women are unemployed. This project on women, environment, and ecological agriculture ought to be included. We want to be involved from the beginning. So far, citizens do not understand what is happening around them. Everything goes much too fast, and the citizens we work with demand that things be slowed down. Citizens would first like to understand what it is all about.

Indeed, in regard to local meetings with residents, these critical reflections were expressed in concrete communicative practices. Some female citizens from ORWO who represented short-term employed women opposed the Circle's representatives by arguing that citizens were too far removed from ideas of development and thus unable to identify, recognize, or support the new ideas. Other citizens were fearful and confused about the effects of pollution, and they complained about chemical smells, chronic bronchitis, slow or retarded bone growth, and various skin diseases. They also complained about the construction of a new incinerator in their vicinity and the lack of information about the health risks connected with a revived chemical industry. And they ridiculed the idea of a recreational park with a lake, referring to the region as *Bad Bitterfeld* (Bitterfeld Spa).

Conclusion

In many ways, the debate over reinventing environment and memory in the Dessau-Bitterfeld-Wittenberg region emerges as a microcosm of the larger fields of political culture operative in postsocialist East Germany. In this sense, the Circle and its representatives reflect the dominant logic of a postindustrial, capitalist system that has gained hegemony in the former GDR. Seeking a thorough break with what is regarded as an irredeemably compromised past, the Circle expects to inaugurate a thoroughly new age through the external imposition of a technologically progressive modernization. If the Circle's activities epitomize the domineering extension of West German specificity to the *neue Bundesländer* (new provinces), the Reformed Bauhaus functions as a locally grounded alternative, seeking to preserve and reinvent regional specificity through strategies of creative historicization. In this sense, the work of the Reformed Bauhaus embodies a frequent stance taken by East German intellectuals seeking to defend a degree of cultural distinction in the reunified Germany. This configuration renders the debate over the reconstruction of Dessau-Bitterfeld-Wittenberg's landscape and ecology a principal site of contestation and refiguration of East and West.[19]

In contrast to both groups' positions, however, citizens in the region—and women in particular—maintain that they have been altogether excluded from the debate. Most of the people I interviewed during my fieldwork were unemployed or were about to lose their jobs. They expressed that what matters most for them in these uncertain times was secure employment and healthy families. In regard to these immediate problems, it seems that neither the Reformed Bauhaus's "new environmental imagination" nor the Circle's "managed environmental imagination" offers adequate responses to the needs of the population of the Dessau-Bitterfeld-Wittenberg region. The chilly reality of their world should not be obscured when reflecting on the cultural contest over landscape, environment, and memory that is currently being waged in Saxony-Anhalt.

NOTES

I am most grateful for the generous support received from the International Research and Exchange Board; the Women's Studies Program and Women's Studies Research Center at the University of Wisconsin–Madison; Petra Bläss; Professor Rolf Kuhn, director of the Bauhaus in Dessau; Dr. Harald Kegler; and Dipl. Ing. Birgit Schmidt. I also thank all the women and men who participated and provided ethnographic information in various meetings with local mayors. I particularly appreciate the editorial suggestions from Daphne Berdahl, Martha Lampland, Matti Bunzl, and John Borneman, who helped in honing main propositions. My special gratitude goes to David John De Soto, without whose intellectual support and companionship my ethnographic research would be less meaningful. Last but not least, I am most grateful to Mary Jo Heck for her critical readings of this essay.

1. After German reunification, the districts of the former GDR became reorganized according to the federal system of the Federal Republic of Germany (FRG). Saxony-Anhalt became a new federal state within the FRG.

2. Birgit Schmidt, an eastern German engineer, urban designer, and researcher, provided valuable assistance during observational excursions at the Goitsche coalfield and along the Johannes sewage pit.

3. This development reflected the reunification politics of the West German government and its efforts to introduce a market economy in eastern Germany. As a consequence of the introduction of the West German mark as Germany's common currency and the actions of the *Treuhandanstalt* (a government-run company

created to sell East German property) most of the industrial production in Dessau-Bitterfeld-Wittenberg had been demolished and discontinued by 1991. With this stoppage of socialist industrial production, eastern Germany became (an imperfect) part of a capitalist, postindustrial, political economy. In the case of Dessau-Bitterfeld-Wittenberg, this politics of ecology and environment assumed a postsocialist specificity because the environmental calamities of the last decades had not developed within the historical context of a postindustrial capitalist economy. Instead, in Dessau-Bitterfeld-Wittenberg, a structural break occurred after socialism, leaving behind not a postindustrial capitalist society but a postindustrial socialist society. This postsocialist society currently exhibits a rupture with socialism: a fractured environment, an afflicted ecology, a shattered local economy, and a fragmented sociocultural region (Dahn 1994; Angelus and Neumann 1994; Nick 1995; C. Luft 1996; H. Luft 1997).

4. Unless otherwise noted, all translations are by the author.

5. As an *eingetragener Verein* (e.V.), the *Initiativkreis Bitterfeld/Wolfen* has the official status of a voluntary association.

6. The World Exhibition to be held from June 1 until the end of October 2000 in Hannover, in western Germany, has the theme "Humanity, Nature, Technology."

7. The practice of flooding dugout construction sites—called *Baggersee*—was undertaken in both the former GDR and the FRG. A *Baggersee* is often used as a recreational lake for water sports and fishing. However, to flood former coal mines of such magnitude without the necessary knowledge of possible groundwater contamination would be a new practice for eastern Germany.

8. The series included a celebratory book commemorating the hundredth birthday of the coal mine called Johannes. Yet, when visiting the former brown coalfield during my fieldwork, I was informed that in the wake of decades of capitalist and socialist chemical disposal, Johannes had turned into Europe's most contaminated pit-seepage lake, flowing with shining chemicals that have given it the name Silbersee (Silver Lake).

9. The former socialist society also had *Vereine*, but these clubs were not organized on a voluntary basis (that is, within a civil society that was independent of the state), as was the case among *Vereine* in the FRG, where members voluntarily pay membership fees (Eidson 1990). In the former GDR, *Vereine* were directly connected to a person's place of employment—collectives, state factories, and so forth—and were generally financially supported by the place of employment.

10. The Reformed Bauhaus uses two opposing landscapes in public presentations and in its politics of culture and consciousness-raising. One of these is the former industrial brown coalfield of the Goitsche (that is, the abandoned "moon-landscape"); the other is a landscape that the Reformed Bauhaus has named Ferropolis. Ferropolis is also referred to as the *Stadt aus Eisen* (Iron City). This name refers to the huge dredgers and other large-scale industrial tools that were left behind on the former GDR coalfields in Gopa-Nord. The Reformed Bauhaus's battle in cultural politics includes its demand that Ferropolis be officially designated as one of Europe's grandest outdoor, modernist, industrial

landscape museums. The alternative landscape, that of the previous Garden Empire symbolizing an enlightened vision, is concretely demonstrated in the Wörlitzer Garden Park, or Gartenreich, which—for the Reformed Bauhaus—illustrates the legacy of the reformist practices of Duke Leopold III.

11. Some recent Reformed Bauhaus projects include the restoration of Piesteritz, the first car-free settlement in Germany; the modernization of the Plattensiedlung Wolfen-Nord; the restoration of the working-class settlement Zschornewitz; the restoration of the Cranach Gardens in Wittenberg; and the redirection and restoration of the river flow in the center of Wittenberg. The Reformed Bauhaus intends to include these projects in Expo 2000.

12. Some women referred to a specific working-class culture that they connected to the *Bitterfelder Kulturpalast,* which for them symbolized a socialist cultural-renewal attempt. This specific East German socialist renewal, which became known as the *Bitterfelder Weg,* developed in Bitterfeld between 1959 and 1964. The main socialist goal expressed in this concept was to unite art and everyday life for artists and workers. East German artists and writers were encouraged to move to Bitterfeld and to work in factories (a kind of participant observation). In Bitterfeld-Dessau, workers were invited to participate in the creation and production of art. Prominent East German authors wrote novels about their experiences in factories and their observations of the working class. See, e.g., Maron 1981; Heiduczek 1977; Neutschs 1968.

13. In 1996, a year after my fieldwork, women from the ökologische Landwirtschaftszentrum in Bitterfeld reported that in August 1996 the unemployment rate in Dessau and Bitterfeld had reached 25 percent. On the basis of observations and my personal communication with Saxony-Anhalt's federal Parliament representative in 1997, I determined that the unemployment rate was expected to increase sharply thereafter in the Dessau-Bitterfeld-Wittenberg region since many transitional short-term jobs would be terminated in 1997. In the spring of 1997, the women's NGO, the *Bitterfeld-Wolfen Fraueninitiative,* wrote that 52 percent of the county's population was unemployed, with women's unemployment ranging between 70 and 80 percent (Ungefroren 1997). The women's NGO currently holds public town meetings to encourage both women and men to take initiatives to develop grassroots projects that would create at least some short-term jobs. This women-led NGO was founded in 1996 and has so far initiated fourteen work projects; among them is the women-led, ecologically oriented agridevelopment that reappropriated a former socialist and collectivized state farm. In regard to the state's development and statistical information after socialism, see esp. Ministerium für Raumordnung 1996.

14. Interviewees preferred that fictitious names be used in the text.

15. Hugo Junkers (1859–1935) was a professor, inventor, and technician. As an industrial pioneer in Dessau, he founded one of Germany's most important military and commercial aviation industries. After World War I he became a pacifist and joined the left-liberal Democratic Union. Following the seizure of political power by the National Socialists, his factories were confiscated, and he was expelled from Dessau. In March 1945 most of his former factories were destroyed by Allied air attacks.

16. The "Old Dessauer," Duke Leopold von Anhalt-Dessau (1676–1747), was the grandfather of the reformist duke, the founder of the Garden Empire, Duke Leopold III. The Old Dessauer was a field marshal and served in the military under the Prussian soldier-king Friedrich Wilhelm I and under Frederick the Great. In 1988, during the 775th commemoration of the founding of the city of Dessau, a statue was erected in honor and remembrance of the Old Dessauer. The reformist duke was not mentioned during the ceremony. For further studies on the Garden Empire, see Niedermeier 1995a, 1995b; Ahrbeck and Hirsch 1970; Hirsch 1989.

17. The term *Wessie* is used by eastern Germans to convey a form of oppression created by the behavior of western Germans who assume that they know the eastern German situation much better than do the eastern Germans themselves.

18. ORWO, or Original Wolfen, refers to the Bitterfeld-Wolfen film and chemical industrial conglomerate of the former GDR. The film industry (Agfa) began there in 1897. In the rational-socialist industry of the former GDR, ORWO employed twenty-one thousand people, and in the film-producing branch alone there were almost nine thousand female employees. During my research, which included visits and interviews with women there, only six hundred of the fifteen thousand male and female employees remained after reunification. Most of these six hundred were in short-term, transitional employment and were occupied with demolishing most of the complex's 580 buildings, with the declared understanding that the workers would be laid off after these factories were torn down. Although I was not permitted to talk with the women while they were working, after work the embittered and depressed women complained about their humiliating situation, noting that they felt "numb" (Behnk and Westerwelle 1995).

19. By the late summer of 1996, both the Circle and the Reformed Bauhaus had won the right to exhibit their projects and visions for the future at Expo 2000. So far, projects by women have not been included among the entries.

The Shape of National Time: Daily Life, History, and Identity during Armenia's Transition to Independence, 1991–1994

Stephanie Platz

Between 1991 and 1994, the following joke became popular in the Armenian capital city, Yerevan: "The history of Armenia begins with Grigor the Illuminator (Grigor Lusavorich') and ends with Levon the Terminator (Levon Anjatich'). This joke is a play on words, in which Grigor, the revered saint and national hero credited with bringing Christianity to Armenia in the fourth century A.D., is opposed to Levon Ter Petrossian, the first president of post-Soviet, independent Armenia. The joke ironically evokes a contrast between the act of illumination, through which Armenia acquired its identity as the first Christian nation, and the darkness produced by a devastating energy crisis, which plagued Ter Petrossian's first presidential term. The acts of giving light—*lusavorel*—and disconnecting the lights, as in a power outage—*anjatel*—metaphorically frame Armenian history in the current era. Independence from the Soviet Union, according to the joke, is not a rebirth of the nation, as had been anticipated during an Armenian independence movement only two years earlier. Rather, the Armenian leadership's inability to produce energy and illuminate the present represents the nation's metaphorical dark end.

This joke captures a transformation in other contexts in Armenia during the years of transition to independence. The transformation concerned Armenians' use of time in daily life and their conceptualization of history in relationship to their own national identity. In the early years of independence, political and economic change, in combination with the effects of the war in Azerbaijan and the consequent energy crisis, brought a cataclysmic paralysis of the urban and industrial infrastructure. This paralysis—a phenomenon to which I refer as demodernization—dramatically affected communication, transportation, and labor and thereby Armenian society. Further, demodernization altered the daily habits and frameworks for interaction of most Armenians by changing their use of space and time in their personal everyday life (*kents'agh*). Changes in the experience of daily time corresponded to changes in the imagination of historical time, which, according to some, had ended, ruptured, or begun to go backward. In the first three years of Armenian independence, crisis conditions laid bare a conjuncture of practice and ideology, habit and construct, experience and understanding from which notions of Armenianness emerged. This conjuncture is best observed along axes of space and time—metaphors of place (distance and proximity), duration (the speed of passing time), and directionality (progress versus regress)—as expressed in Armenian accounts of the transition.

Relationships among material, technological, and social change have long been identified by social theorists. In Marx's terms, relations of production in labor and in procreation are linked in a "double relationship," whereby modes and relations of production shape social relationships and consciousness, naturalizing the latter in the process (1978, 157). These naturalized forms of individual and collective social consciousness are the origins of the differences that circumscribe identity (1978, 159). More specifically, the consequences of industrialization—which brought new modes of transportation, communication, labor organization, and political organization—for society, collective action, the family, the individual, and consciousness have been noted by analysts of modernity and postmodernity alike (Anderson 1983; Deutsch 1953; Schivelbusch 1979; Tilly 1986; Robertson 1994; Harvey 1990). States, too, have recognized the "double relationship" between material and social relations. Urban planners and intellectual elites have attempted to transform society and social consciousness by transforming technologies of transportation, communication, and production in daily life and by treating architectural units as tools of "subversion" in efforts to force social change (Holston 1989; Baburov et al. 1971; Brumfield and Ruble 1993; Le Corbusier 1964, 1986).

Accordingly, the minutiae of daily life often reflect social responses to technological change. For example, industrialization and land reform in Russia at the end of the nineteenth century led to changes in status among individuals, which resulted in shifts in pronominal usage (Friedrich 1979, 80). These phenomena also resulted in the social and moral reorganization of the family, as the incidence of nuclear families grew in response to opportunities for private landownership, so that "obligations to distant relatives were often ignored and the relationships themselves sometimes slighted" (Friedrich 1979, 184). Throughout the urban, industrialized world, economic relations have structured and gendered distinctions between public and private spheres, linking the experience of large-scale social changes with transformations in the experience of the private, individual self: "The new urban agglomerations in which factories were concentrated extended the division of social space and time into a private sphere of family and a public one of work and politics. . . . This social division of time and space gave rise to our particularly modern conceptions of the private and gendered person" (Friedland and Boden 1994, 8–9). Thus, conversely, the rapid, catastrophic deindustrialization of Armenian urban society can also be shown to affect social relations, space, and time to a similar degree, with similar consequence for the identity of both the person and the nation.

In Armenia, the demodernization of urban life between 1991 and 1994 offered an opportunity for the examination of the intersection of individual and national identities. Individuals' unquestioned dispositions in action and interaction were revealed in their accommodation of technological crisis. The matrix of such dispositions has been described as the "strategy-generating principle enabling agents to cope with unforeseen and ever-changing situations [and] the source of these series of moves which are objectively organized as strategies without being the product of a genuine strategic intention" (Bourdieu 1977, 72). This matrix of dispositions, or habitus, is spatially and temporally contingent, though historically durable and transposable. At the same time, it mediates the experience of identity and reproduces a social world that is recognizable as itself. Representations of the group and of the self emerge from the intermingling of space, time, and practice and then serve to structure perceptions and experience, providing a framework through which "we learn who or what we are in society" (Harvey 1990, 214). In the Armenian crisis of demodernization, the reconfiguration of basic categories of space, time, and practice urged the rearticulation of personal and national identities. Expressions of identity in the context of cataclysmic spatiotemporal change, via habit or habitus, illustrate processes of recognition and identification that operate beyond rhetorical constructions of the nation or the nation-state but that nevertheless influence those constructions.

In this essay, I demonstrate links between the experience of space and time in everyday life and conceptualizations of the nation and its history. These links have implications for understandings of the formation and nature of national identities. The narrative proceeds chronologically. After a discussion of Armenian daily life before independence, with particular attention to kinship relations as situated in domestic space and time, I briefly introduce some political and economic parameters of the transition that are relevant to changes in popular consciousness, along with a depiction of what I call demodernization. Ethnographic illustrations of the impact of demodernization on the practice of kinship in domestic space-time lead to musings on a reciprocal relationship between habit and ideology in the experience of identity.

Soviet Domestic Space and Urban Armenian Daily Life

Armenia was one of the most densely populated[1] and technologically developed republics of the Soviet Union. In the 1970s, a policy of urbanization more than doubled the population of Armenia's capital city, Yerevan, in a drive to meet Soviet requirements for the building of a metro system.[2] In a single decade, the population grew from approximately five hundred thousand to more than one million (the necessary quota for a metro), bringing hundreds of thousands of villagers to the city. In the 1980s, 55 percent of the Armenian gross domestic product came from the industrial sector, which included engineering, light, and chemical industries, among others.[3] By 1990, more than 60 percent of Armenia's population lived in Yerevan and its industrial environs.[4] This rapid industrialization and migration severely overloaded the existing urban infrastructure and exacerbated shortages of food, housing, and services that were endemic to Soviet society.

Such shortages necessitated continuous interdependence among relatives and acquaintances at the same time that rural patterns of interdependence were being imported to the city. For example, as in other parts of the Soviet Union, one woman might wait in line for eggs, purchase enough for two families, and then divide the eggs and trade with a cousin, who had waited in line for coffee. Consequently, while members of a single extended family (*gerdastan*) may have been settled in diverse parts of the city, the newly developed transportation system, in combination with the existing communication infrastructure (telephone and telegraph), permitted daily contact among relations and fellow villagers. Accordingly, patterns of intense interdependence among relatives and neighbors, characteristic of village life, were revived and enacted in Yerevan, resulting in a sometimes permeable boundary between kinship (*barekamut'yun*) and "neighborship" (*harevanut'yun*).[5]

During the Soviet era, kinship constituted an important part of Armenian daily life and identity. Although Soviet and Western sources on kinship under state socialism have sometimes argued that extended family traditions had been eradicated with the implementation of Soviet policy (Creuziger 1993, 24; Girenko 1984), ideologies of traditional kinship persisted and were associated with images of national identity portrayed in daily discourse. Patriarchal and patrilocal kinship practices characteristic of Armenians in eastern Anatolia in the early twentieth century (Hoogasian-Villa 1982) and the early decades of Sovietization (Kilbourne Matossian 1962) continued to shape popular thought about appropriate behavior. Armenians conceived of their traditional kinship as a static and enduring model that was distinctly and uniquely Armenian. Regardless of whether this kinship was actually remembered or was invented to establish social continuity (Hobsbawm 1983, 2), individual identity was both constructed and understood with reference to a traditional extended family, even when actual behavior diverged from the ideal. Indeed, according to the results of a 1993 survey, 94.2 percent of Armenians possessed an extended family and considered it necessary to their happiness (Poghosian 1993). Further, the performance of kin-based duties and emotions determined whether individuals were considered "un-Armenian."

Concepts of Armenianness and of the family were mutually reinforcing, both because kin-based roles (such as bride, mother-in-law, and patriarch) were thought to be characteristically Armenian and because the Armenian nation (*azg*) derives from lineages composed of extended families. In many ways, kinship was an image of Armenian "communion" to which each individual was connected equally: kinship was central to the daily imagining of the nation (Anderson 1983, 15–16). Consequently, married sons lived with their parents, and their mothers were responsible for food preparation. Daughters and wives in an extended family household were generally responsible for housework and child care, while the senior male of the household and his sons were responsible for the family's income. Exceptions to these traditions were perceived to be anomalous though in fact they were not uncommon. However, divergence from kinship stereotypes was regarded as "un-Armenian," a negative or derogatory epithet I heard used to describe sons who did not live with their parents, sons who smoked in the presence of the head of the household (patriarch, or *nahapet*), and married couples who resided with the wife's parents. While urban infrastructure in Armenia enabled sustained closeness and interdependence of kin, which in turn permitted the endurance of practices thought of as traditional, Soviet housing did not reflect or accommodate the reality of Armenian kinship practices.

In 1987, 77.7 percent of all housing in the Soviet Union was state owned; private homes, located on state-owned land at the city's periphery, often received an incomplete array of state-owned utilities (Vysokovskii 1993, 275). Families could apply for housing officially only through their place of work. A young man or woman who wanted to move to Yerevan from a village and who had no relatives in the capital city could find temporary dormitory housing through the university, a technical school, or a work training program, usually with difficulty. Professional organizations and institutions, such as athletic teams, factories, research institutes, and state-owned stores and businesses, provided apartments for their workers. The Ministry of Construction made housing available to these institutions.

Armenians frequently discussed how this system worked inefficiently and unfairly. When Yerevan's population doubled in the 1970s, the Ministry of Construction could not produce enough housing for the growing population. The heads of nuclear families who applied for separate quarters often were placed on waiting lists for as long as twenty years, and young couples continued living with family and friends. The inequities of housing distribution have long been a topic of urban folklore, particularly in regard to the fact that certain employers provided better situated housing and better accommodations than did others. For example, university professors, KGB employees, military families, and other employees of prestigious state institutions were placed quickly in buildings maintained by their employers. These buildings were generally older, with more spacious apartments, and were located in the center of town rather than on the expanding outskirts. Furthermore, once having received apartments, Armenians, like other Soviet citizens, had no legal or practical rights to their residence (Vysokovskii 1993). Thus, Armenians had little flexibility or security in matters of housing, which led to a kind of pseudo-ownership.

Armenians found many paths for circumventing the housing laws and housing shortage and for domesticating state-owned space. Although the direct renting of apartments among individual citizens was illegal, a lively rental market flourished. A married couple with children might legally divorce, entitling one of the spouses to apply for a new apartment. Then, continuing to live together in one apartment, they might rent the other out to supplement their income. Similarly, adult children might continue to reside in cramped quarters with their parents and married siblings and rent out the apartment to which they were legally entitled. Though children were entitled to inherit the apartments of parents and grandparents, nieces, nephews, and other relations were ineligible to inherit family property. In cases like these, aunts and uncles might legally adopt their siblings' children, giving them inheritance rights to apartments.

Such machinations were often elaborate because they were dangerous. Illegally renting out an apartment was classified as speculation and was punishable by imprisonment. However, such practices increased steadily throughout the 1970s and 1980s as state control weakened and urban populations grew. Fearing the observance of neighbors, renters and landlords would frequently masquerade as relations to decrease the suspicion of those living in less spacious accommodations who might be jealous. A delicate yet elaborate web of secrecy and trust surrounded the housing arrangements of urban citizens in Soviet Armenia.

At the same time that Armenians were circumventing the rules of rental in pursuit of profit, they were also converting pseudo-owned Soviet living space into homes. By the early 1990s, most Yerevan residents lived in high-rise buildings erected during the Khrushchev and Brezhnev eras. Apartments are small and closely conform to building standards dictated by communist urban planners and social engineers in Moscow. Most have one or two bedrooms in addition to a central living room, a narrow kitchen, a bathroom, and a separate toilet cubicle. All were originally fitted for water, electricity, natural gas for cooking, centrally supplied heat, and either centrally supplied hot water or an individual gas hot water heater (*kalonka*). Most buildings are only one apartment deep, meaning that there are windows on either far end of a single residence, according to Soviet building standards: "The basic plan for an apartment divides it into two sections: rooms for daytime use and others for night-time use. Furthermore, for the privacy of a married couple, it is essential to be able to subdivide the space into two ample areas for husband and wife" (Baburov et al. 1971, 67). Because Soviet design was premised on a nuclear family, including a single married couple and young children, basic units never met the needs of multigenerational, patrilocal Armenian families.[6] Consequently, Armenians became famous in the Soviet Union for their propensity to remodel their apartments from within and to build illegal additions to state buildings from without. The universality of remodeling (*remont*)[7] among Armenians is well illustrated by a Soviet-era joke:

> *Q:* "Why aren't Armenians allowed to stay in the Hotel Rossiya in Moscow for periods longer than two weeks?"
> *A:* "Because after two weeks, they start enclosing the balconies!"[8]

Aleksander Vysokovskii has called this investment of personal energy to transform state housing into a home "place-making" (1993, 276).

In fact, this form of domestication or place-making (the enclosure or winterizing of balconies characteristically adorning one facade of a building) was so prevalent that a majority of apartments have been enlarged in that way. Yet while the transformation of balconies into rooms expands the apartment itself, it does not improve privacy or the division of space in an apartment because the balconies are always attached either to a bedroom or to a living room, with windows to the interior. A balcony room might become a bedroom for a child or a young, married couple, or the interior walls might be removed to enlarge a living room—to the detriment of a building's structural integrity.

In a multigenerational, one-bedroom household, sleeping arrangements reflect the inadequacy of Soviet urban housing. In one family, the married couple shared the sole bedroom, the husband's mother slept on a divan in the kitchen, his married son and his wife slept on the sofa in the living room, and the grandchildren slept on a winterized balcony. In a two-bedroom apartment, it was common for newlyweds to have their own bedroom, while grandparents and the groom's siblings divided sleeping space among the kitchen, living room, and balcony. In a one-room household with which I was acquainted, a divorced woman shared a bed with her daughter, her friend slept on the sofa, and her friend's mother slept on the winterized balcony. Such sleeping arrangements were fluid and necessarily changed with every birth, death, and marriage. Consequently, a distinction rarely emerged between private and common spaces: most sleeping spaces were converted into common spaces by day, precluding "ownership" of rooms.

Given the overcrowding of urban apartments, many Soviet Armenians struggled daily to maintain a sense of privacy. Young couples and groups of friends would spend evenings in cafés or in the city's extensive parks; adults might socialize with colleagues at the office after the end of the workday; and children would play together in the building courtyard. Men might congregate to play backgammon outdoors, in a garage, or on a balcony, while female neighbors might gather nightly to watch the evening news together, share household tasks, and drink coffee. The Yerevan public transportation system functioned quite effectively, and school friends, married women, and kin were able to communicate and visit regularly despite being separated by up to ten kilometers of urban landscape.

Visiting and entertaining were two components of a significant tradition of hospitality. It was both appropriate and respectful to visit the homes of neighbors, colleagues, and acquaintances—alone or with one's own kin or companions—and visits were invariably met with the "spreading of a table" (*seghan gts'el*). If not a full meal, consisting of tens of platters of diverse dishes served consecutively, a table might minimally include alcohol for ritual toasting; sliced vegetables, bread, and cheese; or fruits, cookies, and candy. As in other parts of the Caucasus region, hospitality included a reciprocal obligation under which "to fail or refuse to give hospitality is unthinkable; to decline to take it (or more generally, to fail to maximize others' opportunities to offer it) is ill-mannered and offensive" (Nichols 1994, 74). The reciprocal obligation entailed in this hospitality was both salient and compelling: guests and hosts respected each other by enacting their roles appropriately and further perpetuated the show of respect by switching roles in future visits. To fail to behave appropriately as a host or guest or to fail to return a visitor's respect with a subsequent visit could lead to offense and dishonor. Significant events, visits, and anniversaries were commemorated at the table, and respects were paid among individuals and between families through visits on both official and unofficial occasions. Spontaneous visits among old and new friends were obligatory: Armenians frequently criticized me and each other with the complaint "Why don't you visit us?" To fail to make a spontaneous visit to an acquaintance's home could be interpreted as a sign of disaffection. Armenian women facilitated this tradition by constantly preparing large quantities of excess food in case a guest might appear. Correspondingly, it was considered shameful to be unprepared with food and drink when receiving a surprise visitor.

Yerevan residents frequently visited family in villages, and village residents came regularly to Yerevan, resulting in the permeable, fluid boundary between the city and the country. Hospitality and visiting, like multigenerational residence, were important components of Armenians' descriptions of themselves as a close (*motik*) people who value closeness (*motikut'yun*). Until the 1990s, urban conditions in Yerevan not only permitted but also facilitated the interdependence, interconnection, and closeness of people in daily life. Though a fully industrialized, modern city, Yerevan's transportation and communication infrastructure allowed many kin and social networks imported or reconstituted from villages to flourish at the same time that it enabled the maintenance of relations with kin still in the villages as well as permitted new networks based on neighborhoods and the workplace to develop. Understandings of Armenianness depended simultaneously on perceptions of Armenia as a modern, industrially developed, and "advanced" society with good economic and technological standing within the Soviet Union and on attachments to pre-Soviet traditional practices, such as kinship, that were thought to resemble and to support continuity with the national past.

Movement, Crisis, Independence

The transition from socialism began earlier in Armenia than in other Soviet republics. Change began in 1988 with the Karabakh movement, a mass movement in support of national self-determination. The movement was triggered by conflict between Armenians and Azerbaijanis in Nagorno-Karabakh, a predominantly Armenian-populated autonomous region (*oblast*) within the neighboring republic of Azerbaijan. Unprecedented in Soviet history in both nature and its scope, this movement brought hundreds of thousands of Armenians to demonstrate in Yerevan for the transfer of Nagorno-Karabakh from Azerbaijan to Armenia, for the fulfillment of constitutional rights, and, eventually, for the redress of historical grievances and independence from the Soviet Union. Meetings of the movement bolstered enthusiasm and expectations for independence and for two years prior to independence (1988–90) fostered a euphoric pan-Armenian solidarity (Abrahamian 1993, 103–9; Dudwick 1994, 168) that many people anticipated would replace the corrupt relations of bureaucratic authority that characterized Soviet society.

In the same period, armed conflict in Nagorno-Karabakh itself escalated into a war of secession between Karabakh Armenians and Azerbaijan, with Armenia playing a strong role in support of its ethnic brethren across the border. In retaliation, Azerbaijan placed sanctions on Armenia in the form of a total economic blockade, which effectively interrupted the flow of natural gas and oil into landlocked Armenia. The impact of this blockade was all the more severe because Armenian environmentalists, in concert with national activists, had pressured the government to shut Armenia's nuclear power plant following a devastating earthquake in December 1988. Beginning in November 1991, the flow of energy into Armenia decreased and then stopped. The lack of energy halted industry and dampened the political aspirations and expectations of the Armenian people. With Turkey's border closed to the west in solidarity with Turkic interests in Azerbaijan, the Iranian border closed to the southeast as the legacy of Soviet policy, and all land routes through Georgia subject to sabotage in the chaos that immediately followed independence, Armenia underwent a catastrophic energy crisis. This crisis was exacerbated by the disintegration of the Soviet Union as Armenian state ministries and institutions found themselves suddenly independent of Moscow's fiscal and logistical support.

Thus independence began with an energy crisis that resulted in irregularly rationed electricity and long periods of total blackout, a permanent end to heat and hot water (previously provided by the state), and the halt of Armenian industry. Without energy, only a small number of new private businesses functioned, while many state employees of factories and other institutions were indefinitely laid off. The impact of the energy crisis on the Armenian state is reflected in statistical data compiled between 1992 and 1994.[9] In the short interval between 1988 and 1993, Armenia's gross national product underwent a five- to sixfold decline,[10] and by 1994, only 30 percent of Armenia's industry was functioning. Though Armenians had enjoyed one of the highest standards of living in the Soviet Union, unemployment now rose to the highest level in the Commonwealth of Independent States at the same time that estimates indicated that 94 percent of the population lived below the international poverty line by April 1994.[11] Prior to the introduction of the Armenian national currency in 1994, prices rose as much as 100 percent in a single day. Even after the stabilization of the dram in 1994, an estimated 80 percent of the population could not afford the minimum amount of basic food,[12] and the average family continued spending 80 percent of its monthly income on food.[13] During the same period, the Armenian Ministry of Economics estimated that the cost of minimal nutrition for an individual was thirty-five times the amount of the average monthly wage,[14] which was somewhere between one and two U.S. dollars.[15] To make matters worse, in 1993, approximately one-third of Armenia's entire population was estimated to be homeless,[16] including more than three hundred thousand refugees from the war in Nagorno-Karabakh and more than five hundred thousand who had lost their homes in the 1988 earthquake.[17] Without energy, the Armenian government was unable to generate significant revenue through industry or export, to alleviate unemployment, or to provide regular municipal services such as public transportation, garbage collection, mail delivery, telephone repair, and pest extermination. These events and circumstances came as a blow to the majority of Armenians, who had participated in the effervescence of the movement only one year before and who had elected their movement leadership to state office in 1991.

Catastrophic Demodernization: Daily Space-Time in Transition

The privatization of property and housing began after the 1990 election of President Ter Petrossian to Parliament and the 1991 Armenian referendum on independence. Privatization ushered in the opportunity for families and individuals to own houses and apartments at last. Armenians rushed to pay nominal fees entitling them to legal ownership of formerly state-owned apartments. Ironically, the sudden and dramatic impact of Azerbaijan's total blockade of Armenia denied the population the empowerment of ownership by transforming the familiar into the unfamiliar and thereby making individuals into strangers in their own homes. The changes in infrastructure brought by the energy crisis transformed urban landscapes, domestic spaces, personal identities, and historical memory.

By 1991, the vast majority of Armenia's population lived either in towns or cities like Yerevan, in the arid Ararat Valley, or at higher altitudes, as in Gyumri and Spitak, where the land is also barren and rocky. Only in northern Armenia, at lower altitudes, does the climate allow for any significant forestation that might produce lumber. Thus, Yerevan's landscape changed rapidly as the decorative trees that adorned it were cut down to be burned in homes for heat or for cooking. Lumber brought from outside of Armenia was scarce, and indigenous resources were quickly depleted. Eventually, when people had burned everything that was expendable at home and had exhausted all the lumber supplies available to them, they began to burn the wooden boards from park benches and any other bits of wood found around the city. Not only did deforestation and smoke-blackened walls transform the city's outer appearance, but the consumption of municipal lumber severely inhibited the flow of people through the parks and cafés, where they once went for privacy.

Other factors also began to make the city's streets and parks less welcoming and navigable to pedestrians. As municipal resources dwindled, the city curtailed many of its services, such as garbage collection and pest control. Piles of garbage around dumpsters on street corners grew higher and wider, often blocking passage with their size and stench. The garbage attracted wild dogs—released, many speculated, by owners who could no longer support them—and rats, which combined with the lack of street-lights made the dark city streets dangerous in the evening. Such changes in the urban landscape dramatically altered the motion of people through it.

Early in the crisis, the combined effects of decentralization and the blockade meant that goods necessary for survival were unavailable among the dwindling supplies at state stores: flashlights, candles, batteries, space heaters, thermoses, kerosene lamps, propane tanks, and camping stoves were scarce and valuable commodities in the city. Few people had enough initial capital to open stores, and even if they had, it took several months for official approval from the local government and for trade partners abroad to be identified and relations established. In the interim, enterprising individuals began hawking wares on the streets, at the markets, and even inside state-owned shops and department stores. "Little tables" (*seghanikner*) emerged everywhere, selling imported food products, candles, soap, and other necessary goods and literally lining the streets until being outlawed in 1993. The tables, too, altered the flow of pedestrian traffic through the city, in many cases completely blocking the sidewalks.

As a new, commercial elite eventually began to form, flashy shops opened around the city, selling a random collection of luxury and status items mixed with appliances, tools, and food products. The availability of these goods almost instantaneously began to stratify society visually by distinguishing the nouveau riche from the increasingly impoverished. Networks of roadside entrepreneurs began selling fuel (including benzene, propane, diesel, and kerosene) from trucks at the same time that state-owned gas stations closed. Few could afford fuel to drive cars, and the state itself was forced to curtail public transportation—metro, bus, and streetcar—for lack of financial resources. These and other similar developments transformed the urban landscape, rearranging the loci of commerce, changing the daily patterns of motion through the city, and altering its overall appearance.

Within a changing city, private homes began to change as well, and the physical space of the domesticated home eventually ceased to resemble itself. Changes to the physical space impaired the ordered functionings of the home, which had constituted an organic "phenomenon of circulation" (Le Corbusier 1964, 30). Thus, changes in this space had implications for domestic life because the home and the family had "each received the imprint of the other" (Halbwachs 1980, 130): images of the created home both represented the family as an entity in relations with the outside world and distinguished domestic space from state space. As the winter weather reached record cold temperatures in 1992 and 1993 and indoor temperatures dropped below freezing, most families installed homemade gas and wood-burning stoves in their living rooms. This installation required many changes to the apartments themselves. Cement blocks or stones had to be placed under the stove so that its heat would not burn the floor, and beds were often arranged in a single room so that all family members could sleep near a source of heat. When food was prepared on a stove in the living room, the kitchen ceased to be a place where women would gather to talk and share chores. On cold winter days, when workplaces and schools were closed, entire families might sit in relative darkness, around a stove in a single room, sometimes joined by neighbors, friends, or kin. However, gatherings became largely impromptu or coincidental as phone lines went down and public transportation flagged, impeding communication.

Gradually, as unemployment and inflation grew, many families began to burn their collections of books and eventually pieces of their furniture for heat in the winter, further altering the configuration of domestic space. Valuable items, such as jewelry, crystal, china, and art, which once domesticated the space and incorporated it into the realm of social relations, were sold at prices far below their value so that families could afford food and fuel. Alterations to the domestic environment such as these had severe consequences for the flow of people through space and for relations between individuals and families. Two important symbols of social status—material wealth in the form of crystal and jewelry and hospitality in the form of elaborate banquets held for weddings, funerals, graduations, or impromptu gatherings—were voided by financial hardship, the rearrangement of domestic space, and the lack of cooking fuel. Thus, relations among neighbors, friends, extended families, and colleagues began to change as embarrassment about the inability to be hospitable grew.

People became reluctant to visit one another and to participate in customary hospitality (*hyurasirut'yun*): on the one hand, they did not want to induce their loved ones to go to an expense they could not afford or to be shamed by being unable to respect their visitors with the hospitality of food and drink. On the other hand, people also did not want to incur the reciprocal obligation of returning hospitality to someone they had visited because they could not offer the traditional excess. Despite the mutual goodwill underlying Armenians' decisions not to visit one another spontaneously, individuals could not avoid taking offense instinctively at friends and family who failed to appear. Often, such offenses grew incrementally into estrangement so that a chance encounter between friends in the street could be awkward and embarrassing for all who had been unintentionally negligent in their reciprocal obligations and who were reluctant to admit the shaming and shameful reasons why they had not visited. In many cases, such estrangement influenced individual and collective identities by contradicting the ideal of closeness conceived as an inherent part of being Armenian. In other cases, hardship intensified closeness within residential households by bringing individuals together in smaller spaces, over longer periods of time, and thereby augmented interdependence.[18]

Transformations of the physical and social configurations of city and home altered the patterns of implicit and explicit action of individuals on which identity in everyday life was based. Without cooking gas, women began to prepare food on electric hot plates and space heaters when electricity was available. In the winter, food would not spoil without refrigeration, but in summer, an elaborate calculus was required for maximizing the cooking time allowed by one or two hours of electricity without producing an excessive quantity of food that might spoil without refrigeration. Water had to be constantly stored in tubs, buckets, pots, and pans so that it could be heated during the hours of electricity. Because hours of rationed electricity and water were not scheduled by the state, it was usually necessary for at least one family member to stay home to collect fresh water during the day. Cooking, bathing, and laundry could only be accomplished when electricity and water were both present, so many women began to stay home from work as the result of the new demands of housekeeping, severely disrupting their habitual activities and motion between private and public realms.

These changes had consequences for personal identities. For example, it had been customary for unmarried girls and young women to bake elaborate cakes for social gatherings while their mothers and grandmothers were responsible for preparing meals. A good baker acquired a good reputation and made a desirable wife, it was thought. Without gas to fire ovens, young women were unable to demonstrate their talent. It was openly discussed that the inability to bake might make it more difficult for girls to attract husbands. Similarly, many adult women had taken enormous pride in being good hostesses, cooks, and housewives. The inability to exercise these talents represented a crisis of meaning and identity for women who could no longer exhibit qualities that distinguished them within their families and among friends and acquaintances.

The energy crisis had further consequences for adults of all ages and both genders. Lack of energy in many workplaces meant that employees were indefinitely laid off, and many husbands and wives found themselves at home together, day after day. Many reported that unemployment made them feel useless and, even worse, that their lives had been reduced to an "animal-like" existence and they could not "recognize" themselves. People who had taken pride in their skill at work now lacked an important context for experiencing their individuality. Elderly people were sometimes unable to go out because the lack of electricity halted elevators in all of Yerevan's high-rise buildings, and climbing as many as thirteen flights of stairs proved too strenuous. In 1992, schools and universities began to close for the winter months, and thus an entire family (*entanik'*) might find itself at home on a weekday. Socially embedded identities began to fade outside of socially demarcated places. Domestic roles and relations began to change as those unaccustomed to constant togetherness struggled to maintain private identities in a new context, without the balancing forces of public identities experienced in work and social environments. Similarly, the speed of passing time was perceived to slow with the boredom of relative idleness, inactivity, and monotony.

For example, in one family with which I stayed, a man in his mid-twenties, finding himself at home during the day for the first time in his life, began helping his grandmother prepare meals in the kitchen, much to the consternation of his immediate male relatives. Implicitly acknowledging the embarrassment inherent in a man doing "women's work," he left the kitchen hastily when guests, visitors, or neighbors arrived. His cooking came not from a new interest in the activity itself but, as he said, from boredom as a result of the idleness of sitting at home. He also admitted that at home, he recognized for the first time the extent of his ailing grandmother's difficult work in preparing meals. This burden moved him, and he wanted to help her, at the risk of damaging his own masculine identity. In another household, a husband and provider for a large extended family whose laboratory was shut began sitting in the kitchen with his wife, widowed sister-in-law, and daughter to stay warm throughout the day. In self-mockery, he began to wear his wife's pink sweater to stay warm and to symbolize the emasculation he felt at being confined to a "female" realm by freezing conditions.

Sitting together in the dark and cold, it became a common practice for families to discuss the conditions, political rumors, and memories of the recent Soviet past. All life experience was divided between before and after. Discourse came to be universally characterized by constant temporal referencing: events, feelings, and states of being "before the war" (*paterazmits' araj*), "before the earthquake" (*yerkrasharzhits' araj*), "before independence" (*ankakhut'yunits' araj*), and in "Soviet times" (*sovyetakan zhamanak*) were continuously juxtaposed with the time after these markers, such as "after the earthquake" (*yergrasharzhits' heto*). Over and over, older people would repeat that life was better in the Soviet Union—that "life was better before"—because there was always a "guarantee" in the form of the state. In response to greetings, Armenians of all ages and backgrounds recited, "There is no light, there is no bread, there isn't anything [*luys ch'ka, hats' ch'ka, voch' mi ban ch'ka*]". Young and old alike would recite new prices in comparison to old ones and complain, "This is not life," "There is no life," and "There is no way out." As one man eloquently explained to me, "existence doesn't exist."

Unmarked by familiar occurrences and interactions, life ceased to be recognized as itself, and individuals ceased to feel that they were themselves. Stripped of its social fabric and contingent on particular spatial and temporal contexts, existence became "animal" and "inhuman," as much because of the absence of markers of domestication as increased preoccupation with survival at the expense of other more human kinds of activity. The apartment, stripped of distinctive features that transformed it into a home, also ceased to be a place. Time lost the texture given to it by work, interactions, and events, so that the present moment became unmeasurable and unrecognizable. Without the "structuration" of place and moment (Giddens 1979, 66) by unreflexive, habitual social action, life, existence, and even history seemed to be at an end. At the same time, experiences and conceptualizations of space and time, "co-constituted" in activity (Munn 1992, 97), changed with habits. Armenians described themselves as backsliding to the Middle Ages (*mijnadar*), to an unfamiliar, premodern world.

In this way, the energy crisis soon acquired national dimensions as it pertained to identity. The blockade revoked what had been called a "frontier" of the industrial age: the night (Friedland and Boden 1994, 8). In wintertime, without electricity, it became dark indoors by 5:00 P.M., and families would gather around a single candle or lamp along with a single heat source or sit in total darkness to conserve resources. The length of the day was cut in half, and nighttime passed unnoticed by recorded time, as activity and sight ebbed with the sun. Whereas a 1986 poll showed that 90 percent of Armenians depended on television for news,[19] now, without television and radio, access to news was limited, particularly because energy shortages also presented obstacles to the regular printing and distribution of newspapers. The absence of these media, which would otherwise connect Armenians to the outside (*durs*), to international time, and to each other, made distances greater both within and outside of Armenia and in making the past seem farther away in time. Where *outside* had once been the term used to refer to every place outside of the former Soviet Union, it now came to include all former Soviet territories outside of the Republic of Armenia. Armenians, "inside," felt cut off from the "outside" world and from each other. With phone lines down and without transportation, relatives on the other side of the city, in the nearest village, or abroad were equally far away and inaccessible. Because a transcendent connectedness had been essential to Armenian identity, changes to the familiar distances binding people, places, and things eroded perceptions and experiences of identities, just as the advent of mass transportation had destroyed local identities by collapsing distances in Western Europe more that a century earlier (Schivelbusch 1979, 45).

Ironically, isolation itself became common to Armenians—isolated from one another—uniting them "inside," in contrast to the "real" world in "real" time, "outside." While isolation eroded the Armenian closeness between individuals, it nevertheless began to distinguish the nation from non-Armenians and outsiders. Time passed without witnesses to verify its passage, and Armenians began to treat the nation as a macrocosm of themselves and to describe their personal experience through the metaphor of the nation. For example, isolation and disconnection were conveyed by the popular, comic expression, "Armenia is the most independent country in the world, because nothing and nobody depends on it."

Semantic games, such as this play on the meaning of *independence,* were one vehicle through which Armenians increasingly began to identify their experience as historical and national in everyday discourse, as in the joke with which this essay began. Another joke made use of the fact that Levon Ter Petrossian had been trained as a scholar of the ancient and medieval Near East and had worked at the national manuscript library (*Matenaderan*) before joining the leadership of the national movement in 1988. It suggested that Armenian history ends with the energy crisis: "Why does Levon want to kill all Armenians?" "So he will know another dead language!"

As conditions worsened, political rumors, jokes, and national expressions circulated. For many Armenians, the energy crisis seemed to be the end of history, and the rapid, cataclysmic changes brought by independence and the energy crisis made daily life, the city, relations, and the home unrecognizable. Recognition, contingent on the reproduction of space-time relations, contributes to the processes of identification by which personal identity is constructed. In the absence of a familiar spatiotemporal matrix, the nation—with its legally defined territory and geopolitically defined history—becomes one means of fixing a place and a moment. The energy crisis simultaneously challenged the imagery of national identity, for example, by impeding the practice of hospitality and united Armenians in shared loss: the nation, rather than the individual or the family, was felt to be backsliding.

Kinship and *Kents'agh,* Tradition and Modernity

Demodernization between 1991 and 1994 was sometimes accompanied by the dislocation of relations among neighbors, friends, kin, and compatriots, which, according to most, could never have happened "before." Interactions occurred out of place, reconstituting collectivities and thereby disrupting socially situated processes of identification. Such dislocations or estrangements further reveal the precise interconnections between basic categories of space, time, relationships, and identities among people, particularly as they pertain to ownership and change.

For example, in one semiprivatized apartment building in the center of Yerevan, a top-floor apartment caught fire and burned, damaging the roof and exposing the floor and, consequently, the lower stories, to the natural elements. While some apartments in the building were privatized, others were not, resulting in varying levels of interest in the damage and the reluctance of certain neighbors to contribute to repairs. Consequently, the financial burden on the owners of privatized apartments became too extreme for sufficient repair funds to be raised. Alienation resulted from attempts to locate blame and responsibility, and families were offended by the accusations of others. While a few years before, the state would have arrested the arson and sponsored reconstruction, neighbors were suddenly pitted against one another in the struggle to make and maintain their homes.

Prior to independence, neighbors had often been allied against the Soviet state, helping each other with goods, labor, bureaucratic connections, and even money, particularly in their place-making and domesticating efforts. I was frequently told that in the past, neighbors had left their apartment doors open and that there was a constant flow of traffic between apartments, as if neighbors were members of one family. Neighborship was valued much like kinship and was considered something particular to Armenian society. One of the first questions asked of travelers returning home from abroad, along with "Is there Armenianness there [*hayut'yun ka*]?" was "Is there neighborship there [*harevanut'yun ka*]?". Therefore, when families closed and locked their doors against the threat of rodents or crime during the crisis, neighbors felt offended, though no offense was intended. Despite intellectual comprehension of new, shared circumstances, neighbors unconsciously and unintentionally felt hurt and disoriented by the reinforcement of the boundaries between private spaces. Neighbors slowly ceased to recognize or identify with each other and became likely to accuse each other when conflicts of interest arose.

As the state-based infrastructure dwindled to almost nothing, poor conditions damaged buildings, phone lines, electrical wiring, and plumbing. In one building, rats gnawed through a main telephone cable and neighbors were forced to collect money for the necessary replacement. Previously, the city would have been responsible not only for repairing the cable but for collecting garbage and exterminating pests before such damage could occur. Now, residents had no alternative but to invest in the property themselves. Yet some residents were in a state of financial distress, while others had found lucrative business in trade after independence. On this account, it was rumored, repair organizers asked certain families to contribute more than others. Such rumors led to debate and conflict based on assessments of who was "responsible" for damage and repairs as well as perceptions that those collecting funds for repairs were overcharging some families and thereby profiting. Attributed guilt led to theft from garages on the premises, hostilities, and to irreparable rifts between families, whose members swore they would never speak to one another again.

It is ironic that several of these neighbors claimed on different occasions that they could never live outside of Armenia because they could not survive without neighborship. In fact, the state had recently given one woman a larger apartment for her family, but she declined to take it because, she said, she knew she could not find such good neighborship anywhere else, even in Yerevan, and she valued neighborship above physical comfort. Despite the fragmentation of her social world and the new, practical conflicts arising with her neighbors, she persisted in representing her experience in the ideal terms of Armenian closeness.

Thus, ownership and deterioration of property began to affect the parameters of spatiotemporal contexts of interaction. Ownership redefined space in state-owned buildings, erecting distinctions between "ours" and "theirs" among neighbors who had previously shared common responsibility and dispossession with respect to the state. Concomitantly, Armenian independence, marking the relaxation of state control, began to redefine time, dividing it into opposing categories of "before" and "after." In the time before, the world was known: prices, places, and relations were constant, and the meanings behind words and actions were transparent. After independence and the onset of economic crisis, the world was in flux:

value, location, and meaning all became opaque. The redefinition of space in ownership and the redefinition of time after independence intersected in the practice of neighborship, resulting in the disruption of social relations, which were manifested in criticism and conflicts. Because Armenians considered closeness and neighborship characteristic of themselves and of Armenianness, changes in neighborly relations, reflecting newly divided spaces in a new era, elicited discussion of the nation and of national character. In this way, daily interaction among neighbors, including conflict and disagreement, acquired significance for the experience and representation of national identity.

While conflict and dispute have sometimes been considered to strengthen social ties by reinforcing shared values and reifying customs and conventional behaviors (Gluckman 1982, 54), conflicts like those among Armenian neighbors failed to establish the "nature of right-doing" (Gluckman 1982, 18) because fields of meaning had shifted with spatiotemporal circumstances, leaving actors with dissimilar points of reference. Within families, as among neighbors, new physical relations of proximity and distance led to shifts in the balance of authority and honor, resulting in further narratives of estrangement and causing shifts in the experience of Armenianness. The following story demonstrates the dislocation of kin relations across the urban-rural divide.

In one extended family, objective obstacles to the fulfillment of reciprocal hospitality obligations led to a rift between households and challenged the kin-based identities of all involved. A young woman, Seta, was engaged to marry a young man whose parents were deceased. Though according to tradition the groom's family would host the wedding party, under the circumstances the responsibility fell to the bride's parents. However, due to the closing of Seta's parents' place of employment, money was tight, and they were unable to host a large party. Not wanting their kin and guests to incur travel and reciprocity expenses, they invited only the senior generation of representatives of each household in the extended family to the wedding party.

When one relative brought all his children, uninvited, other kin were shamed that they had willingly spared the expense of bringing their children too. Jealousies and accusations of favoritism and inhospitality flew back and forth among households. Despite sincere intentions to spare each party's pride, hosts and guests had each unwittingly violated the reciprocal obligations of respect entailed in traditional hospitality. Bad feelings solidified as the lack of phones and transportation prevented communication among the households, whose members' failure to visit one another now appeared to be a sign of disrespect and dishonor. Each perceiving that the other had willfully failed to visit or communicate with them, closeness within the extended family disintegrated to the point that previously close relations did not speak for two years.

In this way, the new economic and infrastructural circumstances of independent Armenia contributed to the expansion of literal and figurative distances between some households and within some families, making the family that bridged the gap between city and village a part of the past—of the time "before," when Armenians, by their own account, were "close, human," and more like themselves. The weakening of ties within some families altered the ways in which national identity was experienced in everyday life. The persistence of Armenian ideals of closeness, kinship, and neighborship at a time when they could not be enacted deepened the division between before and after and exacerbated the sensation that the present moment had somehow been detached from the flow of historical, chronological time. Ironically, demodernization interrupted the enactment of kinship traditions, understood to be of and continuous with the national past. While demodernization was experienced as regression, Armenians experienced the discontinuity of long-standing daily habits as a rupture in the fabric of national, historical time. Polyvalent concepts of tradition and modernity provided metaphorical images of directionality in the history of the nation.

National Historical Time: Repetition, Rupture, or Regression?

Demodernization resulted in the sensation, expressed in popular jokes as well as in private discourse, that history had begun to "go backward" and that, unlike the rest of the modern Western world, which was interconnected in a linear, progressive motion, Armenia was retreating to a "premodern" or "medieval" past. In some versions, history retraced its own recent steps, while in others it jumped back over centuries. By certain accounts, history simply ended or went back to the beginning, forcing the nation to "start again from zero" (*ts'royits' enk' sksum*). Whereas the continuity of Armenian historical experience had been emphasized during the Karabakh movement before independence, demodernizing changes after independence precipitated the conceptualization of a break, or reversal, in the fabric of history, distinguishing this tragic moment from others. Nevertheless, in most cases, the Armenian nation, not the individual, was the subject of this motion.

Between 1991 and 1994, the myriad changes and hardships resulting from demodernization interrupted relations within extended families by altering the spatiotemporal frameworks within which individuals interacted. Lack of heat, homelessness, and displacement caused large families to cohabit in ever-smaller domestic spaces, while emigration left thousands of homes and apartments vacant and affected the dynamics of both domestic authority and division of labor. Failures in the infrastructures of transportation and communication disengaged the center from the periphery at the same time as they made intracity transportation and communication difficult. Young men went abroad by the thousands to try to earn money to support their families at home. Distances and intervals literally expanded at the same time that Armenians felt history had contracted as the result of incomparable rapidity of political and economic change and emotional responses to irreparable losses.

Spatiotemporal expansions and contractions such as these channeled memory and linked extended family experience with narratives of national survival and identity. As changes in the experience of space and time transformed contexts of interaction, individuals became isolated from one another. This isolation affected everyday life and personal identity. At the same time, the shared experience of isolation produced a heightened awareness of the nation as the subject of change; postindependence demodernization bound the individual to the fate of the nation, in the definition of national membership and imperatives. The tension between individual isolation and national membership was expressed in multiple new visions of the nation that contrasted with the preindependence euphoria but continued to unite Armenians in their misfortunes. As opposed to the national ideology propagated by the Karabakh movement, which mobilized the population around the promise of a unified, independent Armenia, postindependence associations between tragic experience and national identity were rooted in the experience of spatiotemporal discontinuities in daily life and did not result from political mobilizations of sentiment.

The use of spatiotemporal imagery to describe national experience after independence reveals the fertile associations of the experience of space, time, and habit with the experience of identity. A language of motion and directionality came to dominate descriptions of the nation in daily conversation. Popular discourse expressed the opinions that history and the nation were "going backward" (*het enk' gnum*), which Armenians illustrated with the apparent, ironic reversals of many of the individual goals of the national movement prior to 1991. Abrupt changes in the experience of space and time precipitated crises of both personal and national identity that were reflected in daily discourse about history and the nation during the early years of the transition. Although scholarship has shown how consciousness of nations can result from mixed degrees of "artefact, invention and social engineering" (Gellner 1983; Hobsbawm 1990, 10), that nationalities have been "organized and mobilized by the work of intellectuals and politicians," and that, in the Armenian case, mass sentiments have been mobilized around a national ideology "created by an intellectual elite" (Dudwick 1993, 270; Suny 1993a, 1993b), the Armenian experience of crisis during the early years of transition illustrates that the lived habits of everyday life, too, impinge on the experience of collective identity.

Rupture and regression were symbolized for many by the reversal of the goals of the Karabakh movement and the proto-Karabakh environmental movement. The latter had demonstrated against Soviet development and environmental policy, which it considered "ecological genocide." Participants demanded the closure of the Nairit rubber plant, which polluted the air and was deemed responsible for health problems ranging from cancer to infertility, and of the Metsamor nuclear power plant after the earthquake because it presented a "genocidal" hazard to the Armenian nation. After 1991, Armenians found themselves pressuring their independent government to reopen these facilities.

The initial steps of the national movement, once conceived of as pro-Armenian victories in a struggle with the Soviet state, now ironically turned against the Armenian nation in the era of independence. The ironic power of this inversion even caused some, once opposed to the atomic station and rubber plant, to reinterpret history and to reremember the shutdown of Metsamor and Nairit as conspiratorial actions by a forward-looking Soviet state. Armenians found a similar tragic irony in the fact that while their mass demonstrations supported the transition to a free-market economy as a component of national self-determination, the official advent of capitalism in Armenia was accompanied by the near-total deindustrialization of the economy and society. High hopes for free trade and economic growth were replaced with the reality of a total blockade and the return to a Soviet style of barter.

Underlying accounts of rupture and regression, reference to national history persisted both in hyperbolic form, as in the joke about Grigor the Illuminator and Levon the Terminator, and in domestic conversation. For example, while visiting a multigenerational family of eight, I watched the youngest son in the household play with hot wax from a candle that lit the room during a power outage. "You are a real Armenian," his grandmother told him, "because Armenians have always loved fire." The whole family began to participate in the conversation, contributing different bits of historical knowledge. The boy's mother reminded her children of the fact that the Etchmiadzin Church, the seat of the Katholikosate of the Armenian Church, was built on the site of a pre-Christian, pagan fire temple. Her oldest son explained that during the pogroms against Armenians in the Ottoman Empire, Turks would light fires to distinguish whether orphaned children were of Armenian, Turkish, or Kurdish descent: if children were attracted to the fire, Ottoman officials knew they were Armenian.[20] Stories of Armenians' attraction to fire in ancient, medieval, and modern times lasted for almost an hour and encouraged listeners to persevere in the face of hardship, as their ancestors had done previously in different episodes and eras defined by popular historical consciousness. At the same time, the incorporation of historical imagery into discussions of daily life suggests a complex relationship between history and memory.

Every day, Armenians continued to use history to talk about themselves and their circumstances. Armenian history was used both to distinguish before from after and to establish a link between them. Both uses were processes of location by which individuals identified themselves. Thus, out of the disruption of shared familiar frameworks, such as the home, the apartment building, the workplace, or the city street, multiple new frameworks were created via history, situating individuals and groups with respect to each other in historical space-time. The act of sharing memories of a time before and of the historical past (Connerton 1989, 17) itself reconstituted community by defining common origins.

In the years 1991 to 1994, demodernization, which transformed experience of space and time, and discontinuity in the enactment of everyday routines threatened the identification of actions and individuals as properly Armenian. Yet the ubiquitous discussion of national characteristics mapped out a historical and territorial context that reframed the placeless and timeless interactions of people in daily life. Through the representation of history, Armenians resisted rupture and regression by constructing a national space-time through social memory. In the face of adversity, Armenian identity itself, propagated through discourse as a perpetual ideal, enabled Armenians to locate themselves in historical time and national space.

While in 1997 Azerbaijan maintained its blockade of Armenia, the reopening of Armenia's nuclear power plant with international assistance in 1996, the opening of the Iranian border, the inauguration of diplomatic and trade relations with Iran, and the institution of numerous reforms and assistance programs have restored a degree of normalcy to Armenian daily life. The impact of the crisis years on Armenian identity under improved conditions and economic development should be the subject of future research.

NOTES

1. Second after Moldova.
2. Population requirements for the building of a Soviet subway were mentioned to me by more than one source. I have, however, been unable to verify the accuracy of this popular belief.

3. According to the industry brief of the United Nations Industrial Development Organization entitled "Armenia: Towards Economic Independence and Industrial Reorganization," August 1990.

4. According to Soviet statistics, the population of Yerevan grew from 767,000 in 1970 to 1,019,000 in 1979 to 1,148,000 in 1985. Thus, by the 1980s more than one-third of Armenia's population lived in Yerevan (Walker 1991, 63).

5. I use *neighborship* as a neologism in English to approximate the meaning of the Armenian term and to distinguish the concept from the English *neighborliness,* which connotes a more formal civility that is not intended by the Armenian usage.

6. For a discussion of the failure of Soviet planning to accommodate the needs of the Russian family, see Ruble 1993, 253.

7. *Remont* is the Russian word, used in colloquial eastern Armenian.

8. This joke was shared with me by Levon Abrahamian in 1991.

9. The news sources in this section were obtained through the Armenian Information Service (AIS).

10. According to IMF estimates, the Armenian GNP dropped from $16.5 billion to $2.7 billion during the same five-year period (Noyan Tapan, July 18, 1994 [AIS, July 19, 1994]).

11. According to the Centers for Disease Control, *Los Angeles Times,* April 12, 1994 (AIS, April 13, 1994).

12. BBC World Broadcasts, January 11, 1994 (AIS, January 11, 1994).

13. According to UNICEF, BBC World Broadcasts, January 7, 1994 (AIS, January 7, 1994).

14. Noyan Tapan, March 4, 1994 (AIS, March 7, 1994).

15. Hayastani Hanrapetutyun, May 10, 1994 (AIS, May 10, 1994).

16. TASS, December 6, 1993 (AIS, December 6, 1993).

17. UPI, December 7, 1993 (AIS, December 8, 1993).

18. It should be noted that Armenian colleagues have reported to me that they knew of individuals who, busy before the transition, found the crisis to be an opportunity to refresh close ties with family and friends by sharing hardship and passing time together. For example, one group of schoolmates and friends from childhood reported that the crisis gave them opportunities to convene and refresh old ties (Levon Abrahamian, personal communication, July 1993). I recognize the wide variation in individual experiences of crisis but did not encounter in my fieldwork examples of this particular crisis solidarity or of the relationship between crisis solidarity and national identity.

19. Cited in Dudwick (1994, 235) from Arutiunian and Karapetian (1986, 86–90).

20. This is an unusual version of a popular legend about the way in which conquering Seljuk Turks distinguished the nationalities of their hostages in Anatolia in the Middle Ages. For a full version of the legend, see Emin 1983.

Memory, History, and Remembrance Work in Dresden

Elizabeth A. Ten Dyke

Introduction

This article is concerned with an intersection of memory, history, and material culture in the former German Democratic Republic (GDR). The *Wende*[1] brought about a massive transformation in virtually every aspect of GDR culture and society, eventually leading to the collapse of the state and the unification of East and West Germany in October 1990.[2] During and after the *Wende* many East Germans experienced the sensation of being hurled into a painful confrontation with their personal, cultural, and national histories.

While some East and West German intellectuals, artists, and politicians called for and initiated an *Aufarbeitung der Vergangenheit* (working-through of the past) that was modeled on the post–World War II *Aufarbeitung*,[3] many ordinary men and women engaged themselves with memory and history in ways that were personal and unique. In this article I present two examples of what I call "remembrance work": an eyewitness account of rioting and violence at Dresden's main train station during the first week of October 1989 and a home "museum" of the GDR created by three students in a spare room in their apartment. In recent years social scientists have produced a considerable literature on history and memory. Through a discussion of some of its major themes, I show that this literature offers useful perspectives that facilitate an understanding of the report and the museum. But I also find that some of its categories prove inadequate when confronted with complex ethnographic description such as that included here.

Social scientists often assume a contrast or opposition between individual and collective memory. The latter is understood to contribute to group cohesiveness and stability (Connerton 1989; Fentress and Wickham

1992; Halbwachs 1992; Middleton and Edwards 1990). The production of consolidating memories through different media (printed literature, commemorative ritual) has been explored, with particular emphasis on periods of national unification (Anderson 1983; Hobsbawm and Ranger 1983).

Pierre Nora (1989) explores consequences of the introduction of alternative historical representations. By raising questions about the past, he argues, critical historiography has led to the loss of "natural memory" (the "traditional" or "ancestral") as well as to the end of the construction of coherent national identities through shared, unfragmented history. "To interrogate a tradition," Nora writes, "is no longer to pass it on intact" (1989, 10). The creation of "lieux de mémoire" (sites of memory), including museums and archives, is evidence of the perceived need to preserve "artificial" memories at a moment when the "acceleration of history" and the emergence of "mass culture on a global scale" have eradicated natural memory (Nora 1989, 7).

Even though museums may serve a necessary function by retaining the past, historical representations contained therein often become the subject of considerable social and political argument (Aagaard-Mogensen 1988; Karp, Kreamer, and Lavine 1992; Berdahl 1994; Bunzl 1995). Such debates suggest that the present period is marked more by the fragmentation of social groups than by their consolidation within nation-states. Along these lines, John R. Gillis (1994) argues that the present period (beginning in the 1960s) is better characterized as postnational than national. Museums and archives no longer adequately conserve the past because "the reality is that the nation is no longer the site or frame for memory for most people" (Gillis 1994, 17; see also Kearney 1996). As Gillis notes, "there is good evidence to show that ordinary people [are] shopping for that which best suits their particular sense of self at the moment, constructing out of a bewildering variety of materials, times, and places the multiple identities that are demanded of them in the postnational era" (1994, 17–18).

As nations fragment or simply become increasingly irrelevant to growing numbers of sub- and transnational individuals and groups,[4] the representation of the past through memory and history is central to the construction of identities and the assertion of present and future material and ideological claims. As different groups acquire or lose power and prestige in complex societies, certain memories and histories emerge as dominant, while others may evolve as oppositional, alternative, or marginal (Popular Memory Group 1982; Swedenburg 1991; Watson 1994; White 1992; Berdahl 1997). As part of this process, memories and histories may become the focus of struggle in and of themselves (for example, through conflicts over commemorative ritual) (see Gal 1991; Lampland 1990).

This brief summary of relevant social science research suggests the importance of explicating the particular contexts in which practices and processes of memory are found and of exploring the politics of the representation of the past. This article also begs the question of the fruitfulness of conceiving memory through such dichotomies as individual-collective and dominant-oppositional. After a brief explication of the circumstances in which I encountered remembrance work in the former GDR, followed by a discussion of the report and the museum, I return to these themes in my concluding discussion.

Discovering *Schätze* (Treasures)

Even when an anthropologist carefully plans a visit or interview, its tenor and course are shaped by the motives and personalities of the participants as well as the immediate and historical contexts of the encounter. As one of very few Americans residing in Dresden during 1991–92, I was the object of a great deal of curiosity and desire. This made it easy for me to collect oral history interviews (for my doctoral dissertation) because many respondents were eager to have "die Amerikanerin" visit their homes. Respondents frequently quizzed me on the GDR and the *Wende,* correcting me when they felt my views were inaccurate or misguided. Because my personal experience of the GDR was limited to the period beginning with November 1989, many respondents assumed the role of instructor or interpreter, teaching me what they felt I should know.

This process led many men and women who were preserving histories of the GDR to share their collections with me. Over and over during interviews respondents abandoned me and my tape recorder to rummage through personal possessions, reappearing with boxes or bags full of items left over from their lives under state socialism. These artifacts included medals awarded for superior performance at work, newspaper clippings, tape recordings of radio broadcasts, photographs, favorite or most despised books, neck scarves from the Young Pioneers (a nationwide youth group), and more.

Repeatedly confronted with evidence of the human penchant to amass things from the past, I began to recognize this behavior as significant and the collections themselves as fascinating and provocative. In fact, in my field notes I began to refer to such collections as *Schätze* (treasures) not because they had any significant material value but because they represented an ethnographic treasure trove for me. Respondents, conversely, usually called the objects *Sachen* or *Gegenstände* (things, possessions), as opposed to *Erinnerungsstücke* (souvenirs). Despite this apparently neutral lexical choice, the men and women with whom I spoke often had very strong and, as will become clear, significant feelings about the objects. While showing me the items and explaining their many meanings, these people sometimes expressed pleasure, delight, or pride. More often than not, however, they also exhibited ambivalence, a detached coolness, even astonishment.[5]

The Report

Herr Beck (a pseudonym) and I met on February 13, 1992 (the forty-seventh anniversary of the bombing of Dresden), on a city sight-seeing tour concerned with the history of Jews in Dresden. At Dresden's oldest Jewish cemetery, the end of a fascinating tour conducted by a member of the local society for Jewish history, we began talking. After I explained that I was conducting research on how people recall and record the past, he paused for a moment, then said, "You know, I wrote a report about the rioting at the main train station during October 1989. Just a small thing." He consented to allow me to read the report, and we made a date for two weeks hence.

Herr Beck lives in a small brick house on a quiet, residential street in Dresden. Walking down the sidewalk to his front gate, I was struck by the fact that the surroundings resemble a suburban cul-de-sac more than an urban neighborhood. However, as I soon learned, the idyllic setting belies the pain of Herr Beck's memories.

Herr Beck greeted me at his front door and gestured that I should present the bouquet of flowers I had brought, a customary hostess gift, to his wife, who invited me to join them for coffee. When I mentioned that I was struck by the charm of their neighborhood, we began speaking about Dresden and its sites, monuments, and history.

"What exactly are you doing in Dresden?" Herr Beck then asked. "What period of history are you interested in?" I replied that I was not so much interested in a specific period of GDR history as I was in the ways history was explained to me—that is, how life experiences shape historical understanding and interpretation. When Herr Beck suddenly pushed his chair back from the table and left the room, I felt that I must have said something terribly wrong. Nervously, I made small talk with his wife while I waited for him to reappear. When he finally returned and showed me what he had retrieved—several books and a file folder containing an application for the rehabilitation of political prisoners—I realized I had said something very right.

Born in 1928, Herr Beck had just turned seventeen when World War II ended. After the war he was imprisoned by the Soviets in three different locations, including the so-called *gelbem Elend* (golden misery) in Bautzen, the yellow brick detention center and prison later used by the Stasi (state security service).[6] In 1947, just before his nineteenth birthday, he and hundreds of other political prisoners were shipped by train and bus to a Siberian detention center, where he was held for an additional two years. He showed me a book by George Kennan, *Und der Zar ist weit: Sibirien 1885* (And the Czar Is Far: Siberia 1885) (1981). An account of a tour undertaken in 1885 specifically to study the Siberian exile system, it included a map that Herr Beck used to point out the route he was forced to take as a prisoner in February and March 1947 from St. Petersburg to an area near Lake Baikal. He observed that, in 1947, sixty-two years after the book was researched, conditions were exactly the same—primitive.

"Have you ever heard of the Werewolves?" he wanted to know. "They were a youth group organized during the Nazi period to defend the Fatherland, primarily in the east against the Russians," he explained. Some Werewolves were very young, he continued; he was imprisoned with a boy who, at thirteen, had been sentenced to twenty-five years. However, Herr Beck had never been a Werewolf; he had gone to one meeting but never joined. For that reason, the Russians could not convict him. He was imprisoned nonetheless and now wonders whether he can be rehabilitated and compensated when no conviction was rendered against him.[7] He was in the process of corresponding with relevant authorities on the question and he had joined two newly organized groups—one for former inmates in Bautzen, the second for victims of Stalinism.

Herr Beck showed me another book, Jürgen Kuczynski's *Dialog mit meinem Urenkel* (Dialogue with My Great-Grandson) (1984). The author, an influential and controversial East German historian, critically interrogated socialism by imagining questions he thought his great-grandson might someday ask him and then answering them. Herr Beck explained, "It was partly because of this book that I decided to write the report. When my grandchildren ask me some day, 'Grandpa, where were you and what did you do?' I will have an answer."

We turned finally to the report. Dated October 7, 1989, it was approximately six pages long, handwritten and accompanied by a hand-drawn map and a newspaper clipping giving the "official" version of the same events. We reviewed it line by line, pausing frequently so that he could explain.

On October 4, Herr Beck, who worked as an engineer in a local factory, heard from colleagues that something was amiss at the train station. Immediately after work he went there to see what was going on because, as he explained, he felt he had a responsibility to be a witness. Thousands of Dresdners had gathered at the station to stop empty trains that were traveling to Prague to collect East Germans from the West German embassy there and transport them back through East Germany to the West.[8] The platforms were blocked by masses of people who wanted to board the trains to flee the GDR; even young families were there, with children carrying stuffed animals. One man lay on the tracks; a train roared through, apparently running over one or both of his legs. The police moved in to block stairs to other tracks. Only people with valid tickets were permitted through. A plea was issued over the public-address system: "*Verehrte Bürger* [Honored Citizens]! Please go home and apply to emigrate. Your petition will be granted in three days!" It was greeted with whistles and catcalls. Herr Beck commented on the ridiculousness of the plea, observing, "The majority of people didn't want to flee East Germany but rather wanted reform!"

The train station was ordered cleared. A chain of uniformed officers pressed forward, pushing people backward and toward the exits. Those who resisted were beaten, pulled off the ground by their hair, and arrested. Eventually the station was cleared; then it filled up again. Another attempt was made to clear it. This time the police beat their clubs against their shields, making a deafening noise that frightened and intimidated the crowd. Outside, teenagers threw stones at the station, shattering some windows. A water tank arrived to blast the crowd with a fire hose. A truck followed the water tank. A police officer stood up through a port in the tank and waved his gun in the air. He did not discharge his weapon, but Herr Beck said he realized at that moment for the first time that "the German communists would fire on their own workers."

Later in the night an additional three hundred uniformed officers made two lines and pushed people down and through the Prager Straße, the wide pedestrian mall that leads from the train station to Dresden's old city center. The officers beat people when they did not move fast enough, while guests of a nearby hotel stared aghast out of windows overlooking the plaza. Herr Beck stood in front of the hotel and saw at that moment something he said he will never forget—a scene he has not seen described in any account of the demonstrations. A chain of police from the "Workers' and Farmers' State,"[9] protected with shields and riot helmets and armed with rubber clubs, stood aggressively ready. Dresden's massive, red granite statue of Lenin and two workers towered behind them, the clenched, raised fist of one of the workers a salute to the power embodied by the Communist Party, exercised in that moment by the police. "It was grotesque," was Herr Beck's only comment. Ironically, at a different point that night, some people began to sing the anthem of the international working class; Herr Beck said that he sang along with passion and commitment for the first time in his life: "Arise ye persons of starvation, arise ye wretched of the earth . . ."

As the afternoon light faded, Herr Beck and I leaned closer and closer over his report, discussing it in detail. Frau Beck announced that dinner was ready and invited me to join them. As we talked more about the *Wende,* they frequently disagreed over matters of fact. When was *Gruppe der 20* formed? When were the meetings with Mayor Berghofer? When were the discussions in the churches?[10] I listened as Herr and Frau Beck attempted to confirm the accuracy of their memories, and then I asked how they felt about the future. They were grateful, they said, that Frau Beck was still employed (Herr Beck had accepted early retirement), but their needs were modest and they were not concerned about their own financial security. They were worried for their daughter, whose training in socialist economics had become obsolete overnight, and they were very concerned about the social costs of German unification. Unemployment, homelessness, and poverty had emerged since the *Wende,* and they had no frame of reference for understanding these conditions except the American movies they had seen since 1989, all of which were grossly violent and offered no resolution.

The Museum

Michael, Karl, and Sabine (pseudonyms) are students at Dresden's Technical University. Their demonstrated aptitude for technical things (door locks in particular), a pioneer spirit, and a healthy disrespect for authority won them their current apartment on a quiet side street in the Neustadt, an area of Dresden on the northeast side of the Elbe populated in part by artists, intellectuals, and other students. They observed that the apartment was empty, easily broke in, and occupied it; then they won the legal challenge raised against them by the office that administers the property. The apartment, located in an old building whose facade is blackened by decades of soot, has spacious rooms, tall ceilings bordered by elaborate trim, large windows, and a majestic coal oven that presides over the living room. A small child's room is located off to the side. This modest space is stuffed full of FDJ (Free German Youth) shirts, Young Pioneer scarves, *Winkelemente*[11] (flags), and other worldly goods that practically tumble out of the room as if it really were occupied by a teenager who had crammed a short lifetime's worth of material possessions into its tiny space. Yet on more careful inspection, one sees that all the stuff squeezed into the room is carefully and deliberately displayed.

Shelves groan with the weight of East German tape recorders, adding machines, record players, and other electronic devices. Cassettes and records by GDR musicians are stacked next to East German novels, textbooks, pamphlets, manuals, and reference works. A bulletin board is papered with bureaucratic documents ranging from applications to travel abroad to order forms for Trabants and a memo detailing the organization of a professional conference. Photos of Wilhelm Pieck and Mikhail Gorbachev round off the bulletin board display. On the opposite wall hang poster displays on worker productivity and friendship with citizens of other socialist countries. A teacher's pointing stick is carefully positioned to lean against a poster board as if frozen forever in the midst of an imaginary lesson. Shoes and boots fill the floor, along with objects simply too heavy to display at a higher level: a case of unopened bottles of GDR cola, an East German vacuum cleaner, an overhead projector complete with transparencies for a talk on the development of the socialist economy in Cuba, a carpet honoring Erich Honecker and the fortieth anniversary of the GDR. On a small table, household goods, including pudding, rice, flour, spices, canned goods, cigarettes, and toilet paper, are displayed. A complete set of plastic and aluminum tableware that someone received as a wedding gift sits in its original box, invitingly open as if for sale. Magazines and newspapers are piled in the little leftover space. Honecker, gazing resolutely forward from an oversized portrait faded to yellow and green from its once revolutionary red color, presides over the entire collection.

Michael initiated the museum project around 1990, motivated by the awareness that there had been an *Alltag* (daily life) in the GDR that was fading so fast that soon no one would remember it. He, Karl, and Sabine observed that everyone they knew had authentic evidence of this *Alltag* in their homes, but they felt that the separate, individual things would have no special meaning until they were assembled in one place. Only then would they provide a complete impression of what daily life in the GDR was really like. The three students spend most weekends collecting East German artifacts from friends, schools, factories, offices, flea markets, and house sales. Donations are often made spontaneously by people who visit the museum and then return with a crucial missing object. Some of the items—for example, a class diary from Karl's second grade—were "borrowed" and never returned.

"Every piece in this room is more than just the thing in itself," Michael explained when I asked about the collection. "Each piece is an episode. We've created a museum of episodes."

I picked up a copy of *Sputnik*[12] and asked, "What is the story behind this?"

"The *Sputnik-Verbot* [*Sputnik* prohibition]!" they cried in unison without hesitation. Michael continued, "*Sputnik* was a good magazine, a very popular magazine. It was when *Sputnik* was prohibited that it became clear that the GDR had approached a point of irreversible change, perhaps even crisis!"

I asked the obvious question: "Why was the ban so significant?"

Michael and Karl thought for a minute, clearly puzzled, then, with a flash of insight, Karl replied, "because it was so concrete, so black and white. In the months, even in the years preceding the *Sputnik-Verbot,* the GDR had distanced itself from Poland, from Russia, from perestroika. In speeches politicians would make statements like 'We'll stay on the old path.' Then there was the justification of the massacre in China in June 1989. But these statements and justifications weren't really concrete and clear—you had to try to figure out what they meant, what path they indicated this country was going to follow. Then *Sputnik* was prohibited, and it was published in the newspapers: '*Sputnik verboten!*' and suddenly it was clear. The GDR was not going to follow the path of Poland and perestroika."[13]

Karl remembered an article that he thinks spurred the ban. "In it, Stalin was compared to Hitler. That was unthinkable here. Sure, the state had distanced itself from Stalin, but to go ten steps beyond that and say Stalin had been as terrible a dictator as Hitler, well that was too much."

The ban did not prevent them from reading *Sputnik,* however. A friend of Karl continued to get the magazine secretly through an acquaintance from Hungary. It would be circulated from trusted friend to trusted friend, perhaps until it appeared as dog-eared and worn as the copy in the museum.

Other objects have humorous stories. The toilet paper was so rough, I was told, that it irritated your skin. "That was how the state made sure that even your ass was Red," they teased, invoking a common East German joke.

In a murmur Sabine continued, "I remember when people who were allowed to visit the West came back and said the toilet paper there was soft, that it had double sheets and was decorated with flowers. 'My God,' we thought, 'can you imagine?' And we couldn't! We couldn't imagine a world where the toilet paper was decorated with flowers!"

Some of the objects recall stories about the so-called *Versorgungsloch* (gap in supplies) or *Mangelgesellschaft* (shortage society) as well as the social relations East Germans manipulated to obtain coveted goods. According to Sabine, this is the "episode" evoked by a particular mail-order fashion catalog: it was difficult to obtain the catalog, as one had to be a member of a club. It was even harder to order from the catalog, as each catalog had only one order form, and orders were accepted only on that form. When one person in a building received a copy of the catalog, it would be passed from apartment to apartment until four or five families had leafed through it and written down their orders.

"All orders would be placed together on the single form," Sabine explained. "Weeks, perhaps months would go by, then one day a *huge* package would arrive!" Her eyes lit up with obvious delight at the recollection.

Two of the most striking aspects of the museum were the evident care with which all of the articles were displayed, despite the extreme overcrowding, and how lovingly they were handled and shown. Michael glanced around the room then said gently, as if talking to a child, "Look here! That's *Putzi*,[14] the GDR children's toothpaste, it tasted good! There was a special *Putzi* toothbrush that went with it, and a spotted plastic cup—everyone had those!"

Then we sat in the living room at the foot of the great coal stove, drank (bitter) East German schnapps, and talked—about growing up in the GDR, about school, family, teachers, and the church. Michael, Karl, and Sabine recalled some of the choices they had made in the past, such as whether to participate in the *Jugendweihe,* the state's coming-of-age ceremony for fourteen-year-old members of the FDJ in which the gathered youth swore, en masse, their allegiance to socialism.[15] Young people who chose to complete the *Jugendweihe* received months of preparatory instruction in history, political economy, and Marxism-Leninism, among other subjects. The *Jugendweihe* itself was a special day in that "you had to have something nice to wear," and, after the ceremony, relatives gathered for coffee and cake. Gifts were customary, too, and Sabine identified some of the things she had received: "perfume, clothes, a tape recorder." While many young people completed the *Jugendweihe* with little or no inner conflict (one male respondent commented on the instruction, "In one ear and out the other!"), others struggled with the decision. For Christians in particular, the *Jugendweihe,* which included the avowal of one's atheism, presented a direct conflict with confirmation in the church. Sabine decided to be confirmed and to participate in the *Jugendweihe,* explaining that she felt the *Jugendweihe* was just for show and she wanted to guarantee her admission to college.

When asked what motivated the frenzy of conservation work that consumes so much of their time and energy, Michael replied, "Think about the 1930s, about fascism. We ask our grandparents what it was like then, and they don't say anything, or they can't remember. Someday our kids will ask us what life was like in the GDR, and we want to be able to tell them." He recalled a visitor who walked into the museum and said, "It smells like *Konsum!*"[16]

"Is that a nice smell?" I asked.

They laughed and said, "Maybe yes! It wasn't all bad, and, after all, that's the world we grew up in."

Finally Michael, Karl, and Sabine asked me to sign their guest book.

"It is a museum, after all!" they insisted, and I obliged, adding my name along with my comments ("*Toll! Sehr eindrucksvoll!*" [Great! Very impressive!]) to a small notebook already initialed by dozens of others.

The Report, the Museum, Memory, and History

The importance of explicating the unique contexts in which remembrance work takes place is illustrated by the fact that the report and the museum took the forms they did in part because of the circumstances that engendered them.

The fact that the *Wende* occurred at all indicates that the state had failed in many areas, for example, in the provision of material goods and the protection of civil liberties. The state's efforts to provide East Germans with a unifying, national frame of reference for personal and social identity had also failed. One of its primary tools in this project had been history as ideology (see, e.g., Küttler 1992). The report, written in the midst of the *Wende,* stemmed directly from a confluence of processes to which Nora pointed in his 1989 essay: the end of "history" as a legitimizing force for a nation and the emergence of critical interrogation of historical representation.

The museum, created well after revolutionary 1989, suggests the post-national personalization of memory work to which Gillis (1994) refers. After the end of the GDR, the adoption of a pan-German identity was highly problematic for many East Germans, including Michael, Karl, and Sabine. As part of the process of creating viable identities for the present and future, they sorted through and collected material objects and memories to maintain a degree of continuity with the past.

The media, contents, and functions of the report and the museum evidence other contextual influences as well. When we now think of the history of the *Wende,* its end is a foregone conclusion. Hungary unlocked its gates to the West, the Berlin Wall was opened, the GDR collapsed, Germany was unified. But to understand the choices of actors in the fall of 1989 it is important to remember that at that time it was entirely conceivable that the state would resort to the so-called Chinese solution (slaughter the protesters) and that no reforms would take place.[17] The repressive state might have prevailed; the populace would have succumbed. An account of the police brutality Herr Beck witnessed would have been rare and dangerous in any form. In fact, because he feared that the document could endanger him or his family, Herr Beck censored the report as he wrote it. He excluded the fact that he recruited several other men that night to rock and bounce a parked Trabant into the path of an oncoming water tank. Justifying the omission, he explained, "Who knows into whose hands the report might have fallen, and what might have happened to me or my family as a result?"

Despite these concerns, Herr Beck chose to create a written document. When I asked him why, he answered, "It was my history. Because of my history I had to do it." His history includes memories of those who resisted the suffering of the Siberian prison by recording their experiences and communicating them to others. After he was freed from prison, he sought out published literature that would help him understand what had happened to him as a prisoner of war. In attempting to make his life story and choices intelligible to me, he showed me the books and urged me to read them. Thus, in writing the report he transformed his memories into practical action; he followed a cultural model of documentation and reproduced that model for his grandchildren.

Michael, Karl, and Sabine's choice of medium was no more arbitrary or accidental than that of Herr Beck. Their remembrance project was initiated well after the *Wende* had occurred and during a period of transition so comprehensive that no East German was left unaffected. In July 1990 new (West German) currency was introduced; waves of factory closings and mass layoffs were regularly announced in local newspapers. The cost of living increased dramatically; familiar products vanished from stores, which were crammed full of new foods and brands; almost all administrative and bureaucratic aspects of government were overhauled, affecting every person who studied, worked, paid taxes, had health insurance, or received social security. Women in particular suffered severe social, economic, and psychological dislocation as a result of the *Wende*.[18]

The *Wende* also created a practical and ideological void in history. East German history books were dumped in garbage bins, and schools rapidly adopted West German curricula and ideology; the GDR's Academy of Sciences, including sections for historical research, was disbanded, and the Museum für die Geschichte der Stadt Dresden (Museum for the History of the City of Dresden) cordoned off the exhibit pertaining to the GDR with heavy, black drapes. When I asked a curator if I could view the exhibit, she looked at me askance and answered "No!" She then declared, "The old history was false. Now we have to write a new history!"

During this time Michael, Karl, and Sabine observed that the GDR's *Alltag* was vanishing—not only its material culture but also its institutions, including youth groups and work collectives, the social relationships uniquely embedded therein, and the norms, values, expectations, pleasures, frustrations, and disappointments specific to the GDR.[19] The cataclysmic *Wende* had irrevocably transformed a social and cultural universe, and what was once "everyday" suddenly was thrust to the fore as "historic."

This metamorphosis of the everyday into the historic is reflected by the fact that Michael, Karl, and Sabine chose to preserve the GDR's bygone *Alltag,* to fix it in history, in a museum—precisely the kind of place, as Nora observes, where memories are preserved when historical circumstances render a world obsolete. The materials collected by the students demonstrate a sophisticated awareness of the complexity of the past they sought to capture as well as the problematic nature of its representation. They chose objects of everyday life (pudding, toilet paper, a vacuum cleaner, toothpaste) as opposed to, for example, high culture (examples of art, technological achievement, and so forth). They recognized that what was significant was not the objects themselves but the memories they evoked; through the juxtaposition of different memories, visitors could recall the totality of daily life in the GDR. The students even captured memories of the unthinkable—a world where the toilet paper was covered with flowers. When East German friends visit the museum, they also visit Michael, Karl, and Sabine and reminisce together; visitors who are not East German, such as myself, invite "instruction" communicated in the form of episodes and stories.

The report and the museum also illustrate the inadequacy of reducing memory and history to simple oppositions, including individual and collective or dominant and oppositional. Individual or private memory is shaped by collectivities in that remembering and recollection are social practices learned as a normal part of childhood socialization (Nelson 1989). Forms of recollection (such as sequencing events), practices of recollection (such as telling stories in certain contexts), the priority of particular subjects of recollection (such as the self), and ways of conceiving memory are social as well (see Yates 1966; Crapanzano 1980; Carruthers 1990; Comaroff and Comaroff 1992). Thus, even the most private memories must be seen as having social or collective qualities. The report, prepared by an individual, describes a social experience. The museum, created by a small group of friends, is in part constituted through objects that bring to mind deeply personal, though shared, memories.

The reductive categories "dominant" (academic or official discourses) and "oppositional" (popular discourses) (Popular Memory Group 1982) mask the ambiguity and fluidity of memory or of the ways memory and history can be powerful resources for individuals and groups who must continuously revise their identities as well as their social, political, and moral stances in changing and sometimes volatile circumstances.

Herr Beck lived in the GDR with considerable ambivalence toward the state. He went to the train station in part because he felt he had a responsibility to be an eyewitness, and he wrote his report to record gross injustices perpetrated by those individuals (police) whose job it was to "protect" security and order in East Germany. But Herr Beck was also angered by an official account of events at the train station—a newspaper article written before journalists wrested their freedom from the state. In that article, the men and women at the station that night were described as "rowdies" whose actions inconvenienced Dresdners by disrupting local and international rail traffic. The article claimed that security personnel were dispatched to restore order at the train station and assured the public that individuals who participated in the riot had been arrested and would be criminally charged ("Rowdyhafte Ausschreitungen" 1989).

Thus, Herr Beck's remembrance work was not only a report of the violence but also an interpretation of the events that contrasted the state's self-serving distortions. By seizing control of that interpretation, at least for himself, Herr Beck took part in the ongoing, revolutionary process of appropriating discursive authority from the state.

So far, the categories dominant and oppositional do not seem problematic. Herr Beck's report, written in secrecy and fear, was prepared in opposition to the state's narratives (represented by the local press). Yet when the content of Herr Beck's report is examined more closely, a different dynamic emerges. At the train station that night, Herr Beck was faced with the sight of East German police standing armed and ready before the Lenin monument. In an instant this image stripped away socialism's mask (the workers' state) and revealed its face (state-sanctioned brutality against workers), a face Herr Beck already "knew" (from his life experience) to be the "truth" of socialism. It is at this point in his report that Herr Beck wrote about singing the anthem of the international workers' movement. Through this act, East German workers, including Herr Beck, seized a bit of the cultural property of socialism, turning it against the state, which had, over the course of the previous forty years, legitimated itself in part through an ideology of opposition (to capitalism and fascism).

This incident demonstrates that dominance and opposition must be viewed as something far more than static categories; even a theory of the processes through which certain memories become dominant while others are marginalized is insufficient in this case. As ideology and lies, "oppositional" memories can be a tool of dominant discourses (see Watson 1994).

The museum makes a different contribution to struggles with and against dominance and opposition. The radical and unceasing changes that accompanied the *Wende* as well as the harsh realities of the new market economy generated, for some, an almost overpowering longing for the "good old days" of socialism. Life in the GDR may have been hard at times, "but at least you had a job," people said, "you could pay your rent, raise your children, buy a car, and take a nice vacation every year." Such popular, nostalgic sentiments contrasted (or were occasioned by?) increasingly negative representations of socialism in newspapers, on television, and in academic debates. In these "dominant" discourses, one of two narratives often emerged. The state was a Stalinist dictatorship, and ordinary East Germans were the *Opfer* (victims) of *Täter* (perpetrators), including informants who delivered information to the Stasi; or East Germans had a cultural (German) predisposition to acquiesce to authority, and even if they did not actively support the state, they permitted it by failing to resist. In the first case (the majority of) East Germans are innocent victims; in the second case all East Germans are guilty of having (at least passively) sustained a totalitarian regime.

These portrayals of daily life in the GDR echoed themes of prior, passionate debates about the past in West Germany, namely those of the *Historikerstreit* (Historians' Debate) of the 1980s (Maier 1988; Knowlton and Cates 1993). Since the *Wende,* the research, recollection, and discussion of history and memory, whether by academics, journalists, or ordinary men and women, have been central to a new, ongoing *Aufarbeitung der Vergangenheit.*

Theodor Adorno (1986), and Alexander Mitscherlich and Margarete Mitscherlich (1975) were among those authors who initiated the original *Aufarbeitung der Vergangenheit* after World War II with their troubled and searching reflections on Germany's Nazi history. They sought to explain Germans' love for Hitler, their enthusiasm for National Socialism, the extent of their contrition after the war, and the possibility for a renewal of fascism in Germany. Since the collapse of the GDR, the new *Aufarbeitung der Vergangenheit,* like that of the postwar era, has focused primarily on the complicity of people vis-à-vis the state and their individual guilt or responsibility for crimes committed by the state or under its purview. In these debates, the ways the German Socialist Unity Party, the ruling party in the GDR, consolidated and exercised its power have emerged as a central issue, while the motivations of millions of East Germans who collaborated or simply cooperated with the Stasi have emerged as a central problem (see, e.g., Eckert, von Plato, and Schütrumf 1991; Burrichter and Schödl 1992; Hoffmann 1992; Lemke 1992; Faulenbach, Meckel, and Weber 1994).

The museum's episodes provide insight into these debates because they are stories of everyday or habitual practices, the activities through which people construct and reproduce daily life as well as the social and political relationships of their universe (see Comaroff and Comaroff 1992, 22). The episodes confirm what many suspect about East Germans: that only a small percentage of the population actively supported the state, and even fewer protested it. The vast majority of East Germans regularly went to work, cooperating with "political" requirements (by attending May 1 celebrations, for example) only to the extent necessary to protect their peace and quiet and out of fear of imagined consequences (see Dahn 1991). People sought refuge from Marxist ideology and politics in what have been called "niches"—that is, family, gardens, and other private domains.[20]

John L. Comaroff and Jean Comaroff (1992, 22) argue that such activities of daily life, or habitual practices, are so ordinary that they appear to be ahistorical, though in actuality they are the practical expression of specific cultural meanings and social relationships that have emerged over time. The historicity of habitual practices is rendered invisible through their routinization. Because hegemony—the cultural tool of political domination—consists of "things that go without saying: things that, being axiomatic, are not normally the subject of explication or argument," it functions, in part, through such routinized behaviors (Comaroff and Comaroff 1992, 28–29). Alf Lüdtke, a proponent of *Alltagsgeschichte,* or the anthropologically influenced history of everyday life in Germany, similarly explores "everyday activities in which an element of 'repetitiveness' predominates" (1995, 5). He claims that patterned behavior relieves individuals of "constant uncertainty or doubts" and that the routinization of behavior is one of the ways that submission to authority is established and reproduced (Lüdtke 1995, 5).

As a German historian, Lüdtke has also had to address debates about daily life in Nazi Germany; his position is relevant here because the present *Aufarbeitung der Vergangenheit* in the former GDR resonates with similar issues. In particular, Lüdtke's focus on the minutia of everyday life has been equated with reducing history to "tinsel and trivia" (Lüdtke 1995, 12). His work and that of other historians of everyday life ostensibly produces little more than a "sentimental celebration of . . . 'ordinary everyday people'"(Lüdtke 1995, 10). Specifically, Lüdtke and others have been accused of exculpating Germans by failing to ask hard questions about the responsibility individuals bear for their actions or inactions during the Third Reich.

Lüdtke has responded that *Alltagsgeschichte* in fact provides concrete evidence of the ways ordinary people cling to regimes. He explains that "in these experiences [of everyday life], the interconnection between life circumstances and subjectivity is accomplished—and so therefore is that between the strategies of domination and the patterns of hegemony. In the context of experience the conditions of action obtain significance for those involved" (Lüdtke 1983, 52). Viewed from this perspective, habitual practices reveal the context of experience in which hegemonic forces make the obligatory seem desirable, thereby winning not only obedience but, at times, also enthusiasm from ordinary people vis-à-vis a given regime.

Sabine's decision to go through with the *Jugendweihe* in addition to being confirmed in the Lutheran Church illustrates this process. While successful completion of the *Jugendweihe* was not an official prerequisite for admission to the *Erweiterte Oberschule* (*EOS,* high school on the college track), it is fair to say that most young East Germans viewed the *Jugendweihe* as mandatory. As evidence of this fact, consider that in the mid-1980s, when Sabine was fourteen, 95 percent of East German youth participated in the ceremony (Krisch 1985, 155). Completion of the *Jugendweihe* certainly offered evidence that an individual was "socially active"—that is, politically compliant or even enthusiastic, qualities favored by those administrators, bureaucrats, and political functionaries who determined which students would be allowed to study for the *Abitur,* the advanced high school diploma required for admission to college.

Sabine's recollections about the *Jugendweihe* reflect her perception of the relative desirability of the choices she faced: a trade apprenticeship or *EOS.* They also disclose the strategy she employed to ensure admission to college. Yet she felt sufficient conflict between the *Jugendweihe* and Christian confirmation that she created a rationalization for herself. The idea that the *Jugendweihe* was just "for show" reflects a perception pervasive throughout the GDR: as long as an individual "played along" or "participated" (the German word is *mitgemacht*), one could achieve those basic things one desired, such as education, while maintaining one's peace and quiet. These are the memories evoked by the presence of utterly everyday objects in the museum: the perfume, clothes, and tape recorder.

I have called the *Jugendweihe* a choice and said that Sabine made a decision to go ahead with it. Can it still be considered a habitual practice? I answer "yes" for three reasons: first, because the vast majority of East German youth participated in the *Jugendweihe,* it was viewed as a normal, everyday part of growing up even if it was not an activity that individuals repeated over and over in the course of a single life. Second, the *Jugendweihe* stands, in a metonymic relationship, for the culmination of a complex of acts that included joining the FDJ, participating in FDJ activities, and in numerous other ordinary ways succumbing to GDR socialization. Finally, if the habitual practices of individuals can be interpreted as evidence of complicity or guilt (for having propped up a regime), one must explore the extent to which those practices were choices and what compelled or persuaded individuals to undertake them.

In a contribution to debates on the nature of the state in the GDR and the responsibility of East Germans for the state's real or imagined crimes, Jürgen Habermas observes that the Stasi did repress and control the population but that it also served as the state's primary bureaucracy of patronage and privileges. Even more than the Nazis, the Stasi trapped the population in a "bureaucratic net of dominance" or an "ambivalent entanglement, characteristically post-Stalinistic" (Habermas 1992). I claim, and the example of the museum illustrates, that it was not just the Stasi that entangled East Germans in ambivalence and compromise, but the culture of everyday life as well, what Comaroff and Comaroff refer to as the "welter of domestic detail and small scale civilities" (1992, 35).

Thus, the museum represents a history of the GDR that does not coincide with either dominant (condemnatory) or oppositional (nostalgic) discourses. Though some of the objects contained within it evoke pleasing recollections (the toothpaste, the smell of Konsum), they simultaneously bring to mind memories of personal and political difficulties in East Germany. The museum reminds Michael, Karl, Sabine, and their East German visitors that they had to plan carefully and live strategically in a world of limited possibilities to obtain what they desired, including material objects, opportunities, and peace and quiet. East Germans were regularly confronted with the need to decide between undesirable alternatives (completing the *Jugendweihe* or possibly not being admitted to *EOS*) and often had to construct rationalizations or justifications for themselves to balance memories of their compromises with values they held. This representation of the GDR is far removed from simplistic portrayals of East Germans as passive supporters of a totalitarian regime or, alternatively, perpetrators and victims.

The report and the museum are at once deeply personal and wholly social forms of remembrance work. They disclose problems in the dichotomous opposition of dominant and oppositional memories and suggest that memory can be a powerfully paradoxical and thus dynamic cultural resource for individuals and groups who must simultaneously respond to and participate in rapidly changing environments such as those in eastern Germany during and after the *Wende*.

NOTES

1. Meaning "turn" or "change," *Wende* is the term most commonly used to refer to the events of 1989–90 in the GDR.

2. Merkl 1993 and Philipsen 1993 are useful English-language summaries of major events of the *Wende*.

3. A brief discussion of the postwar and post-*Wende Aufarbeitungen* (plural) appears at the end of this article.

4. These groups include indigenous peoples within nation-states, immigrant workers, holders of dual citizenship, or families, ethnic groups and other collectivities whose members reside in two or more nations (see Appadurai 1996).

5. For example, one young man showed me the ideologically laden texts from a high school class and commented, "I just can't believe these are now historic."

6. *Stasi* is short for *Staatssicherheitsdienst*, which is often erroneously translated as "secret police."

7. The applicable law provides for the rehabilitation of people convicted of certain crimes by or under the Socialist Unity Party of Germany, the GDR's ruling political party, and for compensation for loss of freedom resulting from detention or imprisonment.

8. For accounts of the week in Dresden from October 3–9, 1989, see Bahr 1990; Liebsch 1991.

9. The GDR's national motto: *Der Arbeiter- and Bauernstaat.*

10. *Die Gruppe der 20* (The Group of 20) consisted of twenty men and women who stepped forward voluntarily during a standoff between police and citizens on the night of October 8, 1989, and met the following morning with the mayor of Dresden, Wolfgang Berghofer, to discuss issues of concern to Dresdners in general. The substance of their meeting was communicated to thousands of Dresdners in numerous churches throughout the city that night. The group and Mayor Berghofer met again on October 16; a second round of open discussions in churches was held on October 17.

11. *Winkelement* (from *winken*, to wave or signal) is a GDR neologism. The GDR created many such terms as part of its effort to effect an ideological demarcation, through language, from fascism and capitalism (see Röhl 1991).

12. A Soviet magazine published abroad in numerous languages in which articles from the Soviet press were abridged and reprinted.

13. In contrast to the chronology Karl presents, *Sputnik* was actually banned in November 1988, seven months before the massacre at Tiananmen Square.

14. A derivative of the verb *putzen*, to polish or clean.

15. A brief description can be found in Bundesministerium für innerdeutsche Beziehungen 1975, 291. See also Krisch, who comments, "Among the rituals of control and socialization [in the GDR], the most important is the *Jugendweihe*" (1985, 155).

16. A nationwide chain of cooperative stores in the GDR.

17. East German government officials greeted the massacre at Tiananmen Square, which had occurred just a few months previously, with approval.

18. See Markovits 1991–92.

19. One of the pleasures that reportedly vanished was subversive humor. One woman complained to me, "Es gibt keine ordentliche Witze mehr! [There aren't any good jokes anymore!]"

20. The term used in this connection is that of the *Nischengesellschaft*, a society of niches.

"We've Kicked the Habit": (Anti)Politics of Art's Autonomy and Transition in Hungary

Anna Szemere

The crisis and rearticulation of collective and individual identities is a pivotal aspect of postsocialist transition in East-Central Europe. Yet, as Michael Kennedy (1994) has observed, much work remains to be done to explore the cultural politics and self-understandings of different social groups as they have experienced and responded to the transformation of society. Even when the conflicting politics, visions, and ideologies of various groups—mostly of the elites—are discussed, the discursive organization and often inconsistent fabric of their ideas remain unexamined, as does the whole cultural field of which these ideas and visions form a part and from which they gain their significance. Kennedy rightly calls for a more nuanced and culturally contextualized approach to the study of politics and ideas in this intriguing era of multilevel reorganization (1994, 3–10). And to the extent that political rhetoric needs to be embedded in what he calls the cultural schemata of social life (24), I argue that ideas negotiated by subcultural communities must also be viewed in their shifting political and social contexts.

In this essay I explore how underground rock musicians in Hungary mobilized ideologies to make sense of and gain control over their lives in a swiftly changing environment. I focus on musicians' aesthetic assumptions and their political implications and effects. The "high art" paradigm—the idea that art is insulated from other societal institutions, especially politics—served as a form of resistance in the underground art community during state socialism. It translated into a measure of cultural freedom at a time when both the state and part of the public wanted to hear underground music as purely political statements inscribed in the medium of music. Musicians' emphasis on rock's status as art rather than merely another form of antistate commentary was an effective response to the long-standing colonization of culture by politics, a conspicuous feature of authoritarian social systems (Szemere 1992; Verdery 1991; Cushman 1995; Gordy 1997). The decay and ensuing fall of the one-party system undermined the political valence of a position insulating culture and art from the realm of (organized) politics and political ideologies. From the mid-1980s on, the state and its cultural institutions placed few restrictions on manifest forms of dissent and cultural avant-gardism. Paradoxically, the expansion of cultural freedom did not so much empower cultural producers (even though in some respects it certainly did) as it effected a crisis of their collective and individual identities.

The end of the party-state, which had defined societal repression, resulted in a burgeoning public sphere that forced underground cultural producers to reappraise the nature and relevance of their art. What it meant to be autonomous in and through art became profoundly problematic. Not fully articulated, it nonetheless underlay some of the major conflicts, dilemmas, and disputes within the community.

For many observers of transition and regime change in East-Central Europe, the connection between the shifting currency of art paradigms and socioeconomic change might seem a strange, even preposterous, area of inquiry. However, a more culturally sensitive and detailed picture of transition requires close analyses of how social groups and individuals with a significant public appeal in state socialism adopted and discarded ideas and ideal interests (Weber 1977c) as part of their "identity work." By the same token, the study of rapid social transformation, I argue, throws new light on autonomy, its various facets (political, individual, and aesthetic), and their interrelations. Under stable social conditions the contextual embeddedness of art's contested meanings might well remain invisible.

Aesthetic autonomy as a position adopted by the underground community made progressively less sense as its art lost its virtual monopoly over the articulation of difference and dissent (Szemere 1996). Numerous alternative cultural and political movements came into existence and broke up or branched off. Rockers' abandonment of the idea that art had a (relatively) insulated existence in society became apparent when a whole group of prominent musicians left the community to join an alternative religious cult. While for some converts the transition from one type of marginal culture to another was seamless and lasting, others rebelled against the reinscription of authority prevailing in a strict religious organization. In this essay, I examine two musicians' responses to existential crisis and show how these responses epitomize contrasting approaches and enactments of autonomy through music and the arts. This discussion provides the basis for proposing a critique of established approaches to transition as well as to the study of cultural autonomy and politics.

Transition—an Alternative Perspective

A more nuanced and culturally contextualized approach to dislocated identities in East-Central Europe suggests taking a broader temporal outlook on transition than has been established in most discussions of the region since the regime change. Typically, authors treat 1989 as symbolic of a well-defined set of political events, experiences, and legal and structural changes that rapidly transformed the fabric of social life (see, e.g., Garton Ash 1989; Arato 1994). Others highlight the period between 1988 and 1990 (Körösényi 1992) or 1989 and 1991 (Downing 1996) as revolutionary within a larger time interval of social change. While a spotlight on the year 1989 and its immediate precedents and aftermath has helped to bring into relief the most spectacular elements of social and political change—the discontinuity of history—this perspective has failed to capture the continuities, the subtleties, the why and how of social transformation.

In this article I caution against the reification of transition.[1] To use Katherine Verdery's (1996) metaphor, while some socialist countries shed their old skin with a new one more or less in place, others entered postcommunism entirely naked. Despite these differences, however, it is important to emphasize that the relative structural and ideological preparedness of some countries induced ferment in the entire region and precipitated the collapse of the entire bloc. Therefore, it is plausible to situate the actual regime change as merely a phase in a wider set of processes and transmutations.

Hungary and similar countries offer a propitious site for using a different lens to represent social change. In fact, any discussion of a relationship between popular culture and politics here renders a processual approach imperative because of the country's special socioeconomic and political status in East-Central Europe. First, economic reforms beginning in 1968 refashioned a command economy into a hybrid one. Often referred to as market socialism, these reforms are generally viewed as having paved the way for capitalist reorganization after 1989 (Nove 1983; Berend 1990; Kornai 1992; Róna Tas 1997). Second, the introduction of free markets consequently produced less of a shock in Hungary than in other postcommunist societies, where commodification and the rise of consumerism appeared among the most decisive aspects of the postcommunist metamorphosis of cultural life (Cushman 1995; Merkel 1994; Klíma 1994). Some of the structures, policies, and predispositions associated with capitalist production and consumption had been in place at the time of the regime change in Hungary. With respect to popular music, the majority of indigenous rock, for example, had been produced by socialist "entrepreneurs" with an eye to the music's profit potential rather than as a valve to mitigate political tension, as in Mikhail Gorbachev's Soviet Union (Cushman 1991; Troitsky 1987), or as a tool of political reeducation, as in Erich Honecker's East Germany (Wicke 1992).

Third, Hungary's comparative economic liberalism was coupled with the establishment's fairly relaxed cultural policies, which are best described with Herbert Marcuse's (1976) concept of "repressive tolerance,"[2] which provided space, however limited and precarious, for alternative, often highly critical, visions and practices in the intellectual and artistic domain (see Cushman 1995, 207). In contrast to most other Soviet bloc countries, the fall of the party-state occurred as the culmination not merely of the system's crisis but of public discourse about societal crisis. The pertinence of this distinction for this study is that dissenting intellectuals' and artists' ongoing rhetoric of moral and political decay was later co-opted by official discourse. The actual regime change was preceded or even prepared for by a drawn-out and gradual process of "dying"; this process constituted the first stage of transition. The term *transition* may be thus distinguished from *regime change,* with the former connoting a shorter and more intense period during which a large number of fundamentally transformative changes took place.

"We're Gettin' Out of It All": The End of an Era

In 1987 an unusual film entitled *Moziklip* (Movie Clip) was playing in local theaters. A sequence of short musical pieces, it occasioned Hungarian pop musicians to try their hand at a recent arrival from the West, the pop video. The song "We've Kicked the Habit" performed by the rock group Sziámi (Siamese) was featured among them. This video stood out in its ability to capture the Hungarian zeitgeist of the late 1980s. Lyrics have traditionally been an important component of the attraction of indigenous rock songs, especially in the underground. The words to this song, written and sung by a prominent figure of the underground art scene, Péter Iván Müller, are as follows:

We've kicked the habit
We're using nothing
This is the last hour
We'll be sober now.

We're watching the time
It's different from what it used to be
It cares about neither saints nor humans
except for a few men and a woman.

We're heading outward
That was the last straw
We're watching the last watch [*óra*]³
that's still going.

We're watching the time
It's shrunk! It's grown!
Everything happens
at a different pace than before.

. . . .
We're getting out of it all
So you'd better not count on us.

. . . .
We're not afraid of anything
that might come and destroy us
Oi, oi, oi, oi . . .
                    (author's translation)

The visuals attending the music were simple but telling: the group members were shot from bird's-eye view in a small enclosed space resembling a prison yard. In contrast, the music and the lyrics conveyed a whole new and different temporal sensation, a radical change of pace formulated in the paradoxical perception of time being simultaneously accelerated and slowed down: "We're watching the time / It's shrunk! It's grown!"

Integral to the revolutionary experience is the actors' sense of accelerated time produced by charismatic events such as mass rallies and rituals (Arato 1994, 184–85). In 1987 only the foretaste of the revolution could be felt, yet the cultural and political ferment of the country was evident in new or revitalized political movements and dozens of associations, organizations, journals, and clubs appearing in the political arena. According to András Körösényi's periodization of Hungary's transition, this was the "golden age of political reformism," characterized by the growing visibility of reformist claims within both the official and unofficial public spheres. The party-state's political hegemony was severely challenged daily (1992, 1–4).

"We've Kicked the Habit" may be regarded as an apprehensive farewell to a whole era and to the underground music scene, which, as the lyrics suggest, was about to sink along with the decade it memorialized, the 1980s. How was this farewell expressed and what did it involve? Back in the early 1980s, underground rock songs had a unique concern with a postmodern theme, the temporal and spatial disjointedness of social existence in late-socialist Hungary. While musicians articulated the crisis of an entire civilization—anxiety about nuclear threat, global totalitarianization of social life, and so forth—this vision intersected with the motif of a socially and morally bankrupt East-Central Europe. Many songs represented the experience of living "here and now" as anachronistic or "off the map" and the future as an absence that collapsed into the present time, stolen away. But the groups' widely diverse perspectives and styles shared the existential anxiety of late-socialist Hungary's young generation, which located this common set of feelings and experiences in a wider historical context of schisms and absences. This broad commonality of philosophical outlook coupled with a high appreciation for bold creative impulse cemented the rock underground's collective identity (Szemere 1992; Szőnyei 1992; Kürti 1994).

Sziámi's song addresses the imminent social transformation of the late 1980s on two levels. First, it gives a twist to the theme of times being out of joint: what previously had seemed a stationary and familiar condition of disorder was now set in motion, and it turned out to be shifting reality itself. Yet despite hints at peril and insecurity ("We're not afraid of anything / that might come and destroy us"), the song is not without a tint of self-satire and tongue-in-cheek humor. Kicking the habit—a reference to drug use, which earlier songs openly exalted—for the sake of celebrating the last hour (of the year? of socialism? of peace? of a relatively orderly social world? of the underground rock era? of modern civilization?) sounds simultaneously somber and ludicrous. The rhyming clichés ("we're heading outward" [*nekünk már kifele áll*]; "this was the last straw" [*betelt a pohár*])[4] and the puns also counterpoint the fear and insecurity caused by the perception of a disintegrating social world and the unknown lurking behind it.

Second, the song makes clear that the coming of a new era inevitably undermines the foundations of an underground rock community ("We're getting out of it all / So you'd better not count on us"). The sense of rupture and finality prevalent in the songs of the countercultural era now becomes extended onto the rock/art community itself. How can this swan song be related to the existential situation of the underground community? How did the shifting social realities and the attendant uncertainty affect the musicians' collective and individual identities?

"Where Shall I Go: To Disco or to Church?"
The Religious Turn

The dilemma expressed in this quotation comes from a boisterous rap song by the group Európa Kiadó (Europe Publishing House or Europe to Rent) from around 1985. Two years later, the song's composer, Jenõ Menyhárt (1993), claims that half of the rock underground, the inner core of which consisted of about fifty people, chose the church instead of the disco. Several musicians converted by joining the recently formed American-based evangelical Christian cult A hit gyülekezete (Fellowship of Faith).

As Robert Wuthnow (1989) has pointed out, the instability of social environments encourages the rise of social movements as producers of ideologies. The simultaneous production of numerous ideologies in a particular social setting is elicited by uncertainty or disruption in the moral order. Preceding and accompanying the political and socioeconomic transformation of Hungary, there occurred a virtual explosion of ideologies and beliefs embraced and often immediately discarded. They resulted in cataclysmic turns and cleavages within various elective communities. The plight of the rock community is a case in point.

Európa Kiadó's song foreshadowed not only a community's disintegration but the individual's struggle of facing an existential vacuum within it. As the "disco"—a self-mocking reference to the underground music scene—ceased to be a countercultural site, so did rock and roll lose its attraction for many of its adherents. Many musicians' careers came to a halt. As Thomas Cushman (1995, 142–43, 143–48) observed, countercultural rock and roll is "serious play" (Huizinga 1950) as well as a vocation (Weber 1977a, 1977b). With rock's slumping personal and social significance, musicians engaged in introspection and the reworking of their self-identities.

The powerful appeal of the Fellowship of Faith was evident not only within the underground art community but in the broader circle of young and middle-aged intellectuals, including professional politicians, historians, and psychologists. The cult group consisted of seven members in 1979 and grew to more than ten thousand people in 1990. The most widely known alternative cultural and political journal, *Magyar Narancs* (Hungarian Orange), devoted an unusual amount of space to a bitter debate between the community's current and former adherents, between those who joined it and former friends, colleagues, and "fellow alternatives" who found this act of succumbing to religious authority and strict community life thoroughly incomprehensible.

The most widely discussed incidence of conversion was associated with Tamás Pajor, formerly the leader of the popular punk/rap group

Neurotic. In his documentary film *Rocktérítõ,*[5] János Xantus, himself a member of the underground art world, set out to examine what it meant for Pajor to quit rock and roll and become a cult member. The opening scenes portray him as an unrestrained, emotionally disturbed young man on the roller coaster of drug- and alcohol-induced ecstasies and outbursts of rage. His life seemed so asocial and destructive that he literally needed to be saved both spiritually and physically. Then he is seen cleaned up, neatly shaved, and dressed as a businessman. He is now the singer with a group named Amen. It performs at venues such as the recently renamed Christian Rock Café. Even though Pajor asserts that rock and roll is a satanic invention—echoing the most orthodox evangelist views—the music he plays is charged with the same untamed energy as before. He uses the same rock idiom, instrumentation, vocal technique, and bodily movements but now deploys them to celebrate the newfound focus of his life: the Holy Spirit, he explains, has become his drug.

For another charismatic musician, Mihály Víg (1995) of the group Balaton,[6] the encounter with the cult was motivated by his quest to find philosophical and moral meaning in his life as he sensed he was growing older. He began to study the Bible and found "Jesus' texts were quite good." Pajor's conversion served as the immediate inspiration. With his wife, Víg joined the Fellowship of Faith. For a few years he stopped playing music at concerts, although he did not entirely stop composing music. But his infatuation with the fellowship ended in about four months' time. A critical-minded person, before long Víg figured that this biblical community did not live up to its professed ideals of caring for each other and the poor. His antimaterialist sentiments were particularly hurt by seeing Pajor's car alarm system. The group encouraged members to grow wealthy and attracted many young prosperous businesspeople.[7] Víg did not want to belong to what he deemed the Pharisees. The authoritarian style of leadership also alienated him.

He searched his way back to the art community. His participation in Béla Tarr's idiosyncratic, seven-hour-long film *Sátántangó* (Satan's Tango) not only marked his return to the avant-garde art world but offered him a way to comprehend and represent aspects of his own lived experience. Yet while Víg's life became absorbed in the production of the film, he could not break away from the fellowship because of his wife's continuing devotion, which resulted in unforeseen consequences for him and his family.

Sátántangó is relevant to this discussion for several reasons: first, Víg's multifarious contributions to the film, including taking the role of the main character, coauthoring the script, and composing the film's music; second, the ways in which his filmic character and the story spoke to his experience with the fellowship and, more broadly, to the problematic of religious and pseudoreligious movements as a symptom of anomie in contemporary Hungary; third, the fellowship's response to Víg's involvement in the movie; and, finally, the implications of his participation in the film for his assumptions about art as an expressive medium. *Sátántangó* is a story of decay and decomposition, "a black comedy" (Jim Hoberman), the "death dance of the still living" (Zwick).[8] It portrays the life of a village community in the most economically backward corner of Hungary. This village seems to have been thrust into a kind of timelessness, excluded from progress and even from modernity. A former inhabitant of the village returns unexpectedly, arousing hopes for a better life. He talks about a new, prosperous, model ranch that would ensure employment, peace, and security for the entire community. Having pocketed the private funds of some villagers, the man, named Irimiás (which rhymes with the name of Old Testament prophet Jeremiás [Jeremiah]), leads them to the new place, which, however, turns out to be more barren than the abandoned one. And while Irimiás helps find work and accommodation for his protégés, before long he is revealed as a secret-police agent. The exodus thus brings about the ultimate deflation of the community's hopes and dreams.

Based on the evidence of critics' discourse on *Sátántangó,* the poverty, backwardness, and moral bankruptcy of this Hungarian village merely constitute one layer of the film's complex messages (see *Sátántangó* 1994). It is a metaphor for Hungarian society, including the art community itself—a society caught in the state of paralyzed waiting and yearning. Víg played the role of Irimiás. He brought to the movie his own experience of yearning for, commitment to, and rapid disillusionment with the Fellowship of Faith. The community, he implied in an interview, had a great deal in common with the village people of the movie, as did their respective leaders. He depicted the fellowship's leader as if he had been the real-life equivalent of Irimiás. Characterizing Irimiás, Víg quotes a famous passage from the New Testament: "For False Christs and false prophets will arise and show great signs and wonders, so as to lead astray, if possible, even the elect. Lo, I have told you beforehand" (*Sátántangó* 1994, 18). It is difficult to miss the autobiographic moment of his ensuing comments: "Few people are capable of breaking out [*kitörni*] of their story. To digress [*kitérni*]. To convert [*megtérni*]. And even fewer can see beyond the story. It is only others' stories that they are able to contemplate with clarity and from a distance" (*Sátántangó* 1994, 18). Years after his disenchantment, Víg views the fellowship as others' stories: the stories of people afraid of making their own decisions and choices and thus prone to succumbing to charismatic leaders. He now believes that human freedom is incompatible with cult membership.

Engaging in art and living his daily life remained in close association for Víg. Since his wife stayed a devout believer, she conveyed the community's resentment for Víg's quitting. The fellowship was even more angered by his role in the movie, which they evidently deemed sacrilegious. Thus, Víg became the target of the community's persistent harassment. It is impossible to tell how many people from the community actually saw the film and what precise sense they made of it. In the complex play of mirrors constituted by art, reality, experience, and their diverse interpretations by different subjects, Víg had to suffer for his participation in an art project that conveyed as one of its multiple meanings the critique of fanaticism, passivity, and manipulation. His denouncement by the fellowship as an Antichrist resulted in his wife's severe mental breakdown and the dissolution of their marriage.[9]

Pajor's and Víg's stories epitomize the depth of disorientation that this highly creative group of young people experienced as participants in social change. Although there were several other ways to opt out of the rock community besides the religious turn, acts of conversion seem most essential to the self-understanding of the musicians' community and its realignment. Participating in and interpreting them stirred a great deal of emotion among fellow musicians and the alternative crowd in general. Elements of both stories came to be retold and debated not only in magazine articles and the movie *Rocktérítö* but also in several of my interviewees' personal reflections about transition and its impact on the community. These narratives point first to the dynamic of "identity work" and second to the fault lines within the rock community precipitating its breakup.

Víg's and Pajor's conversions share a desperate search to be saved from the underground, a search that for a while sheltered them from a sense of meaninglessness in late-socialist Hungary.[10] But how might their disparate experiences with the fellowship be understood? Pajor's encounter with evangelical Christianity in some respects disrupted his previous identity as a punk/rap rocker. But despite the wholesale change in his philosophical and moral outlook and lifestyle, the music he sang as a cult member remained essentially unaltered.[11] Both before and after his conversion, Pajor used music as a straightforward outlet for his passion, regardless of the source and moral nature of that passion.

Víg did not spend enough time with the fellowship to accommodate his music to its exigencies. Seeking to regain his freedom, he resumed his ties with the avant-garde art world and treated the film *Sátántangó* as a medium of intellectual and emotional inquiry. For Pajor, music became tied to a specific occasion and context. In semiotic terms, he transposed his music-as-sound into a wholly different lifeworld without changing anything about it except its lyrics and performance context. Making music served for him a purpose outside of itself. Conversely, Víg used art as an autonomous cultural form, a self-sufficient activity and cultural entity, both a tool and a symbol of his liberation. The fellowship's threats and persecution in fact reiterated for him such a usage of art as the community reproduced the authoritarian control that he had been socialized to defy as an underground musician in the statist culture of socialist Hungary.

Alternative Subcultures and the Avant-Garde Art Tradition

How did a religious movement like the Fellowship of Faith come to occupy such an important place in the life of formerly underground rock musicians? Why did religious faith and practices become the functional Other of rock and roll at this conjuncture of micro- and macrosocial change? Why was alternative religion a viable option for some individuals but not for others?

In his book *Getting Saved from the Sixties: Moral Meaning in Conversion and Cultural Change* (1982), Steven Tipton has explored the connections, continuities, and disjunctures between the music- and drug-based counterculture and alternative religious movements in the United States of the 1960s and 1970s. The 1960s youth movement, he contends, was an expressive alternative to mainstream culture in that its ethical style emphasized self-expression, sensitivity, intuition, and emotional immediacy. But it gave no moral rules to live by (232–34). This cultural contradiction was particularly conspicuous in the case of the Hungarian rock underground. First, it drew on the more nihilistic ideology of punk rather than the love- and peace-embracing collectivism of the hippie culture. Second, Hungary's rock underground constituted part of and a response to mainstream society's severely anomic processes.[12] Pajor's life before his conversion well exemplifies how the lack of rules in the counterculture drove him to the brink of total self-destruction. He was caught up in a "liminal antistructure" (Turner 1990) existence, which, as I suggested, also comprised the central theme of *Sátántangó*.[13] The state of normlessness was both a condition of everyday existence among artists and musicians and a theme stylized in their art as the human condition. This countercultural position, if translated into a lifestyle, may either induce suicide (see Willis 1978; Vermorel and Vermorel 1978) or function as a catapult into alternative elective communities. For Pajor and Víg, the evangelical Christian cult embodied the latter option.

In what specific social and cultural context did alternative religion exert its influence on the formerly countercultural rock community? In late-socialist Hungary, a variety of cultural and political movements, alternative and other, sprang up. Most important among them were peace and environmental groups as well as communities furthering alternative lifestyles; university-based literary and social science clubs; religious groups within and outside of established churches; and political clubs with a range of views, including nationalist, conservative, liberal democratic, and liberal socialist orientations (Sükösd, quoted in Hankiss 1989, 126–27).

All over Central and Eastern Europe, the birth of an autonomous public sphere and the ensuing transition saw a marked rise in people's expressions of religious belief. Meanwhile, the prestige of dominant historical churches—Catholic, Reformed Protestant, and Lutheran—waned, especially in Hungary and in Poland. As Iván Varga (1994) contends, the conservative structure and outlook of established churches, as well as their various degrees of co-optation by the socialist party-state, resulted in a loss of their credibility for most believers. These churches proved unable to respond adequately to what systemic social change only exacerbated, a pervasive condition of anomie.

New religious movements and sectlike communities, Varga maintains, were the only religious organizations to enjoy a growing influence in postcommunist Hungary. These new groups seemed more apt than their established counterparts to offer solutions to people's existential, moral, and social needs, particularly those of the young (1994, 116). These communities had been oppressed, and some of them, like the Jehovah's Witnesses, were even outlawed by the state. In this effort the state often acted in concert with the large, authoritarian-minded Christian organizations. As a result, the plight of small sectlike communities found political and moral support in the early 1980s within the highly secularized circles of dissidents, the democratic opposition (Broun 1988, 157).

The broad trend of rising interest in spiritual matters along with the low prestige of organized religion accounts for what surprised several musicians even within the avant-garde rock community—namely, that some of its most charismatic figures quit rock to embrace evangelical Christianity. Taoism or Buddhism sporadically informed individual musicians' perspective without, however, transforming their self-identity or creative outlook. In fact, as was the case with Western counterculture, these influences colored their art rather than subverted it. The militancy of fundamentalist Christians tended to thwart such a seamless confluence of religion and art. Just as Pajor asserted, the fundamentalists deemed rock and roll Satan's tango. Giving up their intransigent position, most cults no longer reject the music-as-sound but the lifestyle and mentality associated with it.[14] Tipton notes that alternative religions sustain essential continuities within both the counterculture and mainstream cultural traditions. In this sense, they "lay out a relatively detailed picture of reality that is analytically complete in its own terms," thereby supporting an "explicit, unified ethic" (1982, 233). This argument seems valid for the religious scene in Hungary of the late 1980s, where the fellowship stood out because of its authoritative ethical style. But whereas unconditional faith and obedience to authority were acceptable for Pajor, they were not for Víg. As the film *Rocktérítő* testifies, Pajor's conversion from a Neurotic to an Amen musician was smooth because he experienced a structural homology between the emotional effects of drugs and faith. Tipton views this phenomenon as the fellowship's translation of psychedelic ecstasies into devotional ritual ecstasy (1982, 236). This trait of evangelical Christianity helps explain why some former rebels such as Pajor willingly subjected themselves to the cult's extremely restrictive ethic.

Why was Víg not thus transformed? Why were his art and identity as artist impervious to the fellowship's doctrines and practices? Part of his resistance may be attributed to his family background. Víg comes from an educated, middle-class home. Defying authority—state authority, in this case—is part of his family heritage, of which he seemed quite conscious. Consider how he introduced his life story:

> *Víg:* I was born in '57. Right after '56. My father was fired after the events of '56. He'd been a conductor at the State Folk Ensemble. . . .
> *Szemere:* Did your father take part in the events?
> *Víg:* No. But instead of rehearsing with the ensemble, he turned on the Radio Free Europe, saying, "Okay, let's ditch [*elblicceljük*] this rehearsal now because everyone's interested in what's going on." After this [a composer] denounced [my father], and the next thing he knew was that he was laid off.

Even more important, in terms of an explanation, is Víg's long history of involvement with amateur art-based fringe movements. He dropped out of high school in the early 1970s. At sixteen he was already a drug abuser, alternating glue sniffing with the combined use of alcohol and prescription drugs. Like Pajor, he was a deviant youth, but his deviance followed a distinctly middle-class intellectual pattern. In the mid-1970s he joined temporarily a leftist countercultural commune inspired by Western precedents. Even though he made a living by menial jobs, he immersed himself early on in the politicized art world of young avant-gardists—filmmakers, drama groups, protest and folk musicians, and so forth—whose oppositional character was forged in a climate of constant threats and persecution (see Forgács 1994, 15–27).

Víg's life story thus gives a clue to understanding his later conflict with the fellowship.[15] Moreover, it illuminates why this conflict came to be crystallized in and through his art activities. Through his family background and his peers, Víg became socialized into a distinctly Central/Eastern European cultural tradition—the avant-garde art tradition—that construed art as an aesthetically complex code imbued with critical or subversive potential. In James Scott's terms, it operated as a "hidden transcript"—that is, "a critique of power spoken behind the back of the dominant [group]" (1990, xi). But art's critical function did not automatically relegate it to an underground position. And when it was so relegated, art constituted more than merely an oppositional code, the secret language of subordinates. It was a medium of interrogation and introspection as well, a realm removed from that of everyday life and politics. Despite its subversiveness—perceived as political in the suppressive state culture of Eastern Europe—it always aimed at autonomy. It attempted to carve out a space of its own and to determine its own traditions, conventions, and rules.

At a specific intersection of cultural and political change, rock music became incorporated into the high-art-oriented avant-garde tradition as a favored medium for the younger generation of bohemians. As "Doktor" Máriás (1995), a young painter and musician, put it, the espousal of rock music ensured what fine arts could no longer achieve by themselves: the open, communicative, fresh character of the avant-garde. The predominance of these traits marked a transition from the ascetic modernism of the local art scene, as Éva Forgács notes, to a more sensuous and subjective style of self-expression that can be associated with postmodernity (1994, 24–27).

Despite this shift at the turn of the 1970s, the community continued generally to associate its music and art with a specific idea of freedom and autonomy that was rooted in, though not restricted to, the discourse of high culture. Musicians and critics were reluctant to consider their movement in political terms and often rejected the idea wholesale. This view was most provocatively stated by Menyhárt (1984) when comparing his politics with that of his songs' censors: "Everyone is more oppositional than me, . . . including the functionary at the record company."

This phenomenon leads to several pivotal theoretical questions: What is the nature of art's autonomy? How is it related to the subversive politics of cultural movements? When and why is art believed to need insulation to be meaningful? In what sociopolitical and historical contexts is the ideology of art's separation from politics mobilized as a source of empowerment?

The (Anti)Politics of Aesthetic Autonomy

Aesthetic autonomy is a contested idea referring to the extent and nature of connections between a representational form called art and the social world at large. In new cultural sociology and cultural studies, aesthetic autonomy and associated concepts such as cultural freedom—and even the concept of art itself—have come to be treated as ideological constructs serving to obfuscate, ignore, or reject the embeddedness of all cultural forms in a web of social relations. (For some of the most eloquent critiques of aesthetic autonomy, see Eagleton 1983; J. Wolff 1987; Aronowitz 1994.) From this stance, the claim for art's autonomy can be traced to the Enlightenment ideals of the integrated individual self and individual freedom.

Marxist-leaning social sciences, feminism, constructivism, and postmodernism have dissected this discourse in Western social and political philosophy as the legitimizing myth of the white, middle-class, heterosexual male social power. In the same way, the notion of autonomous art, as well as the categories and institutional practices surrounding it, has been discredited as exclusionary along the axes of race, gender/sexuality, and social class. Assumptions of autonomy, so the argument goes, encourage hegemonic meanings and uses of art as either cultural capital or pure entertainment because the concept, associated exclusively with Western high art, assumes and reiterates a value-based polarization between "serious" and popular culture (see Bourdieu 1980; Schiach 1989; Willis 1990; Levine 1988).

A closer look at the debate about aesthetic autonomy, however, reveals interesting ambiguities and tensions. In their critique, deconstructors often choose to debate with the most theoretically sterile and narrow versions of artistic autonomy. Furthermore, deconstructors tend to decontextualize the concept by ignoring the variety of social and historical conditions and settings in which the arts' aspiration for autonomy and its philosophical representation evolved. Therefore, they fail to recognize instances when the latter constitute a progressive response or a challenge to oppressive social forces. State-socialist societies, for example, may be seen as a setting where the aesthetic ideology of autonomy and related practices served to resist the colonizing attempts of the state and its crude politicization of culture.

Several theorists working in Central and Eastern Europe have reflected on the complex and paradoxical relationships among autonomy, resistance, and the realm of politics. Novelist and sociologist György Konrád's (1989) idea of antipolitics is certainly pertinent here. Antipolitics is a form of intellectual resistance, but, as the name intimates, antipolitics is outside of or even in defiance of politics. It amounts to personal and artistic self-assertion in the face of institutions, collectivities, and, most important, the state. In a society entirely colonized by state power, Konrád maintains, individuals seeking autonomy withdraw their language and philosophy from politicians. This theory makes it clear that even when antipoliticians are involved in politics, they seek a different name for it or deny it altogether.

A similar problematic is highlighted in both Verdery's (1991) study of three professional intellectual groups' discourse in socialist Romania and Cushman's (1995) book on countercultural rock in Russia. Both authors present the ideology of autonomous creative activity as the backbone of elite groups' construction of identity. Verdery's appraisal of the uses and political effects of this ideology is less celebratory. She pinpoints the elitism inherent in this stance while acknowledging its liberatory potentials vis-à-vis the center—that is, the state.

Cushman investigates the ideology and experience of cultural freedom among Russian rock musicians in the context of transition from communism to capitalism. Intrigued by what he viewed as the paradox of a resistant cultural movement shying away from the idea of being political, he scrutinizes the musicians' own terms of discourse. Even more pointedly than most Hungarian artists in the counterculture, the Leningrad/Petersburg rock and roll community championed the aesthetic ideal of art's independence and transcendence of the everyday and especially of the political: "the very ideas of politics and politicized music took on decidedly negative connotations" (1995, 93). Cushman asks why the prohibition against being political was so strong in the musicians' symbolic critique of their society and its institutions. An interviewee condemning the politicized rock of his fellow musicians answered, "They think that they are fighting against this but adapting such methods of struggle, they become the same. You see? This is interesting. . . . When you begin fighting against somebody with his own means, you somehow grow like him" (106).

It is a powerful reiteration of Konrád's idea of antipolitics. Cushman concludes that politics in Soviet society was too corrupt and banal for the musicians to adopt its terminologies, symbols, and categories. Yet their search for an autonomous space was anything but escapist: musicians saw their distance from politics as potentially revolutionary. Only through such distance could they envision profound social change.

The Russian underground's assumptions about art's social status and meaning also reverberate in the discourse of its Hungarian counterpart.

My interviews centering on social transition were conducive to discussing what it takes to be free in and through art. Freedom is a property of good art, Laca FeLugossy (1993) explained. It comes across to him even in foreign-language songs in which the lyrics are not accessible:

> Language is an extra communicational channel that helps you comprehend the lyrics. But if it's not there for you—the performer's personality, the freedom in the music, or the secret, the oddity—these are the characteristics that give you a clue as to what the songs are about. Those that possess that freedom will offer this clue. You kind of sense how the conventions are being screwed. (FeLugossy 1993)

Freedom lies in the ways artists spurn the conventions of their media. Freedom in art is thus the embodiment of artistic freedom, as is artists' ability to differ from convention-bound society. Péter Magyar (1993) highlights the sensuous and expressive aspects of this idea by referring to flying: freedom "is a life feeling in which you fly and fully experience existence." FeLugossy associates freedom in art with oddity and secret, an idea that is congruous with Csaba Hajnóczy's (1993) opinion that the final meanings and effects of art are always murky. Citing Claude Debussy, Hajnóczy argues for the indeterminacy, ineffability, and openness of textual meanings in Western art.

Ágnes Kamondy (1993) sees art as a complex form of human expression in which the conceptual and the sensuous, will and spontaneity, must be kept in balance. But referring to Polish dramatist Witold Gombrowicz, Kamondy believes that freedom should not be willed too much: "There must be a bit of Buddha and a bit of Tao" in art and "a bit less of the West." This point is important, implying that art as an expressive medium has its own distinct rules, styles, and logics resistant to the excesses of human will. Kamondy's aesthetic concept also includes art's ability to pose difficult and complex existential questions. She took part in some of the same countercultural movements as Víg over the past two decades. But even at her most overtly political, she sought in her art activities not merely a defiant lifestyle but one allowing for a "complex mode of living."

In citing these ideas I do not suggest that people participating in this artistic tradition have had identical views about the nature of art, cultural freedom, autonomy, and their relations to everyday life and politics. Laci Kistamás (1993), for example, contends that the face of countercultural rock was predominantly shaped by its opposition to the party-state and its culture. In contrast, Öcsi F. Zámbó (1993) believes that his artistic activity—both music and visual art—is countercultural regardless of the kind of political system in which it is pursued. His Dadaist provocations target certain human values and forms of behavior that he regards as constants despite and beyond social and political change.

It would be mistaken to assume that individuals' handling issues of art and politics remained consistent over the years. In synchrony with internationally shifting political and cultural trends and climates, Hungary's avant-gardism of the 1960s and early 1970s was far more suffused with revolutionary zeal than the postmodern and often elusive politics characterizing the 1980s fringe movements. Yet underlying the postwar avant-garde of which the rock underground was an outgrowth, a few persistent concepts and assumptions can be traced.

One such assumption is that art, whether conventionally classified as high or popular, is a complex cultural form in its own right. Its meanings are neither transparent nor fixed. Second, art is a terrain separate from "pragmatic everyday existence." Iván Péter Müller's (1993) ideas illustrate this stance despite their cultural relativism:

I think it's very important that there is some rather sharp demarcation line between pragmatic everyday life and poetic life, which is a little elevated. I classify pragmatic culture as part of pragmatic life, which means that certain enormous cultural achievements I regard as nothing different from buying half a pound of bologna at the supermarket. And sometimes the most primary acts of everyday life I consider art. It makes a difference who does them, out of what, and how.

Even as he challenges the distinction between high and popular, Müller does not dissolve the category of art itself. Whatever is understood to be art, it has the capacity to transcend ordinary existence. Even as a "primary act of everyday life," art's meaning is not transparent or banal. The conjecture of an aesthetic realm—which may or may not involve the use of a complex aesthetic vocabulary—transcendence, and autonomy are crucial to musicians' artistic endeavor. To take the argument one step further, this aesthetic ideology was integral to the avant-garde subculture's resistance and identity in state-socialist Hungary. The precept of autonomy served to shield art from being either wholly suppressed or co-opted by the political and cultural establishment.

This lengthy theoretical parenthesis should illuminate why Víg, whose identity owed more than Pajor's to the local avant-garde tradition and its persistent demand for autonomy, resisted and eventually defied the totalizing claims of the evangelical Christian community. The community reproduced an authoritarian society, albeit one based on different principles than state socialism. Víg's entrenched ideal of cultural freedom forbade for him art's instrumental use for ideological persuasion, whether the ideology was oppositional or hegemonic, religious or secular, emergent or residual.

Conclusion: Social Transition, Autonomy, and Politics

In this article I have argued for the salience of taking a broader temporal perspective in studying Central-Eastern European social and political transition. Viewed in this way, transition does not have a clear and unequivocal trajectory—say, from secularism to religion, from resistant cultural politics to commercialism, or from progressive politics to nationalism. Investigating individuals' and social groups' everyday actions and decisions, transition appears as a complex reconfiguration and diversification of the sites where social control and escape, authority and autonomy, disempowerment and resistance, came to be enacted.

I was particularly intrigued by questions of autonomy and social control in the life of creative artists undergoing a momentous crisis of identity as the glue of their community, dissent through art, became undone by political resurgence. These pop artists were compelled to construct new meanings and viable identities to fill an existential void in their lives. The idea of autonomous art espoused by the formerly underground community during state socialism represented resistance against the state. As an ideology it made less sense as transition redefined the nature and meaning of politics and art's status in the politicocultural map.

Thus, while it is possible to argue that the shifts and ruptures in the fabric of marginal culture are symptoms of broader processes of dislocation and relocation in society, I must underscore the complex and nonlinear nature of dislocation experienced by various social groups. I mean to say that the existential blow suffered by the artistic underground, for instance, may be more legitimately compared to the crisis experienced by its political Other, the official ideologues of state socialism (instructors of the Marxist-Leninist doctrine) than to the plight of professional fellow artists. Both the underground rock culture and official state religion lost their specific sites of existence with the collapse of the system. Not only were the university departments and colleges specialized in state-socialist Marxism shut down by the first post-1989 government, but the kind of knowledge in which their proponents' professional identity had been rooted was proclaimed invalid. Consequently, underground rockers and Marxist instructors were faced with similarly onerous tasks of reinventing their public identities.

Several musicians' encounters with evangelical Christianity removed some of them from the art community, whereas for other musicians, fundamentalist religion proved a temporary commitment. I have traced here two musicians' contrasting experiences with the Fellowship of Faith. For one of them, the religious cult group helped reestablish a sacred realm previously occupied by rock and roll. For the other, before long the tightly knit community embodied a threat to individual autonomy previously enacted in countercultural art.

My goal in presenting and interpreting the two musicians' narratives has been to contribute critically to theories of cultural politics and art's autonomy. Prevalent in cultural studies and cultural sociology is an opposition set up between autonomous versus political art as well as the equation of politically consequential art with some often blurry idea of political art. These conjectures resulted in the hyperbolization of the political as well as its vagueness as a signifier.

Although situated, art's autonomy cannot be construed as a fixed category, permanently and invariably opposed to the political, which itself is contextually defined. The meaning and specific forms of either category should not be divorced from the historical process whereby various societal value spheres assume a measure of independence from one another as well as from the center (state). In East-Central European societies, this process of differentiation was slowed down and resisted by an excessively domineering center, the state, that instrumentalized arts and culture by subsuming them under the realm of politics. Cultural producers' struggle for political autonomy became intertwined with if not synonymous with efforts toward institutional insulation and independence from the center. However, the political effectiveness of these efforts, in the sense of genuine transgression, hinged precisely on the actors' ability to view and represent this struggle as nonpolitical or antipolitical.

Despite this paradoxical relationship between autonomy and politics, I do not intend to "correct" native categories with Western analytic ones. If musicians rejected, as they did, the idea and practice of being political, this rejection should be taken seriously because it indicated a deviation in the local meaning and connotations of politics and the political from those established in Western cultural theory (Cushman 1995). To reconcile this and similar mismatches, James Clifford (1986b) has proposed a dialogic and interactive relationship between ethnographers and their subjects with regard to their respective analytic terms. According to Clifford, only through such exchange can ethnographers escape the imposition of their cognitive categories onto a different sociocultural construct.

To overstretch the concept of the political not only causes dialogues to falter between Western and other societies' intellectuals but also washes away diverse nuances of meaning attached to terms such as *resistance, insulation, independence, opposition,* and *counterculture* (see also Grossberg 1992). Finally, the hyperbolization and reification of the political inadvertently imbue all strictly political or antistate art with the aura of progressiveness. After all, racist and right-wing cultural currents (for example, skinhead rock, sexist/racist graffiti, and so forth) are more conspicuously political than most other mainstream, alternative, high, or popular cultural ventures (Lipsitz 1994).

Finally, even though the high-art paradigm lost its valence for the underground community as a form of resistance, it continued as a component of the rock community's habitus, as in Víg's case, to inform individual life choices and cultural practices in postcommunist society. This finding implies that art's autonomy is not merely an ideology furthering cultural and social hierarchy or something strategically mobilized by oppressed artists against an authoritarian state. It is a precept probed and lived by actors in diverse social contexts in which authority and control stifle personal autonomy and the independent exploration of the social world through art.

NOTES

I am grateful to the Joint Committee on Eastern Europe of the American Council of Learned Societies for generously supporting my research. Chandra Mukerji, Richard Madsen, Bud Mehan, and George Lipsitz offered illuminating comments on earlier drafts of this article. I also thank the editors of this volume for giving suggestions for the article's further improvement. I am especially indebted to my interviewees: to Mihály Víg for the confidence and honesty with which he shared so deeply personal aspects of his life story; to Ágnes Kamondy, Jenõ Menyhárt, Péter Magyar, Csaba Hajnóczy, Laca FeLugossy, Béla Máriás, Iván Péter Müller, László Kistamás, and Öcsi F. Zámbó for giving their time, concern, and delightful ideas to this project.

1. It is important to note that the pace of transformation varied from country to country. While Hungary experienced a peaceful and rather gradual change, such was by no means the case in Romania, where a bloody revolution ended Ceauşcu's dictatorship, or in Czechoslovakia, where the "Velvet Revolution" moved Václav Havel from jail directly to the presidential office.

2. I have encountered the effective application of this concept to late socialist society in Cushman 1995, 207.

3. The Hungarian word *óra* has a double meaning: "hour" and "watch," or "clock." This usage plays on the double meaning.

4. The phrase *betelt a pohár* translates as "the glass is full now." The imagery itself is a play on the theme of drunkenness and sobriety, as it ironically counterpoints the suggestion of "kicking the habit." I thank Martha Lampland for making this point.

5. The title is a pun associating Henry Miller's novel *Tropic of Cancer* (in Hungarian, *Ráktérítö*) with conversion (*térítö*) and rock music.

6. Named after Hungary's largest lake, a popular resort.

7. The fellowship has strong personal ties to Hungary's larger liberal party, the Free Democrats' Alliance (SZDSZ). A member of the party's parliamentary faction is known also to be a prominent group member. Rumor has it that the party enjoys financial backing from the fellowship. Considering the fact that the Free Democrats are the most consistent advocate of economic liberalism, one might assume, along Max Weber's theoretical lines, a persistent "elective affinity" between the Protestant ethic and the spirit of evolving capitalism even in postsocialist society.

8. Both critics are quoted in *Sátántangó* 1994, 2–7.

9. A curious parallel may be drawn between Víg's story—note the adjective *satanic* in the film's title—and Salman Rushdie's persecution for his *Satanic Verses* by Iran's fundamentalist Islamic community.

10. As hinted in the analysis of "We've Kicked the Habit," the underground art scene was not a wholesome environment. Many people abused alcohol and drugs, and the community as a whole, one may argue, "lived" the moral and existential crisis of 1980s Hungary. As a result, after transition, a musician referred to the scene as a ghetto that she wanted to forget (Szemere 1997).

11. By *music* I mean sound. The music's overall meaning certainly did not remain unchanged as a result of the radically different philosophical content of the lyrics and the new purpose and context of performance.

12. Between 1960 and the early 1980s anomic processes manifested themselves in persistently rising rates of divorce (especially within the younger population), in decreasing life expectancies among middle-aged and older men, and in the growing percentage of accidents and suicides within overall mortality rates. See Kamarás and Monigl 1984, 69–117.

13. Western rock music history has a set of icons representing this type of "liminal antistructure": Jim Morrison, Janis Joplin, Jimi Hendrix, the Rolling Stones of the 1960s, Iggy Pop, Sid Vicious of the Sex Pistols, and Kurt Cobain. I borrow this term from Victor Turner (1990), who discusses various types of liminal experience in human society. A liminal phase "provides a stage . . . for unique structures of experience . . . in milieus detached from mundane life and characterized by the presence of ambiguous ideas, monstrous images, sacred symbols, ordeals, humiliations, esoteric and paradoxical instructions" (11). Of particular interest is Turner's application of liminality to theater, drawing on power sources suppressed in rational everyday life.

Bernice Martin (1981) effectively used Turner's concept in her account of the 1960s counterculture, examining reformist thought in a broad field of culture and learning, with special regard to rock and roll. She argued that the counterculture's search for alternative or liminal experience by challenging the legitimacy of traditional limits and boundaries (between, for example, students and teachers, patients and doctors, everyday life and holidays, normalcy and abnormalcy, and so on) amounted to the negation of structures. Martin claims that the denial of structures proved to be the source of many countercultural formations' failure to survive and have a lasting impact.

While Bennett Berger's (1981) account of a hippie commune does not suggest the plausibility of the overall antistructure character of countercultures, he also makes the point that longevity in the communes seemed to have encouraged the increase of "structure" and a proximation of "normal" society. The Hungarian art underground, in its decaying phase, clearly gravitated toward the total rejection of structures.

14. This reflects a gradual move by this, itself differentiated, branch of Christianity toward co-opting a whole spectrum of contemporary pop and rock idioms (see Howard and Streck 1996).

15. Unfortunately, I have no comparably rich, firsthand biographical data to explain Pajor's different kind of involvement in alternative religion. The documentary *Rocktérítő* provides a subtle portrayal of his personality at the junction of rock and roll and Christian evangelism but is vague on his sociological background. Unlike Víg's group, Balaton, Pajor's original band, Neurotic, is usually classified as part of the second generation of underground musicians, who displayed a different social class composition than their forebears. Whereas the first generation was dominated by children of the educated middle classes, the second generation included more youth from lower-middle- and working-class backgrounds.

Tropes of Depth and the Russian Soul: Openings and Closings in Post-Soviet Siberia

Dale Pesmen

Pick your nose, pick it and stick
Your whole finger into the hole,
But with the same force to pick
Don't climb into your soul.

Sergei Esenin

Just as Democritos applied the concepts of above and below to infinite
space . . . so philosophers . . . apply the concept "inside and outside" to
the essence and appearance of the world. They think that with deep feelings man penetrates deep into the inside, approaches the heart of nature.

Friedrich Nietzsche

Perhaps Russia is the triumph of the "inner" man, a permanent
reproach to the "outer" man.

Aleksandr Blok

In Russian literature and philosophy, in everyday post-Soviet discourses
of city, nation, morality, and personhood, in the media and in the understanding and use of space, the metaphor of spatial extension, *depth,* has
long been a master organizing principle (see Whorf 1956, esp. 145). This
project, based partially on 1990–94 fieldwork in Omsk, a closed Siberian
city and region that opened in 1991, draws on materials relating to the
mutually influential emotions, poetics and politics of private, public, and
metaphorical spaces, including those of the person. I discuss the pragmatics of and movement between such hybrid and multilayered spaces, both
"deep" and "superficial." I examine material elements of the lived world as

well as imagined and physical geographies in an attempt to explore ethnographically the metaphysics, faith, and (often quite un-Romantic) practices involved in the "deep" aspect of what is called the Russian soul
(*russkaia dusha*)[1] during a time of radical social change.

Cherniavsky (1969, 227) argues that what he calls the Russian soul
myth began a protracted death in the late 1880s; according to Robert C.
Williams (1970, 587) and Jeffrey Brooks (1984, 217), by the turn of the
century *russkaia dusha* was losing its vitality. In Russia, the Soviets have
been blamed for the death of *dusha,* as were, I found, the engineers of perestroika: the soul was often said to be dying or killed by attempts at a market economy, by everyday life, by the powerful. Even a certain percentage
of "optimists," new businessmen and others who were taking vigorous
advantage of social changes, agreed at that time that something was being
lost, albeit perhaps necessarily.

The Russian word *byt* may be glossed as "(mode of) everyday life,"
but attitudes toward the routine it implies have long given it a nuance of
exhaustion and rottenness. Roman Jakobson, in his oft-cited discussion of
byt, called it "an immutable present, overlaid . . . by a stagnating slime
which stifles life in its tight, hard mold" (1987, 277); Nicholas Berdiaev
(1955, 11) called it "a prison in which the human soul is trapped." Soul was
clearly understood and experienced in part in opposition to *byt.* The nineteenth-century Russian notion of the Western soul destroyed by materialism, mechanization, and rationalization included related imagery instrumental in the formation of Russian collective identity, or *dusha,* soul. "If
the West was dying, it was from the disease of *pustodushie,* an empty soul"
(R. C. Williams 1970, 577). Descriptions of how the practical world and
material concerns were felt to constrict and imprison the soul, resulting in
decay, lifelessness, and emptiness, had far from disappeared from Russian
discourse during the early 1990s. Much about both Soviet and perestroika
everyday "worlds" was said to be killing the soul; as nineteen-year-old
Olga told me, "*byt* and *dusha,* it's jailer and prisoner."

I found that *russkaia dusha* was not only the Romantic cliché that
many Russians and others assume it to be but was also a pervasive, important player in both attitudes toward post-1985 changes and the processes
of change themselves. In Omsk, the Soviet Union's death on December 8,
1991, for quite a while seemed distant, temporary, an impostor. Everyday
life was too difficult to allow much expenditure of energy on the subject,
anyway. The USSR's dissolution did not pass with time, however, and it
slowly began to be described by many, as were so many other events, in
terms of injury and pain to and in *dusha,* the soul. In 1992, a woman,
implying that *dusha* had taken on new vitality as a result of the assaults on

it, told me that, whereas Russians had previously thought about soul "philosophically," "now we've really started to think about *dusha,* simply, deeply." Conversely, Oleg, whom I knew as a struggling young business-man and ex-KGB agent, mused with no trace of irony that

> We've changed a lot. . . . Something has happened to that—that *dusha* of ours. If we start living better materially, I'm afraid spirituality will fall. People on a high rung socially, that effect stands in front of your eyes, but it's not interesting to talk to them; people like your average teacher don't have material valuables, but they have other sorts of valuables. You can tell when you sit and drink, have a soul-to-soul talk. It's deeper.

It was precisely *v dushe* (in the soul) and, more importantly, *s dushoi* (with the soul) that social change was negotiated and lived through. In the early 1990s *dusha* was daily invoked and involved in, indexed and was indexed by, sacred and profane contexts such as friendship, kinship, exchange, pain, joy, drinking, the baths, power relations, love, betrayal, and so forth.[2] *Dusha* was a player in perestroika and subsequent changes partially by being an important tool for wrestling with "inchoates"[3] Soviets were facing. I found *dusha* to be a deceptive lexical item, not just a notion or thing but an aesthetics and a revitalized and modified node of discourse, ritual, belief, and practice available to and present for individuals.

A primary value associated with this *dusha* is the alleged impossibility of exhaustively defining or knowing it, its *depth,* its *unfathomable bottom-lessness.* In different contexts I found different value continua of bringing something from a distance, from one inner, outer, conceptual, or cosmo-logical order to another. In a given statement or performance these con-tinua may appear singly, meld together indistinguishably, or be in inter-esting states of tension, as James W. Fernandez (1986, 10) describes. Unlike the continua Fernandez gives as examples, however, those I observed were all, in different ways, strung between poles with more or less the same names: inside and outside. Their complex relationships and for-mal similarities were part of what makes the cultural quality of spaces defined by depth-surface so overdetermined and important.

Closedness as Invisibility: Omsk

> Chto tvoritsia na Rusi ne pokazhet Bi-Bi-Si.
> [What's really going on in Russia you won't see on BBC.]
> Newspaper headline (1992)

Nobody could see [the enigmatic Slavic soul] and yet it was irrefutable. Nobody could deny the Russian nation's superiority which expressed itself in the world beyond the apparent.

Liah Greenfeld

In poetry and literature, veils are associated with unclear apartness, distance, and mystery. Veils conceal, shield, distance from as well as tempt into other worlds. Richard Stites (1992, 84) describes how, in the 1930s, Soviet "borders were sealed even tighter. . . . Migration into cities was closely controlled and elaborate rituals . . . were required to enter into buildings." Entering a building, one encountered an attendant, usually a pensioner. Depending on power relations at the workplace and the individual, the experience could be one of being brutally denied entrance, interrogated, "spied on," or warmly welcomed "home." Such ranges of contingent values, where inside and outside were markedly separated, were characteristic of many veil-like Soviet thresholds. Anna Wierzbicka, in her work on the semantics of Russian *dusha,* described *dusha* as an internal place unknowable to outsiders. As in the proverb "chuzhaia dusha potomki," to others, a person's dusha is dark and unfathomable (Wierzbicka 1992, 50). One afternoon in his tiny kitchen, my friend Grisha, in his thirties, unfolded a metaphor on the topic of *dushevnyi nastroi,* the soul's tuning, disposition, condition, harmony:

> In different situations a violin sounds differently—one of my favorite instruments, one of the most enigmatic. In a violin there is a *dushka,* something invisible to the eye; the whole sound depends on it. It's a little stick,[4] no one sees it. The character of the violin depends on the place, and only the violin master can choose that place. The one who made us placed that in each of us. A violin without a *dushka*—it's not a violin.

Grisha's metaphor invokes a range of related ideas, many of which are explored in the following pages, which touch on the kitchen table's, wardrobes', and closed cabinets' privacies, the Soviet Union's opaque, semipermeable borders and its lore of enigmatic, incomprehensible, or masked social folly, deception, and complexity, Omsk's even more opaque borders, rigid culture of closedness, and huge, central blank spots. Some of these phenomena implied positively valued, and others, negatively valued hidden interiors, defined as they were separated, by ranges of contingent values.

When I began this study of *dusha* in Omsk, I was shocked by the nearly complete absence of mention of this large industrial city in Soviet

Blank spot on Omsk city map

and post-Soviet studies and by its minimal presence in literature, as if
Omsk was, despite its size (population 1.2 million), invisible. Omsk was
hard to see from the outside: from its founding it was a place of military
secrets and exile. During World War II, when military factories and KGB
archives were evacuated there, Omsk became large and officially closed.
Until 1989, rare foreign specialists visiting the refineries rode in vehicles
with blacked-out windows and did not see the city. Areas I saw that were

blank on maps were presented as ones that even now foreigners do not see. Some maps showed smaller cities but omitted Omsk.

Omsk was also hard to see from inside: Omsk acquaintances often directed me east or north to the "real Siberia." Omsk was Eurasian, forest-steppe, mixed ethnic, middle-of-the-road, unreal. One man told me, "Omsk is a navel: geographically in the center of everything but nothing in itself." After being released from labor camp there, Dostoevsky wrote, "Omsk is a nasty little town. There are almost no trees. In the summer it is sultry, with sandy wind; in the winter there are blizzards. As for nature, I saw none. It is a dirty little town, military-ridden and to the highest degree degenerate."[5] One afternoon Mila, a woman in her thirties, asserted that Dostoevsky's statement was interesting because "Nothing has changed. The dirty, dusty, exactly nasty little town is still what Omsk is. Omsk is a black hole; I am . . . living in a black hole. . . . Omsk has one of every possible sort of cultural institution and institute of higher learning, but it has a very thin layer of culture." Mila showed three millimeters between two fingers, adding to her black hole theme those of flying energy and organic growth: "In the far north, south, west, there are strong forces, but here spiritual energy flies away. It can't put down roots in that thin layer." She continued, adding images of physical and psychological constriction, wind, pollution, and irreality:

> If the ceilings are low, if the window looks out on a typical industrial landscape, you can say beautiful words to children, but it affects their psyche. There are talented people in Omsk. People try, produce emotional effort . . . but the cultural soil doesn't get made, there's no sum of that energy. Where does it all go? In the capitals—Moscow, St. Petersburg—the good is not just empty prestige; there is something in the air. Omsk should be different than it is. Seeds get scattered, but nothing grows. It all remains separate bursts of energy. . . . If Dostoevsky came back to Omsk today, I think he would make exactly the same evaluation. Perhaps he would also mention what the refineries dump into the air.

Omsk was hard to romanticize, which made its few legends important to its residents. The commander of White forces in Siberia, Admiral Aleksandr Kolchak, took Omsk from the Soviets in 1918, intending to make it the capital of his Russia. Dostoevsky's 1850s imprisonment in Omsk's "Dead House" is described (not only by Omsk residents but by other sources and by Dostoevsky himself) as the time during which he came to know the Russian soul through his suffering and through contact with the traditions and the folk (*narod*). These descriptions relate Omsk to *dusha* as

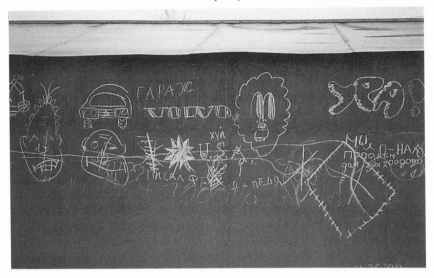

Graffiti on the side of a rusting metal garage in Omsk. (Photograph by Dale Pesman.)

constricted but vast and as a locus of suffering that is also a source of works of genius. But again, constriction and suffering were as often described as precluding internal vastness: "One hope I see," Mila concluded, "would be if they'd take away all borders so that people could interact," masterfully capping her multiply mixed imagery with an image of crossing borders and thereby opening that which is closed.

In 1936 the philosopher Chaadaev described Russia as a desertlike void and Russians as lost souls. Omsk was often described as just such a nothing, unreal, empty, missing something, even aggressively negative. A 1992 joke called Omsk an experiment in how to annihilate city dwellers. When Nina called Omsk a swamp, I thought she was referring, literally, to the cranberry bogs. Then she added that if she shuts herself into her own world at home, it cannot suck her in. Oleg remarked, "What Dostoevsky said is as true now. How can anyone live in these dusty winds? Omsk is not a typical Russian city. It has an empty center."

When Oleg called Omsk's center empty, I assumed he was being poetic, but another man told me why Omsk was, as he said, "the inverse of all other Russian cities." Omsk was founded in 1716 as a military fortress at the meeting point of the Irtysh and Om Rivers. An empty space had been maintained around the fortress for security; the city grew up around it. When the fortress disappeared, Omsk's streets were left radiating out from a void that in the early 1990s was partially park, with an abandoned, rotting heating plant at one end.

Inverting the values of inside and outside, soul and body, could imply even more depth. Physicality could emphasize spirituality, as in, for example, cases when fear was said to have become deeply encoded physically or penetrated to the genes of Omsk descendants of exiles or survivors of repression, or when people expressed how deep their emotions were by describing physical responses.[6] Anna Viktorovna told me, "A *dushevnyi* person does not need many words. He feels biocurrents." Her son, Grisha, said, "So many words would have to be said. . . . *Dusha* is an internal indicator. Something inside pinches, contracts." One way that body could be linked to soul was through pain, by "the involuntary connection of the self with sensations, feelings and desires" (Foucault 1982, 23), and because the flesh has a "deep" invisible inside that, though the center of the person, is represented as unclear, that feels better than it speaks.

Spaces of Transformation

> There is, after all, nothing intrinsically good about the end of any continuum. No culture is so unambiguous . . . that a clever man cannot turn a continuum to his advantage.
>
> James W. Fernandez

Important elements of most perestroika/early post-Soviet Omsk residents' material universes were "wall units," *stenki.* Consisting of glass cases as well as cabinets, drawers, shelves, or wardrobes, *stenki* not only "expressed spiritual values" and "relations to the outer world" (Dunham 1990; Boym 1994a, 285–86) but were, as Munn (1986) has put it, symbolically constituted foci of sociocultural practices. Retired teacher Evgeniia Pavlovna's display cases housed souvenir starfish, postcards of Oriental girls, and books on politics, economics, psychology, and literature. A case might display crystal, a tea service, scribbled notes, cigarette boxes, Coke cans, porcelain figurines, photographs, plastic pigs (if one was born in the Year of the Boar), and perhaps a stack of nearly worthless, smelly, tattered one-ruble bills received at work. A friend in the village, Zhenia, mentioned wall units and Oriental-style rugs hung on walls as the "minimum" for a home. One family I knew had only one tiny room but devoted an entire display case to a German wine bottle, American beer cans, and a Styrofoam McDonald's box. If these cases, as Svetlana Boym (1994a, 280) says, "survived . . . the campaign against 'domestic trash' which ridiculed [them] as . . . bourgeois," it is partially because the specialness they indexed and created by separating some things from the rest of the world was related to

Two shelves in a glass display case (*stenki*) in a family's living room.
(Photograph by Dale Pesman.)

a traditional opposition of superficial material treasures to profound spiritual ones; the cases, themselves material, were actively involved with the immaterial.

This signification of the immaterial could index a range of meanings. Once, as Zhenia, his son's godfather, and I were drinking in his kitchen, Zhenia suddenly raised his voice, telling me, "You've seen everything that's visible. Now I'm going to show you what we have in our *dusha,* but we crap on it." He disappeared, reappeared, rummaged, disappeared outside, and then reappeared again, displaying, in a fluorescent orange cardboard frame, a black and white photo of a mother's brother killed in the Great Patriotic War. Pointing at his chest, he said, "This is the enigma of the Russian soul." He continued, pointing at his head, "But it's not here. Closest to *dusha* is fatherland, motherland, isn't it?" he challenged me, turning to inform his son, who had haplessly wandered in, that his first task in wood shop would be to frame the photo. Zhenia then demonstratively carried the picture into the children's room and placed it in their glass case. The godfather excitedly prompted, "Look at where he put it! In the children's room!"

Such framed portraits used to hang on walls, though in some homes this was no longer fashionable. In Zhenia's instance the uncle, after being pronounced "what we have in our soul" but sinfully ignore, found a marked home in the children's glass case, which resituated him (for that conscious moment, symbolically and perhaps didactically) to a more salient place and, hopefully, to the children's *dushi*.

Different families' glass cases and different cases in the same household related to *dusha* differently. My watch, which I accidentally dropped in the children's room, was placed in the living room glass case, not theirs. When I returned late that night, Tamara got up from bed to tell me that it was in the living room case. For this particular family, the communal case clearly had somewhat different transformative powers than did the children's, which Zhenia had used to forefront in consciousness what he felt had been too deeply buried in (or alternately, distanced from) *dusha*. Placing something in the children's case was reexposing it or resituating it in their *dushi*. Placing things in the living room case was, among other things, like complaining about *byt*, a way to co-opt, to appropriate in the form of depth, of *dusha*, what was felt to be unsouled. But the living room case was also a heterotopia, like Zina and Andrei's bedroom glass cases, that contained books and items in transition: packets of seeds, broken eyeglasses, and other items suspended in readiness to be focused on, planted, repaired, and used up.

In one workplace, humorous collages, ironically intended Soviet banners, and labels from foreign products were pasted on the walls. During a bitter war with the directorate, the walls were progressively stripped to a bare expanse, in the center of which a small, crippled fascist eagle looked in the direction of what was missing. Glass cases of the urban privileged held more imported commodities than one in Zhenia and Tamara's sparsely furnished state farm living room, with its few paperbacks, crystal, cheap lipsticks, and Soviet perfume bottle. But no one inventory could reveal how things went in and came out of this particular case; again, much more than expressions, these displays actively contained—co-opted—specialness, taking in goods "charged [like their sources] with . . . supernatural, sacred, or mystical connotations" (Helms 1988, 114). I mentioned earlier how my watch was placed there—so was my camera. Almost every gift from me, even to the children, was immediately placed there (at least for a while); the eleven-year old son once ran there to deposit a candy bar next to a dead Polish watch. Only later did he return to try the American chocolate.

Glass cases were only one of many changeable ways in which spaces were linked to spirit. A shifting family of tropes of expanse, constriction, depth, and height, related geography and various features of maps to human attributes. Berdiaev (1947, 2) writes, "There is that in Russian soul which corresponds to the immensity, the vagueness, the infinitude of Russian land, spiritual geography corresponds with the physical" (see also Jarintzov 1916, 25–27). When friends would discuss the vastness (*prostor*) of local Siberian landscapes, they always related it to soul. Mila said, "In Siberia we try to do things on a huge scale, but you can't embrace so much space rationally. . . . In general, virtuosity is not soulful; depth is what matters, not surfaces."[7] Mila often described herself as a lemon squeezed out by constricting everyday life:

> *Dusha* is wide, expansive, voluminous, and it's always being forced into some narrow little hole, to crawl in there. It's not by chance that people are saying that *dusha* has been trivialized. . . . If a person grows up in a little room, . . . it's hard for his *dusha* to spread its wings, to grow them. If you unfold to the full scale of your *dusha,* they'll crush you.

Such statements portray expansiveness, in landscape and as "maximalist" impulses, as the image of the most beloved. *Dusha,* denied its true scale by "them," by *byt,* by cramped dwellings, is forced to retreat, a tender center miraculously surviving in a brutal shell of insensitive quotidian reality. The coziness, interiority, and liberty of home and those of the particular other world of the bathhouse, contrasted against a grueling, hostile outside, are images of how life-giving *prostor* was often located inside a confined space. Mila said,

> *Prostor* is a rare feeling that appears even when the size is not large. Internal freedom . . . *prostor* is what coincides with *dusha,* where *dusha* feels in its element. A clear horizon, fields, wheat—it's a lyrical landscape but a typical Siberian one. These fields in and of themselves are not comfortable but coincide with my internal condition, which I try to name using the word *dusha.*

Grisha said, "*Prostor* has a special meaning for people from Omsk. It's when I can throw my glance out to the horizon. . . . And it can be felt with the soul. Lock me in a toilet, but give me a book, . . . and I have *prostor.*" Oleg told me that "Sakharov did his best work in confinement," also indicating, though pretty repulsively, that formal constraints can unlock, rather than kill, vast internal generativity. A less perverse version was the toast "Here's to the open soul in the closed city of Omsk!" This locked-up life force could be seen as overly powerful, potentially explosive: Geoffrey Gorer and John Rickman (1949) and Henry Dicks (1967) claim that Russian women believe that, left unconstrained, the child with his uncontrolled strength will injure himself. I return to this kind of interior, one of those highlighted by changes associated with glasnost.

People's "deepest" essences were sometimes described and related to as if encased in a shell of superficial, diluted, or deceptive entities, such as various "masks" or character.[8] When an eleven-year-old boy who lived in central Omsk associated living on the city's edge with soullessness, I was shocked at his crude association of *dusha* with a concentrically organized map and of "uncultured" village lifestyle with soullessness. Adults sometimes also conflated them: a flippant Muscovite said that the interesting, intelligent people lived in central Moscow; "the periphery is increasingly cultureless wasteland." Then, amazed that I had "survived" in Omsk, he reproduced this structure on the level of the country, saying that in terms of cultured cities there were the capitals and Sverdlovsk; other cities were hopeless.

In some concentric models, generosity rather than entropy was the rule: Mila once described *dusha* as a sun emanating rays of kindness. Moscow and Lenin had been the saturated, holy centers of the Soviet universe, emanating communist virtues that, in the words of a pioneer song, made all children "Muscovites." Moscow, as a socialist center, also issued plans, funds, standards, approval (see Verdery 1993, 173). In an almost inversely valued concentric model based on a Romantic association of *dusha* with the profundity of "simple" Russian life and people (*narod*), the provinces are called *glubinka* (the depths). A mode of talk and action associated with "simple people" implied that only unmannered (or even obscene; see Pesmen 1998) responses or generalizations from *dusha* (*ot dushi*) can index (rather than articulate) Russian experience. A vast soul that Western values and superficial manneredness had not penetrated, poisoned, or caused to shrink, outlying and remote areas—the heartland— partook of centrality. Grisha said, "Omsk is *glubinka,* but the best is always inside, like the pearl in an oyster."[9]

A lovely example of a contest between locations (and thus meanings) of the center is the following odd detail from the biography of chemist Dmitri Mendeleev (1834–1907). Mendeleev, a Tomsk-born *sibiriak,* predicted that Russia's mean center of population would be drawn toward a "new center of Russia," at 55° N, just northeast of Omsk. The prospect of such an "irresistible eastward shift of the Empire's center of gravity" sparked a furious reaction: "'There was a Russia of Petersburg,' wrote one critic indignantly, 'but there can be no Russia of Omsk'" (Hauner 1990, 152–53).

Inside and outside, high and low, however, were not necessarily so crudely opposed. Dostoevsky, Mikhail Bakhtin writes, "moved aesthetic visualization into the depths . . . of the heights of consciousness. The depths of consciousness are simultaneously its peaks (up and down in the cosmos and in the microworld are relative)" (Bakhtin 1984, 288). Dostoevsky's statement about his writing being realism in a higher sense, a depiction of the depths of the human soul, has the same feature.

Wierzbicka (1989, 51–52) writes that *dusha* "suggests [an] inner world . . . an internal spiritual theater." If *dusha* was a theater, performances there did not "simply go on *in* or *through*" it but also constituted or created it as a space (Munn 1986, 11) related to other spaces with "sociological, political, and . . . ideological significance" (Helms 1988, 4). This world, other worlds, Russia, Omsk, rooms, and certain furniture could be such spaces. If one's *dusha* is one's *vnutrennyi mir* (internal world), cities, countries, public transportation, rooms, works of art, and many other domains understood as framed or bounded could be called and treated as "worlds." If Russian nationalists described the Russian soul as a set of antitheses to "rational" Western virtues" (Rogger 1960), opposition and images of opposition to the degradation of *byt* often took the form of irrational and/or passionate actions (Pesmen 1998).

The significance of all these spaces is often linked to suffering and orthodox notions whereby the believer enacts his faith that this world is nothing as part of a process of shifting value to the other (Harakas 1990, 51; see also Pesmen 1998; Ries 1997). *Kenosis*[10] explains some of suffering's value, but it is just part of what was meant when 1990s Russians said that the soul developed, was tempered, ennobled, and gained depth through suffering. Indeed, sympathy, feeling others' pain inside as one's own, was the most frequent definition of *soulfulness* I heard. Both creativity and empathy reveal an important attribute of *dusha:* taking things of the outside world in, experiencing them, can make them of the soul, a life-giving transformation. The implication is that this boundary crossing is the most important, "human," thing a person can do. An acquaintance, Alexandr Ivanovich, said, *"Dusha* is how you perceive the surrounding world." That is, *dusha* internally represents the surrounding world, which gives it life, makes it partake of depth. Grisha's wife, Nadia, called *dusha* "the basis of a person, capable of suffering." This statement resembles Marina Tsvetaeva's assertion that "To be pierced means to have a soul" (Wierzbicka 1989, 51). The high value of suffering relies on a metaphysics based on depth metaphors. Taking something to heart occurs when something encountered in the outer world pierces one and forces one to take it in to where it has certain forms and is subject and object of various typical experiences, one of which is called feeling. Emotion and centeredness are conflated or otherwise, mutually defined and mutually determined; emotion is related to the expression, more or less distorted and unclear, of what is in the depth, the center. A people may be governed by their centers or by something peripheral.

Asad (1983, 306) discusses how body pain was linked in medieval Christian ritual to the pursuit of truth. Emotional pain was, in the context of Russian *dusha,* often treated and experienced physically (for example, in the chest), pursuant to some interaction with the outer world, and as such is linked to pursuit of truth.[11] Moreover, this transformative path to truth is isomorphic with that described in the sixth-century Liber de Penitentia: "how art thou to be cured, if thou do not lay bare what things are hidden within thee?" (Asad 1983, 306). The body is treated as an arena (Asad 1983, 311) in which truth hides and whence it might emerge. People's moral quality depends on the condition of their interior space.

A metaphor for *dusha* offered by Professor Sergei Arutiunov, ethnographer and member of the Soviet Academy of Sciences, indicated this kind of potential- and information-rich center. A book, he said, is paper, glue, ink, but what is the sense of the book? "The essence, the main thing, and simultaneously, nothing at all." One may not yet be able to understand the book or a person's *dusha,* but one may come to understand it. One might formulate this experience of coming to understand as "the further 'in' one sees, the more value appears in one's consciousness" or "the experience of something of value appearing in consciousness means it is emerging from somewhere." This formulation and experience intermingles with a metaphysical belief that something closed can and should be opened and that human interest, soulfulness, wisdom, and consciousness not only reveal but increase and realize the value of the depths by penetrating to them. Paradoxically, the depths may be increased and realized by trying to destroy them, trying to eradicate the structure of a hidden inside different from its outside. *Dusha* demands to be better displayed in consciousness, but its purest form is unclear consciousness or suspicion that assumes that there is more.[12]

Although the form in which some feelings or thoughts are displayed to their experiencer implies distance (inside or outside) and thus authenticity, it may also be inferred (as with veils) that one ought to make closer contact with the implied other world, approach it. Wierzbicka (1989, 45) uses the word *deep* for the aspect of *dusha* of which people are not aware in themselves; indeed, a closed or sleeping *dusha* is deep. Conversely, it was clear in my data that the most extreme depths are problematic cases, as they also verge on soullessness, when a person's acts are not reflected on; feelings are not felt, not displayed to the self. Russian soul was related to critique of Russian reality and a sense of potential for development. *Byt* and routine are soulless partially because they are clear, on the surface of things, and are repetitive, seemingly cannot change, resist transformation. As in Professor Arutiunov's metaphor, the fact that *dusha* is seen as holding something inside it was understood as a possibility to open it, discover something.[13] *Dusha,* then, like Michael Taussig's "space of death," is an arena "where the social imagination has populated its metamorphizing images . . . a space of transformation [giving rise to] a more vivid sense of life" (1987, 5, 7).[14]

One morning Grisha was anxious to share with me his thoughts. Rather than "Dobroe utro" (good morning), appropriating my attention in a businesslike way, he proudly blurted out that "*dusha* and suffering are closer than *dusha* and joy. Because suffering is deeper, it's not visible on the surface, it's harder to understand." I return to this idea.

Showing Our Best Side, or, "If You Have Something, Hide It"

> The Soviet millionaire's principal aim is not to spend money but to conceal it.
>
> Konstantin Simis

If Omsk was described as a void à la Chaadaev, it was also, though rarely, described as nothing as per Professor Arutiunov: nothing merely tangible or superficial. Several Omsk readers mentioned the fact that Pasternak gave the force of powerful mystery in Zhivago's life the form of an "enigmatic" Omsk brother who "brings things out of nowhere" (literally, from under the earth).

Another "magic" source were grandmothers' (usually locked) wardrobes. If a glass display case's power hinged in one way or another on consciousness and visibility, that of opaque-doored furniture derived from invisibility and enigma, an attribute of many generative loci cross-culturally. Anna Viktorovna's wardrobes issued old crochet work, sweaters to unravel for knitting yarn, medicines, money, bottles of vodka (a more potent currency), and books and furs her grandchildren might need in the future. When toothpaste was in shortage, Grisha could not believe that there was none in there, though she had been ill and confined to the apartment. When he was a kid, he told me, the most truly untouchable, unseen, sacred places were his mother's and grandmothers' wardrobes. When Anna Viktorovna died, her wardrobes' contents became potentially visible. Nadia was amazed at the clean, painstaking arrangement of the disparate items.

In the *opaque-doored* compartments and drawers in *stenki* lurked miscellaneous possessions and commodities: papers, photographs, collections, and supplies. Point of view becomes an issue here: for an "outside" audience (however ephemerally defined), closed spaces were miraculously generative; for the "insider," their opacity provided privacy, the internal freedom, so to speak, to accumulate these means to provide for others. Russian women were, after all, called magicians (see Pesmen 1998). Every apartment, one man told me, was a small warehouse: "people have gone crazy: we used to buy a bucket of potatoes; now we have thirty-five bags stashed away at my parents' house." He laughed about how funny it would all look spread out in the open; the supplies' power depended on their being hidden.

Conflicting opinions regarding the morality of accumulation of supplies (contingent on class, age, education, and more individual characteristics as well as on location, the topic of conversation, and any number of other contexts) reveal how having things stored inside can be both good and bad, soulful and soulless. The changes that began in earnest in Omsk during late perestroika aggravated and highlighted these issues. On one hand, Siberian hospitality was a primary way of creating *dusha,* impossible without food and drink to offer guests. A contrasting view maintained that hoarding increasingly rare commodities implied stinginess, calculation, and self-interested materialism. As Anatolii once said, "What's on the surface is not what's in *dusha,* and vice versa." Although this description is part of the formal definition of soul (when defined as the most alive and necessarily good essence of a human), it is also the formal description of hypocrisy and other moral ills. What is within may not be positive, and the expression *bad soul* is not necessarily an oxymoron.

This notion of storing things inside—good and bad—is also related to ideas and practices of secrecy. Russian soul is genetically linked to national identity, for example, so it is not surprising that patriotism is situated (as Zhenia situated it) in the depths of *dusha* and that public acknowledgment of those who fought in World War II usually referred to *dusha.* Patriotism was also the given reason that individual secrecy had been demanded in Soviet-era closed Omsk. If the fortress was Omsk's first soul-like center, the factories that closed Omsk during World War II were another. Andrei called secrets "a sacred, patriotic bond. We worked, ruined our health in the name of that duty."

Factory workers signed vows of secrecy, had periodic security briefings, and could neither go abroad for up to twelve years after their last access to secrets nor have contact with foreigners. Everyone worked in the closed sector or had friends and family who did; the economy of networks of acquaintances further linked open and closed domains. Keeping one's insides in was part of daily life. It is strange, people commented, technology exists that can read license plates from ("our" Omsk) satellites; nevertheless, each of us had to keep secrets. Not so strange, of course, as power and hierarchy reproduced themselves through this secrecy. Oleg said that "the whole system" was based on how fear led to "self-censorship, mistrust, closedness, hypocrisy, betrayal"—in other words, to some form of being different inside than outside.

If some secrets guarded "our best" from outsiders, other secrets, by shielding unattractive things from a guest or other observer (often oneself), making them invisible, created a "best." The taking and displaying of photographs was one aid to careful construction of bests. Glass cases were another. Such displays of the best could have their own depth: a shelf in one family's glass case contained a row of world literature eclipsed by a book on Gagarin, a New Testament, a postcard from me, a portrait of Pushkin, and decades-old portraits of family members. This row was upstaged by a plaster rooster, broken clocks, and a wooden die. When I moved closer, I froze, noticing Brezhnev's face lying flat in the shadows.

When Anna Viktorovna tried to stop Grisha from telling me a trivial detail about a local official's corruption, it was also "showing our best side," in the Soviet *lakirovka* tradition of masking, "glossing over grim reality with a smile" (Stites 1992, 119). Andrei stressed that many secrets hid not something brilliantly done and therefore valuable but an abomination or disgrace, a hidden center of disorder, deception, or immorality. But in a more general statement, he also said, "It's a principle of Soviet life: if you have something, hide it." "Don't stick out" (*ne vysovyvaites'*) was explained as a safety tactic, formerly to avoid KGB attention, later to avoid that of criminals. More generally, it was a tactic for avoiding jealousy and the evil eye. If the hypocrisy of the powerful was formulated as "saying one thing on the podium and doing [or saying] the opposite backstage," every Soviet allegedly also wore role-related "masks" that they took off only at home, in the kitchen, the *kurilka* (any location at a home or at work where smokers gathered), or the *bania* (steam baths), where, I was told, "everyone is the same—naked with washtubs." The kitchen, so central in Russian dwellings, was a private world not unlike the heartland. Such centers' official invisibility, like that of closed, provincial Omsk, gave them soul's centrality.

Being different inside than you were outside could be hypocrisy, when, as eleven-year-old Vitya told me, you are dirty in your soul but deceptively decent outside. Or it could result from protecting what was dearest. Zina told me, "You have to learn to keep . . . within certain frameworks. . . . You could only talk openly in the kitchen. . . . *Zadushevnyi* conversation is when . . . you know you can open your soul." Deep "kitchen conversations" opened up the depths. And what was in the depths tended to be about depth, about being deeply deceived by profoundly corrupt elite or criminals, about unutterable joy, alarm, pain, confusion, delight, fear. Talk about and from the depths was quite formal in that sense.

The marked guardedness and interiority of Russia, Omsk, the home, and the soul also held for power and economics.[15] People explained the success of cover-ups of industrial and ecological disasters by saying, "Remember, you're in Omsk. A closed city is easy to govern because the mess is easy to hide. . . . The KGB, the government, and the factory directors . . . had privacy to do whatever they wanted." Being veiled, power had the right shape for *dusha.* Authority thrived on opacity. Even in 1995, said an acquaintance in the police department, all corporate and *mafiia* bosses were invisible, obscured by a collective, and, as in the *partokrat*-run system with its "rule by telephone,"[16] could not be held accountable.

Anatolii explained how a sense of depth in discourse itself was constructed by practices of closedness:

> Maybe it's not exactly fear anymore. Maybe a person wants to talk, but something still tells him not to. Somewhere there, something is weighing, pushing. The same political figures want to exploit openness. . . . For seventy years everyone talked obscurely. Now if you talk openly, others try to find hidden meaning, subtext in every word. They break their heads for hours wondering what you meant.

But two businessmen proudly discussed the related Soviet "skill" of "talking in code," of "saying one thing so as to be understood as intending something else." This devious double-talk is formally similar to soulful empathy and intuition, as Grisha said, "when you see someone's outside and feel something about his *dusha* inside."

Secrets moved around without losing their value as secrets. A former *partokrat,* giving me official statistics of regional industry, added up petroleum, tires, tractors, chemicals, all nonclosed industries, to sum up at 100 percent, then paused and grinned an abyss of "you know that I know that you know." He then added, "But now, of course, everything's open." What he left out he admitted in his oxymoronic metacomment in its direction. We shared the secret that we were separated and united by secrets.

"Now, of Course, Everything's Open"

> Although the phenomenon existed empirically, it didn't rank as . . . significant; it existed below the social threshold that divides existent phenomena into two groups—those that sort of exist and those that exist without the "sort of." And what happened then? An order came

from Moscow to regard the Partygrad dissidents as existent without the "sort of" because they had manifested themselves on the level of the world press.

Alexander Zinoviev

"Now, of course, everything's open!" A 1983 history of Omsk did not even mention the sprawling military factories that had quadrupled the city's industry. Although residents had always been aware of them, by 1992 "openness" about Omsk's blank spots was hitting the local media in a new kind of display, implying another kind of consciousness. One such article claimed that Omsk's close ties with defense was "one of the 'kernels' of its character" and complained about how the military currently occupied almost a quarter of Omsk's territory. The piece concluded, "A city within a city is not normal." In 1992, more than a year after I first came to Omsk, I was openly told the name of the factory where many acquaintances worked and had worked, a factory that by 1995, however, was being advertised to foreign investors in English-language color brochures.

Feador Tiutchev's poem *Silentium* describes the inexplicability of *dusha* and refers to, as Wierzbicka observes, one tragedy of *dusha:* it is alive, but only inside:

A thought once uttered is a lie.
Burst out and you'll disturb the source.
Live from it and—be still.

Although many people claimed that the KGB's presence had crushed and cramped their internal lives, attitudes toward glasnost (openness) were not as unambivalent as might be expected. First, openness was often seen as an easily manipulated commodity: as Anatolii said, "The same political figures want to exploit openness." The *Moscow News* (No. 42, 1992) quoted former KGB chief Bakatin as saying, "I'm against opening KGB files. . . . It plays into the hands of petty politicians." Openness was a powerful political tool, but more interesting in this early 1990s context is that, as Anatolii said about "talking openly," openness was both categorized as good, attractive, and appealing and seen as too or deceptively good because, after all, nothing can be that simple; there must be something lurking behind it.

Second, depth is interesting. At a 1994 reunion of friends, Grisha proposed a toast, suggesting a meeting every year and adding nostalgically, "even underground if we have to—it's more interesting that way anyway." On another occasion, he told me that democracy was "when an American comes out on the street and screams 'the president is a moron' and nothing happens to him. But you know, so what? . . . It's better if I have to hold some things inside and not say them!" He then continued the violin metaphor cited previously, adding electronics and container images:

> The mystery of your internal world lives inside of you, and you don't want to bring it outside of its soulful membrane. . . . The mystery can be good, and *dusha* rejoices, lives with it. There are also mysteries that give *dusha* no peace. . . . *Dusha* is inside, where, like the light on your tape recorder there or on some electronic equipment made in Omsk, it tells you things. They say Russians have "wide open" souls. Well, . . . a person's soul cannot be thrown open, unfortunately and fortunately. If our souls were open, we'd lose our internal worlds, which form there, which we nurture there, which we can't express. Imagine if I turned out all my pockets and walked around like that. I'd have nothing.

Irina, a teacher, said, "*Dusha* is about my insides, my sufferings, what I live through, my conscience, my love; *dusha* is *ne na pokaz,* not for show."

A friend who visited Russia in 1996 after an absence of several years summarized what she felt to be the most important change in Russia: "You can see everything! It's all right there on the surface!" In 1996, information on the Internet announced "*More Hidden Treasures Revealed:* Imitating the Hermitage's new policy of displaying hitherto-unseen collections and opening up long-closed rooms, [the Ethnographic Museum] has unlocked its . . . special storeroom of treasures to reveal the pearls of its unique collection." Opening the most hidden, exposing "pearls," was in fashion, and yet the new politics of openness often took traditional forms: passion, asking "big questions," and willingness to suffer pain still served as proof that one had a moral soul. During late perestroika, openness was often construed as heroic willingness to suffer or display this passion in public.

On January 23, 1991, I witnessed an amazing contrast between two television stations' news coverage: Moscow (central) news at 9 P.M. had little, really—minor news, a short mention of trouble in the Persian Gulf, and a note on how Vilnius had calmed down (although when it had not been calm, there had been no news of it at all). There was no mention of the currency crisis that had thrown every household into emergency mode. At the other extreme, the Leningrad channel's sportscaster delivered a very brief, expressionless, slipshod sports rundown, then exclaimed that he was aware that people had much more on their minds than sports. Pale with grief and anger, he dedicated almost his entire time to "our poor, miserable money." A 1992 Omsk review of Stanislav Govorukhin's film *The Russia We Lost* stated,

The director does not claim to be dispassionate in his investigation of
. . . "the [Soviet-era] murder of Russia." . . . He is trying to find
answers to the questions of who we are . . . what our mother/land
Russia is. . . . Those who do not wish to experience the pain of metic-
ulously hidden facts being made public criticize Govorukhin. . . .
American-style "objective reporting". . . What a joke! . . . Passion,
evidence of the author's position and heartache, are part of the Russian tradition. . . . An amazing genre has been born: "I cannot be
silent."[17] . . . Russia for us is an enigmatic, unknown country, and,
decided Govorukhin, that is why we live so stupidly.

"Confessions," "revelations," and speaking in an *animated* voice,
characterized the speaker as souled. Confessional and revelatory perestroika reporting styles contrasted markedly to both Soviet reporting, with
its bland, even, optimistic party lines and censored prerevolutionary
reporting, both of which had often omitted items of world importance.
Post-Soviet styles were also, however, increasingly governed by Western
styles. At this junction, *dusha* itself became an issue, forcing itself, as a
style and as a philosophy, into the display space of the media. Clichés were
used in suddenly revitalized and newly discovered context-dependent
meanings, characteristic of a general perestroika and early post-Soviet
revitalization or deironization of *dusha* that ran parallel to its increasingly
ironic use as a cliché.

Stites (1992, 121) writes that the film *Kuban Cossacks,* a favorite of
Stalin, by 1992 had become "the object of a hot debate between critics who
see it as an evil mask obscuring reality and defenders who recall the ray of
happiness it brought them in dark days." This echoes a classic conflict
between tactics for achieving *dusha* and again illustrates an aspect of
dusha's life at a particular historical juncture. One woman said, "A sign of
soul, of culture, is that everything is not on display. Things are worse now.
All the filth that was illegal is now legal, so people in power take the best
for themselves openly—formerly at least they hid it! Nothing is holy for
these people." "Holy" here implies tact,[18] creating an image of something's
absence; if something bad could not be eradicated, one could at least be
sensitive to others' feelings and suppress it.[19]

A young man told me how, on the level of world culture, Omsk residents had been shut off, closed in, a phenomenon he called "both good
and bad." Some people who said that their eyes had been opened after life-
times of deceit were nevertheless repelled by unaccustomedly blatant statements of ugly truths. Some blamed glasnost, which began in the mid-1980s
with revelations about Stalin, for the alleged loss of soul and culture as
much as they blamed Stalin's betrayals themselves; it was a case of killing

the bearer of bad news, as if openness itself had "spat" or "shat" in their souls (or released destructive forces better contained and constrained).

Andrei said: "We were brought up emotionally that the Party was 'honor, mind . . .';[20] then when all of this started to be uncovered, in *dusha* some sort of pain appeared that we had been so deceived. . . . Suddenly this abyss appeared." The question asked in such cases was "*Radi chego?*" "For the sake of what [did we do it all]?" In other words, what meaning remains beneath our actions, what sense, now that it is clear that we were deeply deceived—underminings in a rather vivid sense of the word. "Where has it all gone?" and "Where does it go?" were similar laments, not only, as in Mila's words, about spiritual energy, but about the disappearance of Russia's commodities and natural resources and the fruits of Soviet era labors and enthusiasm, all spirited away into the black hole of other people's depths by their deception. Oleg would often bemoan current events, styles, and revelations by gesturing and saying, "*V glubine dushi* [in the depths of my soul], it's offensive." Closedness allegedly kills soul. Opening, sharing, making conscious and explicit any closed thing, in some contexts a supremely soulful practice, in the same and other contexts may also risk injury to *dusha*.

Another way in which glasnost entailed a transformation of traditional values is that secrets were treated as gifts. In Russia (and "especially in Siberia") gifts were to be given generously, sincerely, from within, with a feeling called "*ot dushi*" (from *dusha*). This was part of an elaborate system of exchange including "human warmth," potatoes, and social status (Pesmen 1996, 1998). Secrets were good gifts: they lived, in Grisha's words, "inside there." Anna Viktorovna was reminiscing about how Omsk had changed during World War II. As she was mentioning the tobacco factory's arrival in Omsk, the doorbell rang. As she reentered the kitchen, on her way past me, she leaned down and, in a rapid undertone, whispered, "and all that rocket [missile] business." It was an intimate moment. Maps drawn for me gratuitously featured the KGB building as an orientation point. During "open" communication in a newly opened city, rapid recitals of products, disasters, and other unspeakable attributes of blank spots would be proffered alongside gossip, a valuable rumor, confession of some emotion, a can of condensed milk from a cabinet, or a porcelain figurine from a glass case, with no particular distinction made between these categories of things "emerging" and passing between people.

Distinctions were more often made, however, between reasons for opening up and to whom things were opened. Nineteenth-century discourse of Russian soul included imagery that referred to the peasant "keeping deep within himself that which the gentry was willing to sell for his own profit" (R. C. Williams 1970, 582). A 1992 article accuses the for-mer KGB of the same sins: the agency was said to be about to sign a con-tract with Crown Books for the publication of secret files, having "decided to do business by exploiting our national heritage." The real sin of this deal was not openness itself but opening, "selling," the national soul to foreigners, for money.

Thoughts in Conclusion

This work has shown a number of essential characteristics of the Roman-tic "Russian soul," in particular, concentric models and metaphors of depth, and has shown them present and, to some extent, revitalized and transformed in the 1990s. I have also shown individually and historically specific ways in which such depth models were tools for interpreting, co-opting, and incorporating social change into *dusha* culture, and vice versa.

One of my aims has been to examine the metaphysics, meaning, and emotions that the network of depth metaphors implies. This network is clearly closely related to and very revealing about depths endemic in wider and non-Russian popular cultures, psychology, and scholarly practices. With a few exceptions,[21] however, Russian soul and its associated notions and practices, such as depth, have been ignored in scholarship. Perhaps, as a cliché, they have been too visible, falling victim to scholars' own unques-tioned assumptions that what is "on the surface" must be less interesting, true, and alive than what is distanced.

Yet these assumptions need to be questioned. My examination of tra-ditions and habits of imagery related to some "alive" centers shows them to be quite complicit with their "dead" nemeses. One such complicity is that, if we see *dusha* (as Fernandez [1986] sees metaphor) as giving form to unwieldy and inchoate pronouns, it clearly weaves a deceptive coherence out of images of emptiness, failure, incompletion, unclear perceptions, communitas, and "forces of disorder," as did Mila in her black hole mono-logue (Fernandez 1986, 181, 206–7; Turner 1969, 42–43). This fabric is made dense by the polysemy of inside, outside, and other spatially imag-ined and lived "nodes of interconnection between separate but intersecting planes of classification" (Turner 1969, 42–43). The deep is a culturally val-ued, appropriated, displayed kind of inchoate; moral and psychological battlefields and physical spaces are constructed as these sorts of situations. Mary Helms (1988, 64) writes that space can express "ideological and cos-mological contrasts between the known, visible, familiar, socially con-trolled and morally ordered heartland, and the strange, invisible, uncon-trolled, disordered, and morally extreme . . . lands 'beyond.'" In the case of Russia, the center, the heartland, was formulated as strange, invisible, uncontrolled, disordered, and morally extreme by being displayed in discourse, in practice, or in space.

Classifying things and treating them as unclearly or incompletely perceived, inexplicable, complex, internally contradictory, irrational, antirational, unattainable, distant, or inexhaustible create, often rhetorically, what is accepted as depth. This depth is a trope of scale that abdicates its job of measuring, implying transcendence using the tools of shared experience, opposition and contradiction, invisibility, hyperbole, and silence, among others. The images and practices of suffering, complaining, and of carnivalized forms[22] reproduced the image of an internal soul that survives despite external social evils.

In everyday life, values attributed to opening, closing, outside, and inside are context dependent. Bringing something from a distance (from one inner, outer, conceptual, or cosmological order to another) could mean very different things, yet all such movements tend to be valued as manifestations into visibility or consciousness (the opposite, consciousness of something's disappearance, is still a kind of consciousness of the thing). Conflation of these experiences into one static or cumulative model, *dusha,* seems to reveal an abomination: negative elements infiltrating and polluting positive ones. The good (one's sense of self, intimacy between people, patriotically cherished information) is hidden, and the bad (moral flaws, accidents, corruption, and other sources of wealth and power) is hidden. Things were unsaid because they defied formulation, were precious or private; things were unsaid because of fear of persecution or in jealous protection of valuable information. What was for any reason impossible to simply put in words was deep. Sacred silences and insides merged in practice with profane silences and insides.

One key to soul's complicity with its enemies is that it internalizes. Shameful, good, pure, and impure are formally treated alike, taken in, and come to be alternate forms of the sacred. A constant, eclectic slide from one center-periphery model to another, one definition to another, and the practice of internalizing things in hopes of structurally redeeming them bring the filthiest into the sanctuary of the purest. Dirty laundry and skeletons enjoy the privileges of pearls, which explains people's sense that those pearls had been cast before swine and that their souls had been soiled, negated, made into loci of pain by individual and historical events.

Depth and *dusha* are also externalizing. Conventions of soulful behavior (such as hospitality, friendship, respect, interest, and other forms of love) and consciousness itself are active in realizing the value of the center; focusing on *dusha* is displaying it, opening it, increasing it. Things were opened as part of sacred and profane exchange traditions; they were opened in a spirit of purification and in hope of progress; they were opened in personal and political gambits.

Paradoxically, *dusha* may be seen as sacrificing its mysterious, internal, defining qualities by being too open. The events of the 1980s and 1990s spoke to this very urgently. During perestroika, exchange, money, self-interest, and horrors of history, particularly those of the Revolution and Stalin-era, were displayed, took consciousness's center stage. Glasnost was to some extent experienced as inescapable representations of internal things and was, as a result, often blamed for alleged loss of soul. It will be interesting to see how discourses and practices of this soul, long (and even self-) characterized as dying or dead, fare in later post-Soviet developments.

Any container created by a secret has a pathetic fact or social or personal scrap at the bottom, or nothing, or there is no bottom but always a deeper level one hasn't found. As Boym (1994a, 278) writes, "The 'secret' is . . . hidden in order to be shared . . . [a] fetishized . . . souvenir, preserved only for the sake of the game." The real value is interiority itself. The soul and other depths are riddled with Bakhtinian loopholes; any search for a final, visible form is sabotaged. Depths tempt yet recede. Trying to catch or open such secrets is falling into their trap.

I have examined some aspects of the Russian soul's formal and informational enigma. Depth, I have shown, is a value that is created and sustained by a great number of sociocultural practices, and any attempt to unveil something hidden only creates more depth by reinforcing or recapitulating the same forms. Ethnographers, philosophers, psychologists, and journalists will unwittingly reproduce this cultural version unless they treat depth not as the way their world and knowledge are *really* organized but as results of an ethnometaphysical belief that surfaces are explained, governed, determined by, and/or epiphenomenal to what is profound or underlying.

NOTES

Thanks to Michael Wasserman for his insights; many thanks also to Daphne Berdahl, Matti Bunzl, Steve Coleman, Tania Fel, Paul Friedrich, Martha Lampland, and Marko Zivkovic.

1. I use the Russian word *dusha* in this article more than the inadequate English gloss *soul.* For comparison of *dusha* and the English *soul, mind,* and *heart,* see Wierzbicka 1992.

2. These topics are dealt with in Pesmen 1998.

3. Cf. Fernandez 1986.

4. The violin's sound post; in French, *âme*.

5. Dostoevsky 1985, bk. 1, p. 171 (letter to his brother, January 30–February 22, 1854, Omsk).

6. The word *nutro* indicates a visceral center and has the same root as the word for *inside, vnutri*. It was used in contexts of strong moral or physical gut reaction. Dal' 1881 defines *nutro* as (among other things) a person's *dusha*, spiritual person, invisible essence; Dal' also defines *nutro* as *prostor*, an open expanse contained within something.

7. See Berdiaev (1947, 2) and Dostoevsky's *Gambler* (1982, 333) for versions of the idea that *dusha*'s "size" dooms attempts at efficiency or elegance. For discussion of this idea, see Pesmen 1998.

8. Similarly, *kul'tura*, a notion with varying but always significant relationships to *dusha*, was sometimes seen as undergoing entropic decay or having diminishing influence toward peripheral areas.

9. *Sokrovennyi* (precious) and *sokrovishche* (treasure) are based on roots for *covering* or *sheltering*. Eliade writes, "The true world is always in the middle, at the Center" (1959, 42).

10. Greek for "self-emptying" (Rancour-Laferriere 1995, 28).

11. In his story *Pripadok* (The Attack), Anton Chekhov describes a student's soul pain: "He could . . . show where it was: in his breast, under his heart; but it was impossible to compare it with anything" (1985, 80).

12. This aspect of *dusha* is treated in Pesmen 1998. When people "sit" and commune, they all turn out to have souls. I have no room here to discuss a primary locus of inside-outside dynamics, that of people considered "ours" and "not ours," a fluid, constantly negotiated grouping, including (but in no way limited to) what Friedrich 1979 has called *ty* and *vy* universes. See Zinoviev 1985 on the complexities of such alliances.

13. Open, *otkryt'*; discovery, *otkrytie*.

14. Similar to *dusha* also in that one "descends into" its transformational locus.

15. Simis describes the invisibility of the powerful and the closedness of goods and services in the Soviet system of concentrically tightening circles (1982, 45). Elsewhere (Pesmen 1996, 1998) I discuss ambivalence to economic openness.

16. My Omsk friends explained Soviet *telefonnoe pravo* thus: a boss calls and gives an order, but there is no documentation of it, so the cause of the action effectively vanishes. Part of a pervasive opacity of power itself.

17. This is a version of a slogan that was far from newborn; it was widely associated with the Revolution.

18. "Genuine tact" was often mentioned as definitive of soulfulness.

19. Silence as a way of treating the sacred and profane predates Romantic depth (and is certainly not limited to Russian culture). Ivanits discusses how Russian peasants feared "that the devil would appear the moment his name [was] uttered. . . . The most frequently used designation for 'devil' was . . . related to the magic line . . . usually a circle, that the unclean force cannot cross" (1992, 39).

20. Andrei omits the main word to which he refers in this Brezhnev-era slogan attributed to Lenin: "The Party is the honor, mind, *and conscience* of our epoch."

Conscience (*sovest'*) was often called synonymous with *dusha;* it also hints from inside at moral truths.

21. Including Cherniavsky, Williams, Wierzbicka, Greenfeld (in passing), and my own work.

22. Bakhtin said these carnivalized forms are "a powerful means for . . . generalization in depth," without which life's "most profound layers" cannot be located and expressed (1984, 157).

Afterword

Martha Lampland

States are changing: states of knowledge as well as states of being. Long-cherished beliefs about the intransigence of elites, the resilience of stagnant economies, the strength of Marxist-Leninist party-states, and the apathy of socialist citizens have been challenged by the transition in Eastern Europe and the former Soviet Union. The time has come to reflect anew on the artificial limitations that have been imposed on the world emerging from socialism. This volume has sought to expand the purview of investigation into the world of transition in Eastern Europe and the former Soviet Union to suggest that the narrow focus on economic institutions and their remaking substantially misrepresents the enormity of change and the significance of continuity in these worlds. The chapters in this book illustrate the broad transformations in place, personhood, and politics that have accompanied the momentous changes in the landscape since 1989–91. In this brief afterword, I suggest directions of research prompted by the work published here.

It perhaps should not be surprising that the loudest voices heard in the West following the transition should be those of economists and political advisers. The study of Eastern Europe and the Soviet Union has been dominated for decades by political economy. Questions of moral order, of culture, of belief were treated as secondary to the analysis of politics or not even worthy of note. The presumption that party-state institutions controlled all aspects of social life precluded the study of everyday experience as having a quality and dynamic of its own. One might imagine that the assumption among Western scholars that politics invaded all realms of society would have resulted in a broad and inclusive study of social life, but the reverse was the case. Politics was seen in terms of the abstract institutional structures of the party, and the doing of politics was analyzed through successive policy shifts. But this left a whole series of questions unanswered. How did people create satisfying lives within the constraints of repression and want? What were the forms of everyday accommodation people designed—with neighbors, bureaucrats, police, priests, and friends—that gave social life its particular texture? Were there domains where the party-state could not exercise its control, and, if so, why? What decidedly local cultural values and moral imperatives structured social life and national politics during the socialist period, despite the constant refrain criticizing foreign political agendas and alien institutions? How had the history of socialism become variously the product of local communities and nation-states, so that the separation of culture from politics at this late date would misconstrue the historical process that actually transpired?

The articles in this collection all consider the dynamics of the transition over the past decade. Yet since these studies take as their primary site of analysis the construction of everyday life, the negotiation of meaning, and the process of social community, they are in complex ways also studies of the socialist period. Just as building the wall in Berlin forced a violent break in history, so too drawing a sharp line between socialism and the postsocialist period violates the complex flow of memory, community, family, politics, and culture in which people live their lives. Thus, these essays serve as interventions in the study of socialism as well as the study of postsocialism, whatever it may be.

How are moral orders sustained? What various sites can be used to study the expression of cultural beliefs and the stabilization of social practices? Alaina Lemon chooses the Moscow metro, an icon of socialist development, to examine how its cars and corridors are colonized by Muscovites. By describing where people sit and how they interact, Lemon shows how morality and community are built. They are not always communities of inclusion, as the anecdotes of racial animosities illustrate. Indeed, Lemon demonstrates in important ways how race is made real. Much ink has been spilled since the transition on the strength of ethnic divisions, but little of this work takes as its starting point the study of race as a social process. While race and ethnicity are embodied forms, the content and meaning of those forms shift and change over time. For this reason, it is vital to attend to the making of race, the living of identity, the restructuring of community. Studies of the region would be far better served by a more theoretically informed treatment of race and ethnicity than has been deployed in recent work.

In a world transfixed by televised news sources and the Internet, it is refreshing to learn that in some instances, people simply gather on street corners and at metro stations to inform each other of momentous events and to debate their significance. Western news reports cited the dominant view that Soviet citizens were indifferent in the face of political upheaval, overlooking the means by which people actually did take part. These prejudices, built on the assumption that the average person on the street has no opinion on politics, is an old saw and must be discarded to understand how societies take shape over time. One more time it becomes necessary to challenge the taken-for-granted assumptions of uncaring masses and ignorant citizens. Scholars have been looking in the wrong places.

Philip V. Bohlman has traveled through Eastern Europe to chronicle the fate of synagogues left to languish for decades. The fortunes of these various sites are strikingly different, revealing much about the way the continued presence of a lost community can be reconciled by those who remain. Strategies include creating museums or making postcards that transform the synagogue into a link to the community's past; in other instances, the past is completely obliterated, in one case by a music studio. Bohlman's voyage raises the question of whose history is at stake here. How will the past be represented, and what means will be chosen to further its legacy? The manner in which musical traditions are recast in choral performances or on cassette tapes demonstrates that the rich variety of liturgical forms and folk music of the region is lost in the rush to manufacture packaged traditions, with businesses in the West reconfiguring the music of the East. This phenomenon again demonstrates the power of appropriating the past of one community to make the present of another. The act of commodifying history (whose history?)—through phone cards, CDs, postcards, and even museums—is a cultural technique that deserves far greater scrutiny in the current climate in which markets bewitch and profits beguile.

Regions east of the Elbe have not been known as the site of provocative studies of sexuality, even though one might say that the twentieth-century fascination with sex was prompted by one of Vienna's most famous residents. Freud's simple question—how does becoming sexual mark one's soul and make one's history?—has not been transformed into a research agenda for social analysts in the region. Simple explanations can be put forward that focus on the illegitimacy—cultural and legal—of nonheterosexual practices, restrictions that seriously constrained thinking about what sex is and could be. But even the study of heterosexuality has been poorly addressed, despite the rich material available in as obvious a source as jokes. I have long thought that the sexual excesses during the 1960s and 1970s in Budapest could have been studied to great effect as a form of political resistance to a puritanical state, not simply the local version of the sexual revolution of the West. To what purposes, after all, do people put sex? Matti Bunzl's analysis of gay tourism is thus a welcome change on this bleak horizon.

And horizons, indeed, are the question. The greater taboo than sex in this piece may be the study of colonialism. In recent discussions with colleagues in Eastern Europe, I have found much resistance to the idea that colonialism could be an adequate lens to study the socialist empire or the history of earlier empires in the region. The primary objection is the assumption that the dynamics of colonialism require communities of very different cultural histories (that is, in classic terms, colonialism is a process of civilizing the native). Hence, European nations could not be included. But if colonialism is defined as the project of dominating a nation or a region through the concerted effort of transforming cultural forms as well as political institutions, then it may very well apply. It would be instructive to see debate considering the applicability of the rich theoretical tradition on colonial practices in other areas of the world to the study of Eastern Europe and the former Soviet Union. Is it possible to identify similar patterns of political dominance and cultural imperialism, and if so, during which historical periods and under what social conditions?

In the end, the study of colonialism is about territory, conquest, and transgression. In an era of globalization—when one can eat Kentucky Fried Chicken as easily as goulash in Budapest, buy Versace in Moscow, and watch *Dallas* in Lvov—new borders are ever in the making. The movement of goods and of people is highly monitored in the global economy despite repeated paeans to open borders and numerous tales of smuggling and contraband. What moves in a global economy and what stays tells much about the powers that be and those that be not. How new borders will be erected in Central Europe should constitute a major focus of scholarship in the years to come.

Dealing with the ravages of socialist industry on the local landscape is a daunting challenge in the postsocialist era. More daunting still is the task of reconciling different visions of modernization. Hermine G. De Soto analyzes the conflicts that can arise among different visions of what a community can and should be: conflicts over industrial expansion, over history, over community involvement. In this context, it should be remembered that the history of social planning and urban design long predates the efforts of socialist regimes to remake the economy and its workers. Indeed, the various strains of modernity that were revealed in the opposing plans of the Circle and the Reformed Bauhaus had also been sources of inspiration to socialist planners, though the implementation of the party's particular brand of modernity has not been kind to the landscape.

At the heart of De Soto's analysis is the question of community control and citizen involvement. It is common to bemoan the destruction of civil society that followed the rise of Marxist-Leninist one-party states, particularly in Eastern Europe. And yet little work has been done to examine the role of local institutions during the socialist period—culture houses, youth clubs, schools, folk ensembles—in fostering a sense of community or regional identity. In contrast to the predominant view of socialist society, residents in the state of Saxony-Anhalt fondly remember local institutions that played a part in the construction and transmission of community spirit. The dismantling of social-welfare services has not only deprived citizens of badly needed financial supports but also destroyed the infrastructure that permitted towns and villages to maintain community centers and clubs.

With all the talk about the rejuvenation of civil society, it is curious that the class politics of civil society are rarely broached. The rhetoric of socialist empowerment of the working class clearly has contributed substantially to the dismissal of class analysis among former socialist citizens. But this fact does not excuse Western analysts—particularly those so keen on the rebuilding of civil society—from their consistent failure to analyze the differential participation of various social groups in the new world of politics and community. Questions need to be asked: Civil society for whom? Who shall be heard in the new community of citizens, and why? Why can the visions and aspirations of women workers be so summarily dismissed in discussions for urban renewal? Are intellectuals and managers the only people qualified to enact civic duties? Why do scholars continue to write about the apathy of the masses without explaining the mechanisms that foster such disillusionment? How secure is the knowledge that the standards for civil society demanded of Eastern Europe and the former Soviet Union are actually upheld in the West? And if they are not, what are the social conditions that prevent them from being achieved?

Capitalism, like its scion, socialism, is built on a progressive vision of the future: new products, ever-expanding markets, and upward spirals of technological innovation. The firm belief in progress does not seem to be shaken by the occasional collapse of markets, downturns in economic fortunes, or massive business failures. Each such instance is localized, an anomaly within the general world system. But what if this catastrophe happens at home? All the hopes of bounty awakened in Armenians by the collapse of the Soviet state were dashed by the dynamics of political and economic transition, complicated by the war and ensuing energy crisis, provoking a profound crisis in collective identity as well as personal relationships. Stephanie Platz describes this process as demodernization, "a cataclysmic paralysis of the urban and industrial infrastructure."

While the various struggles since 1989–91 have prompted studies on the politics of national borders and state making, few have devoted attention to the consequences of these battles on the making of everyday life. And yet, as anthropologists have long been wont to point out, all these grand institutions of states, parties, and nations are built from the ground up, dependent in the final analysis on the smooth workings of kitchen and nursery, field and factory, family and friends. Platz's analysis of the spatial and temporal displacements demodernization effects demonstrates how significant such changes can be, precipitating the demise of community relations, the difficulty of sustaining ties with friends and kin, and, importantly, the consequences of these daily practices on concepts of national identity. Platz shows that concepts of nation and of family are intimately related, as are the axes of space and time in the production of everyday experience. The pains of reproducing one's material existence have interfered with the ability to conceive of a future, for one's kin or for one's nation. While the study of everyday life has received greater scope in recent years, this rich field should be explored further, because, in the final analysis, it is where society is made.

The making of everyday life can be a struggle, even in the best of times. So, too, there is much work to be done in recovering one's past. This is particularly true when the past one wishes to remember is widely scorned as forgettable, regrettable, ugly. As Elizabeth A. Ten Dyke illustrates in her analysis of "remembrance work," the abrupt rupture with a socialist present following on the collapse of the GDR provoked a confrontation with personal memories and public histories. The manners in which people engaged in this project differed and included initiating national debates, writing histories, and building museums. And yet all these tasks share one crucial feature: the refusal to see socialism as irrelevant, to acknowledge that one's past has made one's self in the present and will contribute substantially to the future of the community and the nation.

The politics of representing the past are always contentious, but writing the history of socialism has its own particular problems. Two factors complicate this picture. The state controlled all forms of public representation—school textbooks, newspapers, television, and museums and other institutions committed to building national history—a feature that is shared by other repressive regimes and one-party states. But the Marxist-Leninists also had a particular commitment to the representation of historical progress, as the historical-materialist worldview enshrined a very particular image of social actors, historical movement, and moral progress. Moreover, the heavily ideologized histories written during socialism within the Eastern bloc could be easily paired with the ideologized versions of socialist history written in the West. Thus, the path to recovering the history of everyday life in the GDR after 1989 is a struggle against the political apparatuses of West and East. The history of socialism, in other words, remains difficult to write, and the interventions in this struggle of diary and museum Ten Dyke recounts are both sobering and heartening. But the problem of representing the past extends far beyond the history of socialism alone. Negotiating the maze of memory and grappling with the techniques of representation are recurring problems in all social communities. The historical struggles and ethical dilemmas people face in the course of their lives may differ significantly—the dilemmas faced by those in the GDR being especially stark—but the project of confronting one's past and making it speak for oneself, one's community, and one's future is inescapable. That this project is a cultural resource of great value requires devoting more attention than heretofore to its construction and always incomplete resolution.

The twists and turns of social history fascinate and confound: former punk rockers turning born-again Christians; the withdrawal of censorship silencing protest; the growth of markets destroying the economic fortunes of alternative music. These phenomena were not consequences of the fall of socialism that I would have anticipated. Where, then, to find politics, how is it practiced, and under what conditions is it disabled? How relevant for the study of Eastern Europe and the former Soviet Union are theories—of culture, of art, of politics—that have been developed in contexts where the histories of states, markets, nations, and subjects differ in subtle but crucial ways? Anna Szemere's analysis of punk rock musicians and their divergent paths in the transition suggests that the uncritical use of cultural studies categories developed in the West (and in Britain in particular) will lead to poor readings of artistic expression and resistance in Hungary and other former socialist states. The classic distinction between autonomy and politics does not map onto the social terrain of punk rock in the socialist period, since the embrace of autonomy was the site of political expression. This struggle to resist the state by rejecting the party's colonization of culture was the antipolitics of socialism, so well known but still not well understood. To avoid imposing a range of concepts that distort or mislead, it is important to examine more closely how people make sense of their world and so infuse terms with meanings not shared across the continent.

The study of space and time as crucial structuring principles of social experience has flourished in recent years. Material practices of architecture and urban planning and temporal regimes of work and play have been examined thoroughly and provocatively. But few have traveled to the depths of the soul, as has Dale Pesmen. Her journey has led to kitchens, where talk of the soul flows as easily as do spirits from bottles. She has wandered through cabinets to ponder why Leonid Brezhnev's face still peaks through the glass. Anthropology has long been dedicated to a complex rendering of cultural schema, a subtle sketch of actions and beliefs, an attempt to capture experiences of suffering, pain, truth, and mystery. Yet many spaces remain unexplored, such as the cultural tropes of surface and depth Pesmen identifies lying within the folds of the Russian soul. That these phenomena have been hidden, as was the city of Omsk—obliterated from the map of the Soviet Union—should foster a more active engagement in innovative cultural analysis in the spaces now liberated from obscurity.

In reviewing the work published in this volume, I have raised a number of issues worthy of further study. I wish to point out that nearly all the questions I raised—the making of race, the constitution of class, the production of memory, the living of sexuality—could be posed in a variety of societies, demonstrating that the barriers long dividing East and West may finally be falling away. There is so much to learn, and the practice of social analysis will be enriched by these studies.

But one final barrier that has stubbornly remained in place must be acknowledged. It is the barrier separating scholars of East and West, a barrier sustained by disproportionate financial resources and divergent scholarly traditions. Scholars from institutions in Western Europe and the United States have access to funding that—though limited to smaller and smaller numbers—still makes it possible for some to travel and do research in Eastern Europe and the former Soviet Union on a fairly regular basis. Such resources are virtually unavailable to scholars who actually live in those countries. This absence of research funding is complicated by the fact that wages for academic work continue to plummet in most countries in Eastern Europe and the former Soviet Union, making the practice of scholarly work nearly impossible. Researchers are forced to take on a number of moneymaking projects just to get by, thereby reducing the time and energy available for the labor-intensive activities of an engaged scholar.

In cases where new sources of funding are available, through international competitions or local agencies, scholars in the East are scrambling to learn the entirely foreign technique of grant writing. While not the easiest craft to master, it can be learned. But how to reconcile the differences in approach, in conceptualization, in focus between Eastern and Western scholars? If scholars from the East ask different questions than do their colleagues in the West, will the Easterners be excluded from access to funding on the grounds that they have not demonstrated sufficient rigor, theoretical sophistication, or analytic clarity? The institutional production of knowledge in the East and West has long diverged, not simply because of the heavy weight of Marxism-Leninism. It is true that during socialism, social scientists were trained to address pragmatic questions of social policy; high theorizing was relegated to philosophers. But it is also true that throughout Europe, the boundaries among government service, policy work, and academic employment can be crossed more easily. Conversely, the peculiar history of professionalization in the United States has led to a greater division between academics and practitioners. Moreover, the extensive network of colleges and universities in the United States provides a much larger market for teachers engaged in theorizing and distanced from policy-making than is the case in Europe.

But there is a third aspect to this problem. Social-science training in the United States privileges knowledge that contributes to general conclusions and abstract theorizing. In-depth knowledge of a locale is (at most) a stepping stone to more general observations; concern with regional issues is thought to be a limited project. Thus, scholars who articulate a project in terms that are culturally and regionally specific are seen to lack the broad vision and analytic rigor demanded of well-trained intellectuals. The problem, of course, is that few ask under what social and historical conditions particular theories acquire the pedigree of generality, universality, and abstraction while other ideas come to be seen as too tied to a specific locale. Where does one have to be situated—intellectually, institutionally, culturally—to make general pronouncements about social theory, and what contexts are, by definition, seen to deprive actors of their ability to see beyond their own particularities? I am speaking, of course, of the politics of knowledge production, a theme addressed as provocatively in the literature on imperialism and colonialism as the literature growing out of the feminist movement. These intellectual insights were born in intense political struggles across the globe and remain relevant. Why are some people—by virtue of their gender, race, class, or geographical location—seen to be limited in their capacities to know the world, while others are understood to be fully capable of knowing all? What historical conditions produce knowledge of value; how are other views devalued?

The transition has been far more difficult than was initially anticipated, in part, I believe, because those who called for a return to Europe could not imagine that their reincorporation into the West would be achieved on such unequal terms. While the economic downturn may be reversible, the epistemological divide may be far more difficult to eliminate. As long as scholars in the West continue to demand that people in other regions think like them to join the debate, then this problem will continue. The difficulty of drawing scholars into a more sustained debate is exacerbated by the economic difficulties in the East. Even if some Easterners were prepared to engage in a lively critique of truth claims, methodology, and theory, they lack the resources to do so: time, money, well-stocked libraries, smoothly functioning computer networks, and so forth. The editors of this volume may be guilty of not having done more to incorporate authors from the East. Several of the contributors to this volume do hail from Central Europe, but all of the writers featured here acquired doctorates in the United States.

I would welcome a lively debate on this issue. It is important to address the problems that could result from these disparities, most notably the impoverishment of perspective that comes from excluding alternative viewpoints. I have become keenly aware of the cultural and historical specificity of theory building, studying historical events that bred the theories I have used to explain the selfsame history (Lampland 1995). And yet everyone knows full well that in anthropology, it is common to lift (plagiarize?) theoretical insights from cultures near and far, to transform local categories into analytic terms. The politics of theory making and the culture of imperialism have to become as central an issue in conversations with colleagues across the region as discussions about party politics, new goods and services, and old friends. I say these things even though I feel strongly about the importance of contributing to a lively and productive set of principles called social theory. I value practices, such as graduate education and peer review publishing, common in the United States that enhance analytic skills and strengthen the tradition of criticism in scholarship. In short, I do not advocate replacing one set of ideas with another. The point is to engage in an honest investigation into ideas and their consequences. All would be served by a conversation devoted to widening perspectives, deepening understandings, and strengthening the insights of scholarship.

NOTE

I wish to thank Daphne Berdahl and Matti Bunzl for their helpful advice on this commentary.

References

Aagaard-Mogensen, L. 1988. *The Idea of the Museum: Philosophical, Artistic, and Political Questions.* Lewiston, NY: E. Mellen.

Abrahamian, L. 1993. "The Anthropologist as Shaman: Interpreting Recent Political Events in Armenia." In *Beyond Boundaries: Understanding, Translation, and Anthropological Discourse,* ed. G. Palsson. Providence, RI: Berg.

Abrahams, R., ed. 1997. *After Socialism: Land Reform and Rural Social Change in Eastern Europe.* New York: Berghahn.

Abu-Lughod, L. 1991. "Writing Against Culture." In *Recapturing Anthropology: Working in the Present,* ed. R. Fox. 137–62. Santa Fe: School of American Research Press.

Adorno, T. W. 1986 (1959). "What Does Coming to Terms with the Past Mean?" T. Bahti and G. Hartman, trans. In *Bitburg in Moral and Political Perspective,* ed. G. H. Hartman, 114–29. Bloomington: Indiana University Press.

Ahrbeck, R., and E. Hirsch. 1970. *Studien über den Philanthropismus und die Dessauer Aufklärung. Vorträge zur Geistesgeschichte des Dessau-Wörlitzer Kulturkreises.* Halle, Saale: Martin-Luther-Universität.

Anderson, B. 1983. *Imagined Communities: Reflections on the Origins and Spread of Nationalism.* London: Verso.

Angelus, A., and U. Neumann. 1994. *Die Auswirkung der Restrukturierung der chemischen Industrie in Sachsen-Anhalt auf die wirtschaftliche Entwicklung in den Landkreisen Bitterfeld und Merseburg-Querfurt: Erste Bestandaufnahme im Dezember 1994.* Magdeburg: Gesellschaft zur Förderung arbeitsorientierter innovativer Strukturentwicklung in Sachsen-Anhalt e.V.

Appadurai, A. 1992. "Putting Hierarchy in Its Place." In *Rereading Cultural Anthropology,* ed. G. E. Marcus, 34–47. Durham, NC: Duke University Press.

———. 1996. *Modernity at Large.* Minneapolis: University of Minnesota Press.

Applebaum, A. 1994. *Between East and West: Across the Borderlands of Europe.* New York: Pantheon.

Arato, A. 1994. "Revolution, Restoration, and Legitimization: Ideological Problems of the Transition from State Socialism." In *Envisioning Eastern Europe: Postcommunist Cultural Studies,* ed. M. Kennedy, 180–246. Ann Arbor: University of Michigan Press.

Arbeitsamt Dessau. 1995. "Der Arbeitsmarkt im Monat April, 1995." Presseinformation, Arbeitsamt Dessau, Abt. Statistik.

Aronowitz, S. 1994. *Dead Artists, Live Theories, and Other Cultural Problems.* New York: Routledge.

Arutiunian, Iu. V., and E. T. Karapetian. 1986. *Naselenie Erevana: Etnosotsiologicheskie issledovaniia* (The Population of Yerevan: Ethnosociological Investigations). Yerevan: Itdatel'stvo Akademiia Nauk Armianskoi SSSR.

Asad, T. 1983. "Notes on Body Pain and Truth in Medieval Christian Ritual." *Economy and Society* 12 (3): 287–327.

Aslund, A. 1992. *Post-Communist Economic Revolutions: How Big a Bang?* Washington, DC: Center for Strategic and International Studies.

Avenary, H. 1985. *Kantor Salomon Sulzer und seine Zeit: Eine Dokumentation.* Sigmaringen: Jan Thorbecke.

Baburov, A., et al. 1971. *The Ideal Communist City.* New York: George Braziller.

Bahr, E. 1990. *Sieben Tage im Oktober: Aufbruch in Dresden* (Seven Days in October: Uprising in Dresden). Leipzig: Forum.

Bahro, R. 1995. "Das Buch von der Befreiung aus dem Untergang der DDR: Dabei über das scheinbar abseitige Thema Ökologie und Kommunismus." Unpublished manuscript in possession of author.

Bakhtin, M. 1984. *Problems of Dostoevsky's Poetics.* Minneapolis: University of Minnesota Press.

Barsegian, I. Forthcoming. "When Text becomes Field: Doing Fieldwork in Postcommunist Countries." In *Fieldwork Dilemmas: Anthropologists in Postsocialist States,* ed. H. G. De Soto and N. Dudwick. Madison: University of Wisconsin Press.

Baselgia, G. 1993. *Galizien.* Frankfurt am Main: Jüdischer Verlag.

Basso, K. 1992. "Nostalgia—A Polemic." In *Rereading Cultural Anthropology,* ed. G. E. Marcus, 220–51. Durham, NC: Duke University Press.

Behnk, A., and R. Westerwelle. 1995. *Die Frauen von ORWO: 13 Lebensbilder.* Leipzig: Gustav Kiepenheuer.

Benická, L. 1996. Personal communication.

Benoschofsky, I., and A. Scheiber, eds. 1987. *The Jewish Museum of Budapest.* Trans. Joseph W. Weisenberg. Budapest: Covina.

Berdahl, D. 1994. "Voices at the Wall: Discourses of Self, History, and National Identity at the Vietnam Veterans' Memorial." *History and Memory* 6 (2): 88–124.

———. 1997. "Dis-Membering the Past: The Politics of Memory in the German Borderland." In *A User's Guide to German Cultural Studies,* ed. Scott Dedham, Irene Kacandes, and Jonathan Petropoulos, 209–32. Ann Arbor: University of Michigan Press.

———. 1999. *Where the World Ended: Re-unification and Identity in the German Borderland.* Berkeley: University of California Press.

Berdiaev, N. 1947. *The Russian Idea.* London: Centenary.

———. 1955. *The Meaning of Creativity.* Trans. D. A. Levine. New York: Harper.

Berend, T. I. 1990. *The Hungarian Economic Reforms, 1953–1988.* Cambridge: Cambridge University Press.

Berger, B. 1981. *The Survival of a Counterculture: Ideological Work and Everyday Life among Rural Communards.* Berkeley: University of California Press.

Berry, E., ed. 1995. *Post-Communism and the Body Politic.* New York: New York University Press.

Betts, P. 1995. "The Pathos of Everyday Objects: West German Industrial Design Culture, 1945–1965." Ph.D. diss., University of Chicago.

———. 1996. "The Bauhaus as Cold-War Legend: West German Modernism Revisited." *German Politics and Society* 14 (2): 75–100.

Beyme, K. v. 1996. *Transition to Democracy in Eastern Europe.* New York: St. Martin's.

Bhabha, H. 1994. *The Location of Culture.* London: Routledge.

"Bitterfeld möblet die Umwelt auf." 1994. *Express* (Bitterfeld), February 10, 4.

Bittner, St. B. N.d. "Green Cities and Orderly Spaces: Space and Culture in Moscow, 1928–1933." Department of History, University of Chicago.

Bleys, R. 1996. *The Geography of Perversion: Male-to-Male Sexual Behavior outside the West and the Ethnographic Imagination, 1750–1918.* London: Cassell.

Blunt, A. 1994. *Travel, Gender, and Imperialism: Mary Kingsley and West Africa.* New York: Guilford.

Bogartyrev, O. 1996. "Ne xodi s tolpoj tsyganok za kibitkoj kochevoj." *Moja Gazeta,* Samara, February 24–January 3, 3.

Bohlman, P. V. 1993. "Musical Life in the Central European Jewish Village." *Studies in Contemporary Jewry* 9:17–39.

———. 1994. "Auf der Bima—Auf der Bühne. Zur Emanzipation der jüdischen Popularmusik im Wien der Jahrhundertwende." In *Vergleichend-systematische Musikwissenschaft: Franz Födermayr zum 60. Geburtstag,* ed. E. T. Hilscher and T. Antonicek, 417–49. Tutzing: Hans Schneider.

———. 1996a. "The Akedah and the Embodiment of Music: On the Origins of Music in Jewish Thought." *Makorot/Sources* 2:52–58.

———. 1996b. "The Final Borderpost." *Journal of Musicology* 14 (4): 427–52.

———. 1997. "Fieldwork in the Ethnomusicological Past." In *Shadows in the Field: New Perspectives in Ethnomusicological Fieldwork,* ed. G. F. Barz and T. Cooley, 139–62. New York: Oxford University Press.

———. Forthcoming. *"Jüdische Volksmusik"—Eine europäische Geistesgeschichte.* Vienna: Böhlan Verlag.

Boissevain, J., ed. 1996. *Coping with Tourists: European Reactions to Mass Tourism.* Oxford: Berghahn.

Bollerup, S. R., and C. Christensen, eds. 1997. *Nationalism in Eastern Europe: Causes and Consequences of the National Revivals and Conflicts in Late Twentieth Century Eastern Europe.* New York: St. Martin's.

Bonnel, V. E., A. Cooper, and G. Freidin, eds. 1994. *Russia at the Barricades: Eyewitness Accounts of the August 1991 Coup.* New York: M. E. Sharpe.

Boone, J. 1995a. "Rubbing Aladdin's Lamp." In *Negotiating Lesbian and Gay Subjects,* ed. M. Dorenkamp and R. Henke, 149–77. New York: Routledge.

———. 1995b. "Vacation Cruises; or, The Homoerotics of Orientalism." *PMLA* 110 (1): 89–107.

Bourdieu, P. 1977. *Outline of a Theory of Practice.* Cambridge: Cambridge University Press.

———. 1980. "The Aristocracy of Culture." Trans. R. Nice. *Media, Culture and Society* 2 (3): 225–54.

———. 1991. *Language and Symbolic Power.* Cambridge: Harvard University Press.

Boyarin, J., ed. 1994. *Remapping Memory: The Politics of Timespace.* Minneapolis: University of Minnesota Press.

Boym, S. 1994a. "The Archeology of Banality: The Soviet Home." *Public Culture* 6:263–92.

———. 1994b. *Common Places: Mythologies of Everyday Life in Russia.* Cambridge: Harvard University Press.

Bringa, T. 1995. *Being Muslim the Bosnian Way.* Princeton: Princeton University Press.

Brooks, J. 1984. *When Russia Learned to Read.* Princeton: Princeton University Press.

Broun, J. 1988. *Conscience and Captivity: Religion in Eastern Europe.* Washington, DC: Ethics and Policy Center.

Brown, K. Forthcoming. "Would the Real Nationalists Please Step Forward: Destructive Narration in Macedonia." In *Fieldwork Dilemmas: Anthropologists in Postsocialist States,* ed. N. Dudwick and H. De Soto. Madison: University of Wisconsin Press.

Brumfield, W. C., and B. Ruble, eds. 1993. *Russian Housing in the Modern Age: Design and Social History.* New York: Woodrow Wilson Center.

Buber, M. 1949. *Die Erzählungen der Chassidim.* Zurich: Manesse.

Buckley, C. 1995. "The Myth of Managed Migration: Migration Control and Market in the Soviet Period." *Slavic Review* 54 (4): 896–916.

Bundesministerium für innerdeutsche Beziehungen, ed. 1975. "Feiern, Sozialistische." In *DDR Handbuch,* 291. Cologne: Wissenschaft und Politik.

Bunzl, M. 1995. "On the Politics and Semantics of Austrian Memory: Vienna's Monument against War and Fascism." *History and Memory* 7 (2): 7–40.

———. 1996. "The City and the Self: Narratives of Spatial Belonging among Austrian Jews." *City and Society: Journal of the Society for Urban Anthropology,* 50–81.

———. 1997. "Outing as Performance/Outing as Resistance: A Queer Reading of Austrian (Homo)Sexualities." *Cultural Anthropology* 12 (1): 129–51.

Burke, P. 1989. "History as Social Memory." In *Memory: History, Culture and the Mind,* ed. T. Butler, 97–113. London: Blackwell.

Burrichter, C., and G. Schödl, eds. 1992. *Ohne Erinnerung keine Zukunft!* (Without Memory No Future!). Cologne: Wissenschaft und Politik.

Carruthers, M. 1990. *The Book of Memory: A Study of Memory in Medieval Culture.* Cambridge: Cambridge University Press.

Catton, W. R., and R. Dunlap. 1980. "A New Ecological Paradigm for Post-Exuberant Sociology." *American Behavioral Scientist* 24:15–47.

Chekhov, A. P. 1985. *Pripadok* (The Attack). Moscow: Pravda.

Cherniavsky, M. 1969. *Tsar and People: Studies in Russian Myths.* New York: Random House.

Clifford, J. 1986a. "Introduction: Partial Truths." In *Writing Culture: The Poetics of Ethnography,* ed. J. Clifford and G. Marcus, 1–26. Berkeley: University of California.

———. 1986b. *The Predicament of Culture: Twentieth-Century Ethnography, Literature, and Art.* Cambridge: Harvard University Press.

Comaroff, J. L., and J. Comaroff. 1992. *Ethnography and the Historical Imagination.* Boulder, CO: Westview.

Condee, N. 1995. "The ABC of Russian Consumer Culture." In *Soviet Hieroglyphics: Visual Culture in Late Twentieth Century Russia,* ed. Condee, 130–72. Bloomington: Indiana University Press.

Connerton, P. 1989. *How Societies Remember.* Cambridge: Cambridge University Press.

Corbusier, Le. 1964. *The Radiant City.* New York: Orion Press.

———. 1986. *Towards a New Architecture.* New York: Dover.

Cotgrove, S. 1983. *Catastrophe or Cornucopia: The Environment, Politics, and the Future.* New York: Wiley.

Crapanzano, V. 1980. *Tuhami: Portrait of a Moroccan.* Chicago: University of Chicago Press.

———. 1992. *Hermes' Dilemma and Hamlet's Desire: On the Epistemology of Interpretation.* Cambridge: Harvard University Press.

Creed, G. 1995. "An Old Song in a New Voice: Decollectivization in Bulgaria." In *East European Communities: The Struggle for Balance in Turbulent Times,* ed. D. Kideckel, 25–45. Boulder, CO: Westview.

Creuziger, C. 1993. "Childhood in Russia: Representation and Reality." Ph.D. diss., University of Chicago.

Cushman, T. 1991. "Rich Rastas and Communist Rockers: A Comparative Study of the Origin, Diffusion, and Defusion of Revolutionary Musical Codes." *Journal of Popular Culture* 3:17–58.

———. 1995. *Notes from Underground: Rock Music Counterculture in Russia.* Albany: State University of New York Press.

Dahn, D. 1991. "Conformists Like Me." *New German Critique* 52:50–59.

———. 1994. *Wir bleiben hier oder wem gehört der Osten.* Hamburg: Rowohlt.

Dal', V. 1955 (1881). *Tolkovyi Slovar' Zhivago Velikoruskago Iazyka.* Moscow: Gosudarstvennoe Izdatel'stvo Inostrannykh i Natsional'nykh Slovarei. St. Petersburg, Moscow: Izdanie Knigoprodavtsa-Tipografa M. O. Vol'fa.

Dalton, R. J., and N. Lovrich. 1993. "Environmental Attitudes and the New Environmental Paradigm." Paper presented at the conference on "Critical Masses: Public Responses to the Environmental Consequences of Nuclear Weapons Production in Russia and the United States," University of California-Irvine.

Dávid, F. 1978. *A soproni ó-zsinagóga.* Budapest: A Magyar Izraeliták Országos Képviseletének Kiadása.

Debord, G. 1994 (1967). *The Society of the Spectacle.* New York: Zone Books.

De Certeau, M. 1988. *The Practice of Everyday Life.* Trans. Steven Randall. Berkeley: University of California Press.

Denich, B. 1994. "Dismembering Yugoslavia: Nationalist Ideologies and Symbolic Revival." *American Ethnologist* 21:367–90.

De Soto, H. G. 1994. " 'In the Name of the Folk': Women and Nation in the New Germany." *Women's Law Journal* 51:83–102.

———. 1996. "(Re)Inventing Berlin: Dialectics of Power, Symbols, and Pasts, 1990–1995." *City and Society,* 29–49.

De Soto, H. G., and D. G. Anderson, eds. 1993. *The Curtain Rises: Rethinking Culture, Ideology, and the State in Eastern Europe.* Atlantic Highlands, NJ: Humanities Press.

De Soto, H. G., and N. Dudwick, eds. Forthcoming. *Fieldwork Dilemmas: Anthropologists in Postsocialist States.* Madison: University of Wisconsin Press.

Deutsch, K. 1953. *Nationalism and Social Communication: An Inquiry into the Foundations of Nationality.* Cambridge: MIT Press.

Dicks, H. V. 1967. "Some Notes on the Russian National Character." In *The Transformation of Russian Society: Aspects of Social Change since 1861,* ed. C. E. Black. Cambridge: Harvard University Press.

Dobson, A. 1990. *Green Political Thought.* London: Harper-Collins.

Dohrn, V. 1991. *Reise nach Galizien: Grenzlandschaften des alten Europa.* Frankfurt am Main: S. Fischer.

———. 1994. *Baltische Reise: Vielvölkerlandschaft des alten Europa.* Frankfurt am Main: S. Fischer.

Dölling, I. 1991. "Between Hope and Helplessness: Women in the GDR after the 'Turning Point.'" *Feminist Review* 39:3–15.

Dostoevsky, F. 1982. *Sobranie Sochinenie v dvenadsati tomakh* (Collected Works in Twelve Volumes). Vol. 3, *Gambler, Notes from the Dead House.* Moscow: Pravda.

———. 1985. *Polnoe Sobranie Sochinenii v tridsati tomakh* (Complete Collected Works in Thirty Volumes). Vol. 28. Leningrad: Nauka.

Downing, J. 1996. *Internationalizing Media Theory: Transition, Power, Culture.* London: Sage.

Drakulic, S. 1991. *How We Survived Communism and Even Laughed.* New York: Norton.

Druts, E., and A. Gessler. 1990. *Tsygane* (Gypsies). Moscow: Sovietskij Pisatel'.

Dudwick, N. 1993. "Armenia: The Nation Awakens." In *Nations and Politics in the Soviet Successor States,* ed. I. Bremmer and R. Taras, 261–87. Cambridge: Cambridge University Press.

———. 1994. "Memory, Identity, and Politics in Armenia." Ph.D. diss., University of Pennsylvania.

Dunham, V. S. 1990. *In Stalin's Time: Middle-Class Values in Soviet Fiction.* Durham, NC: Duke University Press.

Dunlop, R., and K. Van Liere. 1978. "The Environmental Paradigm." *Journal of Environmental Education* 9:10–19.

Eagleton, T. 1983. *Literary Theory: An Introduction.* Minneapolis: University of Minnesota Press.

Eckert, R., Alexander von Plato, and Jörn Schütrumf, eds. 1991. *Wendezeiten—Zeitenwende: Zur "Entnazifizierung" und "Entstalinizierung."* Hamburg: Ergebnisse.

Efimova, A., and L. Manovich, eds. and trans. 1993. *Tekstura: Russian Essays on Visual Culture.* Chicago: University of Chicago Press.

Eidson, J. 1990. "German Club Life as a Local Cultural System." *Comparative Studies in Society and History* 30 (2): 357–82.

Elbogen, I. 1993. *Jewish Liturgy: A Comprehensive History.* Trans. R. P. Scheindlin. Philadelphia and New York: Jewish Publication Society and Jewish Theological Seminary of America.

Eliade, M. 1959. *The Sacred and the Profane: The Nature of Religion.* San Diego: Harcourt Brace.

Emin, G. 1983. *Seven Songs about Armenia.* Yerevan: Sovetakan Grogh.

Ernst, A. 1987. *Geschichte des Burgenlandes.* Vienna: Verlag für Geschichte und Politik.

Faulenbach, B., M. Meckel, and H. Weber, eds. 1994. *Die Partei hatte immer Recht—Aufarbeitung von Geschichte und Folgen der SED-Diktatur.* Essen: Klartext.

Featherstone, M. 1995. "Global Culture: An Introduction." In *Global Culture: Nationalism, Globalization, and Modernity,* ed. M. Featherstone, 1–14. London: Sage.

FeLugossy, L. 1993. Personal interview, Budapest.

Fentress, J., and C. Wickham. 1992. *Social Memory.* Cambridge, MA: Blackwell.

Fernandez, J. 1986. *Persuasions and Performances: The Play of Tropes in Culture.* Bloomington: Indiana University Press.

Fitzpatrick, S. 1993. *The Cultural Front: Power and Culture in Revolutionary Russia.* Ithaca: Cornell University Press.

Forgács, É. 1994. "A Valóság Fogalmának Változása a 80-as Évek Magyar Müvészetében." In *A Modern Posztjai: Esszék, Tanulmányok, Dokumentumok a 80-as Évek Magyar kÈpzömüvészetéröl,* ed. K. Keserü, 15–27. Budapest: Eotuus Lorand University, Faculty of Humanities.

Foucault, M. 1978. *The History of Sexuality.* Vol. 1, *An Introduction.* New York: Vintage.

———. 1982. *Discipline and Punish.* New York: Vintage.

———. 1984. "Space, Power and Knowledge" (interview with Paul Rabinow). In *The Foucault Reader,* ed. Paul Rabinow, 239–56. New York: Pantheon.

Frank, B. G. 1996. *A Travel Guide to Jewish Europe.* 2d ed. Gretna: Pelican.

Friedland, R., and D. Boden, eds. 1994. *NowHere: Space, Time, and Modernity.* Berkeley: University of California Press.

Friedrich, P. 1979. *Language, Context, and the Imagination: Essays by Paul Friedrich.* Stanford, CA: Stanford University Press.

———, trans. 1994. *Tiutchev's* Silentium: *The InterGalactic Poetry Messenger.*

Frigyesi, J. 1993. "Jews and Hungarians in Modern Hungarian Musical Culture." *Studies in Contemporary Jewry* 9:40–60.

Gal, S. 1991. "Bartok's Funeral: Representations of Europe in Hungarian Political Rhetoric." *American Ethnologist* 18 (3): 440–48.

———. 1994. "Gender in the Post-Socialist Transition: The Abortion Debate in Hungary." *East European Politics and Societies* 9 (2): 256–86.

———. 1995. "Language and the 'Arts of Resistance.'" *Cultural Anthropology* 10 (3): 407–24.

———. 1996. "Feminism and Civil Society." *Replika*, 75–82.

———. Forthcoming. "Feminism and Civil Society." In *Transitions, Environments, Translations: The Meanings of Feminism in Contemporary Politics*, ed. J. Scott and C. Kaplan. New York: Routledge.

Gallagher, C. 1986. "The Body versus the Social Body in the Works of Thomas Malthus and Henry Mayhew." *Representations* 14: 86–106.

Garb, P. 1993. "Environmental Thinking among Environmental Leaders in Russia." Paper presented at the conference on "Critical Masses: Public Responses to the Environmental Consequences of Nuclear Weapons Production in Russia and the United States," University of California-Irvine.

———. 1994. "Sociocultural Responses to Radiation Contamination in Russia and Some Comparisons with the United States." Paper presented at the American Anthropological Association annual meeting, Atlanta, GA.

Garton Ash, T. 1989. "Reform or Revolution?" In *The Uses of Adversity: Essays on the Fate of Central Europe*, by T. Garton Ash, 218–74. Cambridge: Granta.

Gazda, A., ed. 1989. *Magyarországi Zsinagógák*. Budapest: Müszaki Känyvkiadó.

Gellner, E. 1983. *Nations and Nationalism*. Ithaca: Cornell University Press.

———. 1992. "Nationalism in the Vacuum." In *Thinking Theoretically about Soviet Nationalisms: History and Comparison in the Study of the USSR.*, ed. Alexander Motyl. New York: Columbia University Press.

Giddens, A. 1979. *Central Problems in Social Theory: Action, Structure, and Contradiction in Social Analysis*. Berkeley: University of California Press.

Gillis, J. R. 1994. "Memory and Identity: The History of a Relationship." In *Commemorations: The Politics of National Identity*, ed. J. R. Gillis, 3–23. Princeton: Princeton University Press.

Gilman, S. 1985. *Difference and Pathology: Stereotypes of Sexuality, Race, and Madness*. Ithaca: Cornell University Press.

Girenko, N. M. 1984. "Systems of Kinship Terms and Systems of Social Categories." In *Kinship and Marriage in the Soviet Union*, ed. T. Dragadze. London: Routledge.

GKPIT. *Moskovskij Metropoliten (Metodicheskie rekomendatsii k ekskursii)*. 1984. Moscow: USSR State Committee for Foreign Tourism.

Gluckman, M. 1982. *Custom and Conflict in Africa*. Oxford: Blackwell.

Gordy, E. 1997. *The Destruction of Alternatives: Everyday Life in Nationalist Authoritarianism*. Ph.D. diss., University of California-Berkeley.

Gorer, G., and J. Rickman. 1949. *The People of Great Russia: A Psychological Study.* London: Cresset.

Goven, J. 1993. "Gender Politics in Hungary: Autonomy and Antifeminism." In *Gender Politics and Post-Communism: Reflections from Eastern Europe and the Former Soviet Union,* ed. Nanette Furk and Magda Mueller, 224–40. New York: Routledge.

Graupner, H. 1995. "Sexualität, Jugendschutz und Menschenrechte: Über das Recht von Kindern und Jugendlichen auf sexuelle Selbstbestimmung." 2 vols. Ph.D. diss., University of Vienna.

Greenberg, J. B., and T. K. Park. 1994. "Political Ecology." *Journal of Political Ecology* 1:1–12.

Greenfeld, L. 1992. *Nationalism: Five Roads to Modernity.* Cambridge: Harvard University Press.

Grossberg, L. 1992. *We Gotta Get Out of This Place: Popular Conservatism and Postmodern Culture.* New York: Routledge.

Grove-White, R. 1993. "Environmentalism: A New Moral Discourse for Technological Society?" In *Environmentalism: The View from Anthropology,* ed. K. Milton, 18–30. London: Routledge.

Groys, B. 1993 (1987). "Stalinism as Aesthetic Phenomenon." In *Tekstura: Russian Essays on Visual Culture,* ed. A. Efimova and L. Manovich, 115–26. Chicago: University of Chicago Press.

Gruber, R. E. 1992. *Jewish Heritage Travel: A Guide to Central and Eastern Europe.* New York: Wiley.

———. 1994. *Upon the Doorposts of Thy House: Jewish Life in East-Central Europe, Yesterday and Today.* New York: Wiley.

Guttmann, H. Z. 1989. *Vom Tempel zum Gemeindezentrum: Synagogen im Nachkriegsdeutschland.* Frankfurt am Main: Jüdischer.

Habermas, J. 1992. "Bemerkungen zu einer verworrenen Diskussion." *Die Zeit,* April 3, 82–84.

Hafner, K. 1995. *The House at the Bridge: A Story of Modern Germany.* New York: Scribner.

Hajnóczy, C. 1993. Personal interview, Budapest.

Halbwachs, M. 1980. *The Collective Memory.* New York: Harper and Row.

———. 1992 (1952). *On Collective Memory.* Ed. and trans. Lewis A. Coser, Chicago: University of Chicago Press.

Halter, R., ed. 1991.*Vom Bauhaus bis Bitterfeld: 41 Jahre DDR Design.* Giessen: Anabas.

Handl, M., G. Hauer, K. Krickler, F. Nussbaumer, and D. Schmutzer, eds. 1989. *Homosexualität in Österreich.* Vienna: Junius.

Handler, R. 1988. *Nationalism and the Politics of Culture in Quebec.* Madison: University of Wisconsin Press.

Hankiss, E. 1989. *Kelet-Európai Alternatívák.* Budapest: Közgazdasági és Jogi Könyvkiadó. Published in English as *East-European Alternatives: Are There Any?* Oxford: Oxford University Press, 1990.

Hann, C. M. 1993. "Introduction: Social Anthropology and Socialism." In *Social-*

ism: Ideals, Ideologies, and Local Practice, ed. C. M. Hann, 1–26. London: Routledge.

Hannerz, U. 1996. *Transnational Connections: Culture, People, Places.* New York: Routledge.

Harakas, S. S. 1990. *Health and Medicine in the Eastern Orthodox Tradition: Faith, Liturgy, and Wholeness.* New York: Crossroad.

Harkin, M. 1995. "Modernist Anthropology and Tourism of the Authentic." *Annals of Tourism Research* 22 (3): 650–70.

Harvey, D. 1990. *The Condition of Postmodernity.* Cambridge: Blackwell.

Hauner, Milan. 1990. *What Is Asia to Us?: Russia's Asian Heartland Yesterday and Today.* London: Routledge.

Hayden, R. 1995. "Recounting the Dead: The Rediscovery and Redefinition of Wartime Massacres in Late and Post-Communist Yugoslavia." In *Memory, History, and Opposition under State Socialism,* ed. R. Watson, 167–84. Santa Fe, NM: School of American Research Press.

———. 1996. "Imagined Communities and Real Victims: Self-Determination and Ethnic Cleansing in Yugoslavia." *American Ethnologist* 23 (4): 783–801.

Heiduczek, W. 1977. *Tod am Meer.* Halle: Mitteldeutscher.

Helms, M. 1988. *Ulysses' Sail: An Ethnographic Odyssey of Power, Knowledge, and Geographical Distance.* Princeton: Princeton University Press.

Herzfeld, M. 1997. *Cultural Intimacy: Social Poetics in the Nation-State.* New York: Routledge.

Hirsch, E. 1985. *Dessau: Wörlitz: Zierde und Inbegriff des XVIII. Jahrhunderts.* Munich: Beck.

———. 1989. *Wörlitzer Anlagen.* Leipzig: Brockhaus.

Hobsbawm, E. 1983. "Introduction: Inventing Traditions." In *The Invention of Tradition,* ed. E. Hobsbawm and T. Ranger, 1–14. Cambridge: Cambridge University Press.

———. 1990. *Nations and Nationalism since 1780.* Cambridge: Cambridge University Press.

Hobsbawm, E., and T. Ranger, eds. 1983. *The Invention of Tradition.* New York: Cambridge University Press.

Hockenos, P. 1993. *Free to Hate: The Rise of the Right in Post-Communist Eastern Europe.* New York: Routledge.

Hoffman, E. 1993. *Exit into History: A Journey through the New Eastern Europe.* New York: Penguin.

Hoffmann, C. 1992. *Stunden Null? Vergangenheitsbewältigung in Deutschland 1945 und 1989* (Zero Hours? Overcoming the Past in Germany 1945 and 1989). Bonn: Bouvier.

Holston, J. 1989. *The Modernist City.* Chicago: University of Chicago Press.

Holy, L. 1996. *The Little Czech and the Great Czech Nation: National Identity and the Post-Communist Transformation of Society.* Cambridge: Cambridge University Press.

Hoogasian-Villa, S. 1982. *Armenian Village Life before 1914.* Detroit: Wayne State University Press.

Howard, J., and J. Streck. 1996. "The Splintered Art World of Contemporary Christian Music." *Popular Music* 15 (1): 37–53.

Huizinga. J. 1950. *Homo Ludens: A Study of the Play Element in Culture.* Boston: Beacon Press.

Human Rights Watch—Helsinki. 1995. "Crime or Simply Punishment? Racist Attacks by Moscow Law Enforcement." 12 (September).

Humphrey, C. 1993. "Myth-Making, Narratives, and the Dispossessed in Russia." Keynote speech presented to the Society of the Anthropology of Europe at the 1993 meeting of the American Anthropological Association, Washington, DC.

———. 1994. "Remembering an 'Enemy': The Bogd Khan in Twentieth Century Mongolia." In *Memory, History, and Opposition under State Socialism,* ed. R. S. Watson, 21–44. Santa Fe, NM: School of American Research Press.

———. 1995. "Creating a Culture of Disillusionment: Consumption in Moscow, a Chronicle of Changing Times." In *Worlds Apart: Modernity through the Prism of the Local,* ed. D. Miller, 43–61. London: Routledge.

Hyam, R. 1990. *Empire and Sexuality: The British Experience.* Manchester: Manchester University Press.

Idelsohn, A. Z. 1914–32. *Hebräisch-orientalischer Melodienschatz.* 10 vols. Berlin et al.: Benjamin Harz et al.

Ivanits, L. J. 1992. *Russian Folk Belief.* Armonk, NY: M. E. Sharpe.

Jakobson, R. 1987. *Language in Literature.* Cambridge: Belknap Press of Harvard University Press.

Jarintzov, M. N. 1916. *The Russians and Their Language.* Oxford: Blackwell.

Jeffries, I. 1993. *Socialist Economies and the Transition to the Market: A Guide.* New York: Routledge.

Jessop, B. 1983. *Theories of the State.* New York: New York University Press.

Judson, P. 1993. "Inventing Germans: Class, Nationality and Colonial Fantasy at the Margins of the Habsburg Monarchy." *Social Analysis* 33: 47–67.

Kamarás, F., and I. Monigl. 1984. "A Demográfiai Folyamatok És az Ifjúság" (Demographic Processes and Youth). In *A Magyar Ifjúság a Nyolcvanas Években,* 69–119. Budapest: Kossuth.

Kamondy, Á. 1993. Personal interview, Budapest.

Karatnycky, A., A. Motyl, and B. Shor, eds. 1997. *Nations in Transit, 1997: Civil Society, Democracy, and Markets in East Central Europe and the Newly Independent States.* New Brunswick, NJ: Transaction.

Karp, I., C. M. Kreamer, and S. D. Lavine, eds. 1992. *Museums and Communities: The Politics of Public Culture.* Washington, DC: Smithsonian Institution Press.

Kearney, M. 1996. *Reconceptualizing the Peasantry: Anthropology in Global Perspective.* Boulder, CO: Westview.

Kennan, G. 1981. *Und der Zar ist weit: Siberien 1885.* Berlin: Rütten and Loening. Originally published in English as *Siberia and the Exile System.* London: Osgood, McIlvaine, 1891.

Kennedy, M., ed. 1994. *Envisioning Eastern Europe: Postcommunist Cultural Studies.* Ann Arbor: University of Michigan Press.

Kideckel, D. 1993. *The Solitude of Collectivism: Romanian Villagers to the Revolution and Beyond.* Ithaca: Cornell University Press.

————, ed. 1995. *East European Communities: The Struggle for Balance in Turbulent Times.* Boulder, CO: Westview.

Kilbourne Matossian, M. 1962. *The Impact of Soviet Policies in Armenia.* Leiden: E. J. Brill.

Kirpichnikov, A. 1996. "Korruptsija i Zakon v Russkom Soznanii." *Zvesda* 1:159–69.

Kiss, C. 1963. "Foldalatti Moszkva." In *Moszkva és Környéke,* trans. Miklós Vörös, 88–92. Budapest: Panorama.

Kistamás, L. 1993. Personal interview, Budapest.

Kligman, G. 1990. "Reclaiming the Public: A Reflection on Creating Civil Society in Romania." East European Politics and Societies 4 (3): 393–438.

————. 1992. "The Politics of Reproduction in Ceaucescu's Romania: A Case Study in Political Culture." *East European Politics and Societies* 6: 364–418.

Klíma, I. 1994. "Progress in Prague." *Granta* 47:249–55.

Knowlton, J., and T. Cates, trans. 1993. *Forever in the Shadow of Hitler?* Atlantic Highlands, NJ: Humanities Press.

Kohlbauer-Fritz, G. 1993. "Zur Geschichte der Juden in Lemberg." In *Lemberg/L'viv, 1772–1918: Wiederbegegnung mit einer Landeshauptstadt der Donaumonarchie,* ed. Hans Bisanz, 17–21. Vienna: Eigenverlag der Museen der Stadt Wien.

Konrád, G. 1989. *Antipolitika: Az Autonómia Kisértése* (Antipolitics: The Temptation of Autonomy). Budapest: Codex RT.

Konrad, G., and I. Szelenyi. 1979. *The Intellectuals on the Road to Class Power.* New York: Harcourt Brace Jovanovich.

Konstantinov, Y. 1996. "Patterns of Interpretation: Trader-Tourism in the Balkans (Bulgaria) as a Picaresque Metaphorical Enactment of Post-Totalitarianism." *American Ethnologist* 23 (4): 762–82.

Kornai, J. 1992. *The Socialist System: The Political Economy of Communism.* Princeton: Princeton University Press.

Körösényi, A. 1992. "The Decay of Communist Rule in Hungary." In *Post-Communist Transition: Emerging Pluralism in Hungary,* ed. A. Bozóki, A. Körösényi, and G. Schöpflin, 1–13. New York: St. Martin's.

Kovacs, J. M. 1994. *Transition to Capitalism? The Communist Legacy in Eastern Europe.* New Brunswick, NJ: Transaction.

Kozminski, A. K. 1993. *Catching Up? Organizational and Management Change in the Ex-Socialist Block.* Albany: State University of New York Press.

Krinsky, C. H. 1985. *Synagogues of Europe.* New York: Architectural History Foundation.

Krisch, H. 1985. *The German Democratic Republic: The Search for Identity.* Boulder, CO: Westview.

Kuczynski, J. 1984. *Dialog mit meinem Urenkel.* Berlin: Aufbau.

Kürti, L. 1994. "How Can I Be a Human Being? Culture, Youth, and Musical Opposition in Hungary." In *Rocking the State: Rock Music and Politics in Eastern Europe and Russia,* ed. S. Ramet, 73–103. Boulder, CO: Westview.

Kürti, L., and J. Langman, eds. 1997. *Beyond Borders: Remaking Cultural Identities in the New East and Central Europe.* Boulder, CO: Westview.

Küttler, W. 1992. "Kontexte und Merkmale eines Paradigmawechsels? Das Jahr 1989 und die Konsequenzen für die Geschichtswissenschaft der DDR." In *Ohne Erinnerung keine Zukunft!,* ed. C. Bürrichter and G. Schödl, 65–78. Cologne: Verlag Wissenschaft und Politik.

Lampland, M. 1990. "The Politics of History: Historical Consciousness of 1847–1849." *Hungarian Studies* 6 (2): 85–194.

———. 1995. *The Object of Labor: Commodification in Socialist Hungary.* Chicago: University of Chicago Press.

Landmann, S. 1995. *Mein Galizien: Das Land hinter den Karpaten.* Munich: Herbig.

Lane, C. 1995. *The Ruling Passion: British Colonial Allegory and the Paradox of Homosexual Desire.* Durham, NC: Duke University Press.

Lanfant, F., J. Allcock, and E. Bruner, eds. 1995 *International Tourism: Identity and Change.* London: Sage.

Lass, A. 1994. "From Memory to History: The Events of November 17 Dis/membered." In *Memory, History and Opposition under State Socialism,* ed. R. Watson, 87–104. Santa Fe, NM: School of American Research Press.

Lavigne, M. 1995. *The Economics of Transition: From Socialist Economy to Market Economy.* New York: St. Martin's.

Leifer, A. E. 1984. *Dostoevskii i Omsk: Glavnyi zal omskogo literaturnogo muzeia imeni F. M. Dostoevskogo.* Ed. I. A. Makarov. Omsk: Omsk Region Department of Culture and Omsk State F. M. Dostoevsky Historical and Literary Museum.

Lemke, C. 1992. "Trials and Tribulations: The *Stasi* Legacy in Contemporary German Politics." *German Politics and Society* 26:43–53.

Lemon, A. 1995. " 'What Are They Writing about Us Blacks?' Roma and Race in Russia." *Anthropology of East Europe Review* 13 (2): 34–40.

———. 1996. "Indic Diaspora, Soviet History, Russian Home: Political Performances and Sincere Ironies in Romani Cultures." Ph.D. diss., University of Chicago.

Levine, L. 1988. *Highbrow/Lowbrow: The Emergence of Cultural Hierarchy in America.* Cambridge: Harvard University Press.

Liebsch, H. 1991. *Dresdner Stundenbuch: Protokoll einer Beteiligten im Herbst 1989.* Wuppertal: Peter Hammer.

Lipsitz, G. 1994. *Dangerous Crossroads: Popular Music, Postmodernism, and the Poetics of Place.* New York: Verso.

Lotman, Y. 1994. *Besedy o russkoi kul'ture.* St. Petersburg, Russia: Iskusstvo-SPB.

Lüdtke, A. 1983. " 'The Historiography of 'Everyday Life': The Personal and the Political." In *Culture, Ideology and Politics: Essays in Honor of Eric Hobs-*

bawm, ed. R. Samuel and S. Jones, 38–54. London: Routledge and Kegan Paul.

———. 1995. "Introduction: What Is the History of Everyday Life and Who Are Its Practitioners?" In *The History of Everyday Life: Reconstructing Historical Experiences and Ways of Life,* ed. A. Lüdtke, trans. W. Templer, 4–30. Princeton: Princeton University Press.

Luft, C. 1996. *Die Lust am Eigentum.* Zurich: Orell Füssli.

Luft, H. 1997. *Landwirtschaft Ost kontra Treuhandmodell.* Berlin: Dietz.

Magyar, P. 1993. Personal interview, Budapest.

Maier, C. 1988. *The Unmasterable Past: History, Holocaust, and German National Identity.* Cambridge: Harvard University Press.

———. 1997. *Dissolution: The Crisis of Communism and the End of East Germany.* Princeton: Princeton University Press.

Marcuse, H. 1976 (1965). "[Repressive Tolerance]." In *Critical Sociology: Adorno, Habermas, Benjamin, Horkheimer, Marcuse, Neumann,* ed. P. Connerton, 301–30. New York: Penguin.

Máriás, B. 1995. Personal interview, Budapest.

Markovits, A. S., ed. 1991–92. "Germany and Gender: Effects of Unification on German Women in the East and the West." *German Politics and Society* (special issue) (nos. 24–25).

Maron, M. 1981. *Flugasche.* Frankfurt am Main: S. Fischer.

Martin, B. 1981. *A Sociology of Contemporary Cultural Change.* Oxford: B. Blackwell.

Marx, K. 1978. "The German Ideology." In *The Marx-Engels Reader,* ed. R. C. Tucker, 110–64. New York: Norton.

Matouschek, B., R. Wodak, and F. Januschek. 1995. *Notwendige Maßnahmen gegen Fremde? Genese und Formen von rassistischen Diskursen der Differenz.* Vienna: Passagen.

McClintock, A. 1995. *Imperial Leather: Race, Gender, and Sexuality in the Colonial Conquest.* New York: Routledge.

Menyhárt, J. 1984. Personal interview (with A. Bozóki), Budapest.

———. 1993. Personal interview, Budapest.

Merkel, I. 1994. "From a Socialist Society of Labor into a Consumer Society? The Transformation of East German Identities and Systems." In *Envisioning Eastern Europe: Postcommunist Cultural Studies,* ed. M. D. Kennedy, 55–65. Ann Arbor: University of Michigan Press.

Merkl, P. H. 1993. *German Unification in the European Context.* University Park: Pennsylvania State University Press.

Middleton, D., and D. Edwards, eds. 1990. *Collective Remembering.* London: Sage.

Milbrath, L. 1984. *Environmentalists: Vanguard for a New Society.* Albany: State University of New York Press.

Miller, D., ed. 1995. *Worlds Apart: Modernity through the Prism of the Local.* New York: Routledge.

Mills, S. 1991. *Discourses of Difference: An Analysis of Women's Travel Writings and Colonialism.* London: Routledge.

Ministerium für Raumordnung, Landwirtschaft und Umwelt des Landes Sachsen-Anhalt. 1996. *Landesentwicklungsbericht 1996.* Magdeburg: Reference Öffentlichkeitsarbeit.

Mitscherlich, A., and M. Mitscherlich. 1975. *The Inability to Mourn: Principles of Collective Behavior.* New York: Grove.

Modestov, N. 1996. "V Metro za Podaianiem" (In the Metro for Alms). *Krestianskaia Rossiia,* January 29–February 4. Excerpted in *Moskovskaia Pravda,* April 3, 16.

Moore-Gilbert, B. 1997. *Postcolonial Theory: Contexts, Practices, Politics.* London: Verso.

"Moskovskij Metropoliten im. L. M. Kaganovich." 1954. In *Bolshaja Sovjetskaja Entsiklopedija* (Great Soviet Encyclopedia), 330–32.

Moskovskoe Metro. 1978. Moscow: Moskovskii Robachii.

Mosse, G. 1985. *Nationalism and Sexuality: Middle-Class Morality and Sexual Norms in Modern Europe.* Madison: University of Wisconsin Press.

Moziklip. 1987. Dir. P. Tímár. MAFILM. Film.

Müller, I. P. 1993. Personal interview, Budapest.

Munn, N. D. 1986. *The Fame of Gawa: A Symbolic Study of Value Transformation in a Massim Society.* Cambridge: Cambridge University Press.

———. 1992. "The Cultural Anthropology of Time: A Critical Essay." *Annual Review of Anthropology* 21:93–123.

Nagengast, C. 1991. *Reluctant Socialists, Rural Entrepreneurs: Class, Culture, and the Polish State.* Boulder, CO: Westview.

Nash, D. 1996. *Anthropology of Tourism.* Oxford: Pergamon.

Nelson, K. 1989. "Remembering: A Functional Developmental Perspective." In *Memory: Interdisciplinary Approaches,* ed. P. R Solomon et al., 127–50. New York: Springer.

Neutschs, E. 1968. *Spur der Steine.* Halle: Mitteldeutscher.

Nichols, J. 1994. "Chechen-Ingush." In *Encyclopedia of World Cultures,* vol. 6, *Russia and Eurasia/China,* ed. P. Friedrich and N. Diamond. Boston: G. K. Hall.

Nick, H. 1995. "An Unparalleled Destruction and Squandering of Economic Assets." In *German Unification: The Destruction of an Economy,* ed. H. Behrend, 80–118. East Haven, CT: Pluto.

Niedermeier, M. 1995a. *Erotik in der Gartenkunst: Eine Kulturgeschichte der Liebesgärten.* Leipzig: Edition Leipzig.

———. 1995b. "Das Gartenreich Anhalt-Dessau als kulturelles und literarisches Zentrum um 1780." In *Von Wörlitz bis Mosigkau,* ed. E. Hirsch and T. Heohle, 55–68. Band 55, Dessau-Wörlitz Beiträge V. Dessau: Kulturamt Dessau.

Nora, P. 1989. "Between Memory and History: *Les Lieux de Mémoire.*" *Representations* 26 (spring): 7–25.

Nove, A. 1983. *The Economics of Feasible Socialism.* London: Allen and Unwin.

Nyiri, J. 1992. *Die Juden-Schule.* Trans. H. Linnert and U. Szyszkowitz. Frankfurt am Main: S. Fischer.

O'Connell Davidson, J. 1996. "Sex Tourism in Cuba." *Race and Class* 38 (1): 39–48.

Otsarot Genuzim: Osfe Omanut Yehudie Mi-Galitsyah Meha-Muze'on le-etno- grafyah Ve-le-Omanuyot bi-Levov. 1994. Tel Aviv: Bet ha-Tfutsot 'al shem Nahum Goldmann.

Paperny, V. 1993 (1975). "Movement—Immobility." In *Tekstura: Russian Essays on Visual Culture,* ed. A. Efimova and L. Manovich, 55–79. Chicago: University of Chicago Press.

Perlman, M. 1988. *Imaginal Memory and the Place of Hiroshima.* Albany: State University of New York Press.

Persky, S. 1996. *Boyopolis: Sex and Politics in Gay Eastern Europe.* New York: Overlook.

Pesmen, D. 1995. "Standing Bottles, Washing Deals, and Drinking for the Soul." *Anthropology of East Europe Review* 13 (2): 65–75.

———. 1996. " 'Do not have a hundred rubles, have instead a hundred friends': Money and Sentiment in a Perestroika-Post-Soviet Siberian City." *Irish Journal of Anthropology* 1:3–22.

———. 1998. "The Russian Soul: Ethnography and Metaphysics." Ph.D. diss., University of Chicago.

———. Forthcoming. "Those Who Poke into My Soul: Bakhtin, Dostoevsky, Love." In *Anthropology and Literature,* ed. S. Coleman and D. Boyer.

"Petronius." 1995. "Prager Erlebnisse." *XTRA* 13–14:8–9.

Philipsen, D. 1993. *We Were the People: Voices from East Germany's Revolutionary Autumn of 1989.* Durham, NC: Duke University Press.

Poghosian, G. 1993. *An Armenian's Life in Armenia.* Yerevan: Sociological Research Center of the National Academy of Sciences.

Polanyi, K. 1944. *The Great Transformation: The Political and Economic Origins of Our Time.* Boston: Beacon.

Pollack, M. 1984. *Nach Galizien—von Chassiden, Huzulen, Polen und Ruthenen. Eine imaginäre Reise durch die verschwundene Welt Ostgaliziens und der Bukowina.* Vienna: Edition Christian Brandstätter.

Popular Memory Group. 1982. "Popular Memory: Theory, Politics, Method." In *Making Histories: Studies in History-Writing and Politics,* ed. R. Johnson et al., 205–52. London: Hutchinson.

Poznanski, K., ed. 1994. *Constructing Capitalism: The Reemergence of Civil Society and Liberal Economy in the Post-Communist World.* Boulder, CO: Westview.

Pratt, M. L. 1992. *Imperial Eyes: Travel Writing and Transculturation.* London: Routledge.

Pridham, G., and T. Vanhanen, eds. 1994. *Democratization in Eastern Europe: Domestic and International Perspectives.* New York: Routledge.

Rancour-Laferriere, D. 1995. *The Slave Soul of Russia: Moral Masochism and the Cult of Suffering.* New York: New York University Press.

Rau, Z., ed. 1991. *The Reemergence of Civil Society in Eastern Europe and the Soviet Union.* Boulder, CO: Westview.

"Reactions to Bomb Blast." 1996. *OMRI Daily Digest,* June 13.

Redclift, M. 1994. "Development and the Environment: Managing the Contradictions." In *Capitalism and Development,* ed. L. Starr, 123–39. London: Routledge.

Reiss, J., ed. 1997. *Aus den sieben Gemeinden. Ein Lesebuch über Juden im Burgenland.* Eisenstadt: Österreichisches Jüdisches Museum.

Ries, N. 1992a. "Fables, Anecdotes, Litanies, and Laments: An Ethnography of Contemporary Russian Verbal Performances and the Construction of Self." Paper presented at Soviet Cultural Studies Conference, Columbia University, New York.

———. 1992b. "Mystical Poverty and the Rewards of Loss." *Kyoto Journal* 20:26–31.

———. 1997. *Russian Talk: Culture and Conversation during Perestroika.* Ithaca: Cornell University Press.

Roback, A. A. 1979 (1944). *A Dictionary of International Slurs (Ethnophaulisms).* Waukesha, WI: Maledicta.

Robertson, A. F. 1994. "Time and the Modern Family: Reproduction in the Making of History." In *NowHere: Space, Time, and Modernity,* ed. R. Friedland and D. Boden, 95–126. Berkeley: University of California Press.

Rogger, H. 1960. *National Consciousness in Eighteenth-Century Russia.* Cambridge: Harvard University Press.

Röhl, Ernst. 1991. *Deutsch-Deutsch: Ein Satirisches Wörterbuch von Ernst Röhl.* Berlin: Eulenspiegel Verlag.

Róna Tas, Á. 1997. *The Great Surprise of the Small Transformation: The Demise of Communism and the Rise of the Private Sector in Hungary.* Ann Arbor: University of Michigan Press.

Rosaldo, R. 1986. "From the Door of His Tent: The Fieldworker and the Inquisitor." In *Writing Culture: The Poetics and Politics of Ethnography,* ed. J. Clifford and G. Marcus, 77–97. Berkeley: University of California Press.

Rosenberg, T. 1995. *The Haunted Land: Facing Europe's Ghosts after Communism.* New York: Vintage.

Rotenberg, R. 1995. *Landscape and Power in Vienna.* Baltimore: Johns Hopkins University Press.

"Rowdyhafte Ausschreitungen" (Rowdy Rioting). 1989. In *Deutsch-Deutsch: Ein satirisches Wörterbuch,* by E. Röhl. Berlin: Eulenspiegel, 1991.

Ruble, B. 1993. "From Khrushcheby to Korobki." In *Russian Housing in the Modern Age: Design and Social History,* ed. W. C. Brumfield and B. Ruble. New York: Woodrow Wilson Center Press.

———. 1995. *Money Sings: The Changing Politics of Urban Space in Post-Soviet Yaroslavl.* New York: Cambridge University Press.

Rybár, C. 1991. *Das jüdische Prag—Glossen zur Geschichte und Kultur. Führer durch die Denkwürdigkeiten.* Prague: Akropolis.

Sächsische Zeitung (Dresden, Germany). 1989. October 6.

Said, E. 1979. *Orientalism.* New York: Vintage.

Salner, P. 1993. "Tolerancia a Intolerancia Vo Velkych Mestách Strednej Európy." *Slovensky Národopis* 41 (1): 3–15.

Sátántangó: Krasznahorkai László Regénye Alapján Tarr Béla Filmje. 1994. Budapest: Budapest Film. Film and accompanying booklet.

Schama, S. 1995. *Landscape and Memory.* New York: Knopf.

Schiach, M. 1989. *Discourse on Popular Culture: Class, Gender, and History in the Analysis of Popular Culture, 1730 to Present.* Cambridge: Polity.

Schivelbusch, W. 1979. *The Railway Journey.* New York: Urizen.

Scott, J. 1990. *Domination and the Arts of Resistance: Hidden Transcripts.* New Haven: Yale University Press.

Sedgwick, E. K. 1985. *Between Men: English Literature and Male Homosocial Desire.* New York: Columbia University Press.

Silverstein, M. 1988. "De-Voice of Authority." Paper presented at the American Anthropological Association annual meeting, Phoenix, AZ.

———. 1993. "Metapragmatic Discourse and Metapragmatic Function." In *Reflexive Language,* ed. J. A. Lucy, 33–58. New York: Cambridge University Press.

Simis, K. M. 1982. *USSR: The Corrupt Society: The Secret World of Soviet Capitalism.* Trans. Jacqueline Edwards and Mitchell Schneider. New York: Simon and Schuster.

Slobin, M. 1989. *Chosen Voices: The Story of the American Cantorate.* Urbana: University of Illinois Press.

———, ed. 1996. *Retuning Culture: Musical Changes in Central and Eastern Europe.* Durham, NC: Duke University Press.

Smith, V. L., ed. 1977. *Hosts and Guests: The Anthropology of Tourism.* Philadelphia: University of Pennsylvania Press.

Spartacus International Gay Guide. 1996. Berlin: Bruno Gmünder.

Spivak, G. C. 1989. "Who Claims Alterity?" In *Remaking History,* ed. B. Kruger and P. Mariani, 269–92. Seattle: Bay Press.

Spurr, D. 1993. *The Rhetoric of Empire: Colonial Discourse in Journalism, Travel Writing, and Imperial Administration.* Durham, NC: Duke University Press.

Stark, D. 1992. "Path Dependence and Privatization Strategies in East Central Europe." *East European Politics and Societies* 61:17–54.

Starr, F. S. 1984 (1978). "Visionary Town Planning during the Cultural Revolution." In *Cultural Revolution in Russia,* S. Fitzpatrick, 207–40. Bloomington: University of Indiana Press.

Stephens, S. 1995. "Children and the Politics of Culture in 'Late Capitalism.'" In *Children and the Politics of Culture,* ed. S. Stephens, 3–48. Princeton: Princeton University Press.

Stites, R. 1992. *Russian Popular Culture: Entertainment and Society since 1900.* Cambridge: Cambridge University Press.

Stoler, A. L. 1989. "Making Empire Respectable: The Politics of Race and Sexual Morality in Twentieth-Century Colonial Cultures." *American Ethnologist* 16 (4): 634–60.

———. 1991. "Carnal Knowledge and Imperial Power: Gender, Race, and Morality in Colonial Asia." In *Gender at the Crossroads of Knowledge: Feminist Anthropology in a Postmodern Era*, ed. M. di Leonardo, 55–101. Berkeley: University of California Press.

———. 1992. "Sexual Affronts and Racial Frontiers: European Identities and the Cultural Politics of Exclusion in Colonial Southeast Asia." *Comparative Studies in Society and History* 34 (2): 514–51.

———. 1995. *Race and the Education of Desire: Foucault's* History of Sexuality *and the Colonial Order of Things*. Durham, NC: Duke University Press.

Suny, R. G. 1993a. *Looking toward Ararat: Armenia in Modern History*. Bloomington: Indiana University Press.

———. 1993b. *The Revenge of the Past*. Stanford, CA: Stanford University Press.

Swedenburg, T. 1991. "Popular Memory and the Palestinian National Past." In *Golden Ages, Dark Ages: Imagining the Past in Anthropology and History*, ed. Jay O'Brien and William Roseberry, 152–79. Berkeley: University of California Press.

Szemere, A. 1992. "The Politics of Marginality: A Rock Musical Subculture in Socialist Hungary in the Early 1980s." In *Rockin' the Boat: Mass Music and Mass Movements*, ed. R. Garofalo, 93–115. Boston: South End.

———. 1996. "Subcultural Identity and Social Change: The Case of Postcommunist Hungary." *Popular Music and Society* 20 (2): 19–42.

———. 1997. "Pop Culture, Politics, and Social Change." Ph.D. diss., University of California–San Diego.

Szõnyei, T. 1992. *Az új hullám évtizede (*The Decade of the New Wave). Vol. 2. Budapest: Katalizátor Iroda.

Taussig, M. 1987. *Shamanism, Colonialism, and the Wild Man: A Study in Terror and Healing*. Chicago: University of Chicago Press.

Tertz, A. (A. Sinyavsky). 1992 (1980). *Little Jinx*. Trans. L. P. Joseph and R. May. Evanston, IL: Northwestern University Press.

Tilly, C. 1986. *The Contentious French*. Cambridge: Harvard University Press.

Tipton, S. 1982. *Getting Saved from the Sixties: Moral Meaning in Conversion and Cultural Change*. Berkeley: University of California Press.

Todorova, M. N. 1997. *Imagining the Balkans*. New York: Oxford University Press.

Tomas, D. 1991. "Tools of the Trade: The Production of Ethnographic Observations on the Andaman Islands, 1858–1922." In *Colonial Situations: Essays on the Contextualization of Ethnographic Knowledge*, ed. G. Stocking, 75–108. Madison: University of Wisconsin Press.

Troitsky, A. 1987. *Back in the USSR: The True Story of Rock in Russia*. Boston: Faber and Faber.

Truong, T.-D. 1990. *Sex, Money, and Morality: Prostitution and Tourism in Southeast Asia*. London: Zed.

"Tsygane Shumnoju Tolpoju." 1996. *Lipetskaja Gazeta*, February 10, 7.

Turner, V. 1969. *The Ritual Process: Structure and Anti-Structure*. Ed. V. Turner. Ithaca: Cornell University Press.

————. 1990. "Are There Universals of Performance in Myth, Ritual, and Drama?" In *By Means of Performance: Intercultural Studies of Theatre and Ritual,* ed. R. Schechner and W. Appel, 8–19. Cambridge: Cambridge University Press.

Ungefroren, S. 1997. "Allein ein Jammern bringt Keinem etwas." *Mitteldeutsche Zeitung,* March 3, 9.

United Nations Industrial Development Organization. 1990. "Industry Brief. Armenia: Towards Economic Independence and Industrial Restructuring."

Varga, I. 1994. "Churches, Politics, and Society in Postcommunist East Central Europe." In *Politics and Religion in Central and Eastern Europe,* ed. William H. Swatos Jr., 101–18. Westport, CT: Praeger.

Verdery, K. 1991. *National Ideology under Socialism: Identity and Cultural Politics in Ceausescu's Romania.* Berkeley: University of California Press.

————. 1993. "Ethnic Relations, Economies of Shortage, and the Transition in Eastern Europe." In *Socialism: Ideals, Ideologies, and Local Practice,* ed. C. M. Hann, 172–86. London: Routledge.

————. 1996. *What Was Socialism, and What Comes Next?* Princeton: Princeton University Press.

Vermorel, F., and J. Vermorel. 1978. *Sex Pistols: The Inside Story.* London: W. H. Allen.

Víg, M. 1995. Personal interview, Budapest.

Vinaver, C. 1985. *Anthology of Hassidic Music.* Ed. and annotated by E. Schleifer. Jerusalem: Magnes Press of Hebrew University.

Vysokovskii, A. 1993. "Will Domesticity Return?" In *Russian Housing in the Modern Age: Design and Social History,* ed. W. C. Brumfield and B. Ruble. New York: Woodrow Wilson Center Press.

Walker, C. J., ed. 1991. *Armenia and Karabagh: The Struggle for Unity.* London: Minority Rights Publications.

Watson, R. S. 1994. "Memory, History, and Opposition under State Socialism: An Introduction." In *Memory, History and Opposition under State Socialism,* ed. R. Watson, 1–20. Santa Fe, NM: School of American Research Press.

Weber, M. 1977a (1948). "Politics as a Vocation." In *From Max Weber: Essays in Sociology,* ed. and trans. H. H. Gerth and C. Wright Mills, 77–129. London, Henley and Boston.

————. 1977b (1948) . "Science as a Vocation." In *From Max Weber,* 129–57.

————. 1977c (1948). "The Social Psychology of the World Religions." In *From Max Weber,* 280.

Wedel, J. 1992. "Introduction." In *The Unplanned Society: Poland during and after Communism,* ed. J. Wedel, 1–20. New York: Columbia University Press.

Werner, E. 1976. *A Voice Still Heard. . . . The Sacred Songs of the Ashkenazic Jews.* University Park: Pennsylvania State University Press.

Whisnant, D. E. 1991. "Sandinista Cultural Policy: Notes toward an Analysis in Historical Context." In *The Politics of Culture,* ed. B. Williams, 175–217. Washington, DC: Smithsonian Institution Press.

White, G. M. 1992. *Identity through History: Living Stories in a Solomon Islands Society.* New York: Cambridge University Press.

Whorf, B. L. 1956. "The Relation of Habitual Thought and Behavior to Language." In *Language, Thought and Reality.* Cambridge: MIT Press.

Wicke, P. 1992. "'The Times They Are A-Changing': Rock Music and Political Change in East Germany." In *Rockin' the Boat: Mass Music and Mass Movements,* ed. R. Garofalo, 81–92. Boston: South End.

Wierzbicka, A. 1989. "Soul and Mind: Linguistic Evidence for Ethnopsychology and Cultural History." *American Anthropologist* 91:41–58.

———. 1992. *Semantics, Culture, and Cognition: Universal Human Concepts in Culture-Specific Configurations.* New York: Oxford University Press.

Wildenthal, L. 1993. "'She Is the Victor': Bourgeois Women, Nationalist Identities, and the Ideal of the Independent Woman Farmer in German Southwest Africa." *Social Analysis* 33:68–88.

———. 1994. "Colonizers and Citizens: Bourgeois Women and the Woman Question in the German Colonial Movement, 1886–1914." Ph.D. diss., University of Michigan.

———. 1997. "Race, Gender, and Citizenship in the German Colonial Empire." In *Tensions of Empire: Colonial Cultures in a Bourgeois World,* ed. F. Cooper and A. L. Stoler, 263–83. Berkeley: University of California Press.

Williams, B. 1991. "Introduction." In *The Politics of Culture,* ed. B. Williams, 1–18. Washington, DC: Smithsonian Institution Press.

Williams, C. J. 1996. "Russia Slowly Building a Middle Class." *Los Angeles Times,* May 18.

Williams, R. C. 1970. "The Russian Soul: A Study in European Thought and Non-European Nationalism." *Journal of the History of Ideas* 31:573–88.

Willis, P. 1978. *Profane Culture.* London: Routledge and Kegan Paul.

———. 1990. *Common Culture: Symbolic Work at Play in the Everyday Cultures of the Young.* Boulder, CO: Westview.

Wischenbart, R. 1992. *Karpaten—Die dunkle Seite Europas.* Vienna: Kremayr and Scheriau.

Wolff, J. 1987. "Foreword: The Ideology of Autonomous Art." In *Music and Society: The Politics of Composition, Performance, and Reception,* ed. R. Leppert and S. McClary, 1–13. Cambridge: Cambridge University Press.

Wolff, L. 1994. *Inventing Eastern Europe: The Map of Civilization on the Mind of the Enlightenment.* Stanford, CA: Stanford University Press.

Wuthnow, R. 1989. *Meaning and Moral Order: Explorations in Cultural Analysis.* Berkeley: University of California Press.

Yates, F. 1966. *The Art of Memory.* Chicago: University of Chicago Press.

Yerushalmi, Y. H. 1982. *Zakhor: Jewish History and Jewish Memory.* Seattle: University of Washington Press.

Zámbó, F. 1993. Personal interview, Budapest.

Zinoviev, A. 1985. *Homo Sovieticus.* Trans. C. Janson. Boston: Atlantic Monthly Press.

———. 1990. *Perestroika in Partygrad (Katastroika).* Trans. C. Janson. London: Peter Owen.

Contributors

Daphne Berdahl is assistant professor of anthropology at the University of Minnesota. She is the author of *Where the World Ended: Re-unification and Identity in the German Borderland* (1999). She teaches and writes on culture and consumption; the anthropology of modernity, history and memory; and gender and nationalism. Her present work concerns the relationship between mass consumption and the changing definitions, understandings, and practices of citizenship and nation building in reunified Germany.

Philip V. Bohlman is associate professor of music and Jewish studies at the University of Chicago. An ethnomusicologist, he has done fieldwork in Israel, North America, Central Europe, and, most recently, Eastern Europe. Among his major publications are *"The Land Where Two Streams Flow": Music in the German-Jewish Community of Israel* (1989) and *"Jüdische Volksmusik"—Eine europäische Geistesgeschichte.* He serves as series editor for Recent Researches in the Oral Traditions of Music and Chicago Studies in Ethnomusicology.

Matti Bunzl is the Aaron and Robin Fischer Professor of Jewish Culture and Society and assistant professor in the anthropology department at the University of Illinois at Urbana-Champaign. His research interests range from the literary and cultural fields of fin-de-siècle Vienna and the history of anthropology to the anthropology of contemporary Austria and Central Europe. His articles have appeared in such journals as *Cultural Anthropology, History and Memory, History of Anthropology, German Quarterly,* and *City and Society.*

Hermine G. De Soto received her Ph.D. in anthropology from the University of Wisconsin at Madison, where she is a research fellow in the women's studies program and research associate at the Center for Russia, East Europe, and Central Asia. She has edited the volume *Culture and Contradiction: Dialectics of Wealth Power and Symbol* (1992) and is the coeditor of *The Curtain Rises: Rethinking Culture, Ideology, and the State in Eastern Europe* (1993). She is currently completing a coedited volume entitled *Fieldwork Dilemmas in Disintegrating Postsocialist States* and is working on *East German Transformations: Politics of Gender, Identity, and Environment.*

Martha Lampland is associate professor of sociology at the University of California at San Diego. She is an editor of the *Journal of Historical Sociology* and the author of *The Object of Labor: Commodification in Socialist Hungary* (1995) as well as articles in the *American Ethnologist, Eastern European Politics and Societies,* and *Hungarian Studies,* among other publications.

Alaina Lemon is assistant professor of anthropology at the University of Michigan. She received her Ph.D. from the University of Chicago in 1996; her dissertation is entitled "Indic Diaspora, Soviet History, Russian Home: Political Performances and Sincere Ironies in Romani Cultures." Her research and teaching interests include racial and national ideologies, language, performance, visual anthropology, criminality, and exchange in Russian conversation, literature, and film. She has written articles for such publications as *Theater Journal* and *Cultural Anthropology.*

Dale Pesmen received her Ph.D. in anthropology from the University of Chicago, where she completed a dissertation entitled "The Russian Soul: Ethnography and Metaphysics." Her articles have appeared in the *Irish Journal of Anthropology, Anthropology of East Europe Review,* and James Fernandez, ed., *Beyond Metaphor: The Theory of Tropes in Anthropology* (1991). She will also be a contributor to a forthcoming volume on anthropology and literature edited by Steve Coleman and Dominic Boyer. She has published translations from Russian to English of stories, verse, and plays.

Stephanie Platz is assistant professor and holds the Alex Manoogian Chair in Modern Armenian History at the University of Michigan. She has previously worked as a program officer for the John D. and Catherine T. MacArthur Foundation and for the International Research and Exchanges Board in Armenia and Georgia. She is currently revising her dissertation, entitled "Pasts and Futures: Space, History, and Armenian Identity, 1988–1994," for publication, and she has published several articles on Armenian historical consciousness and national identity.

Anna Szemere received her Ph.D. in sociology from the University of California at San Diego; her dissertation is entitled "Pop Culture, Politics, and Social Transition." The author of several articles on Hungarian rock music and social identity, her work has been published in Lawrence Grossberg, Cary Nelson, and Paula Treichler, eds., *Cultural Studies* (1992), and in such journals as *Popular Music and Society.*

Elizabeth A. Ten Dyke is adjunct assistant professor of anthropology at Hunter College. A 1997 graduate of the Ph.D. program in anthropology of the City University of New York, her dissertation is entitled "Dresden: Paradoxes of Memory in History." Her research interests include comparative work on struggles over history in divided or once-divided nations. She is the author of articles in *Political and Legal Anthropology Review* and in Kelly Boyd, ed., *Encyclopedia of Historians and Historical Writing* (forthcoming).

Index